Information Technology Auditing

An Evolving Agenda

Jagdish Pathak

Information Technology Auditing

An Evolving Agenda

160401

 Springer

Jagdish Pathak
Odette School of Business
University of Windsor
Windsor, N9B3P4
Canada
E-mail: jagdish@uwindsor.ca

Library of Congress Control Number: 2005921591

ISBN 3-540-22155-7 Springer Berlin Heidelberg New York

Springer is a part of Springer Science+Business Media
springeronline.com

© Springer-Verlag Berlin Heidelberg 2005
Printed in Germany

Cover design: Erich Kirchner
Production: Helmut Petri
Printing: Strauss Offsetdruck

SPIN 11012511   Printed on acid-free paper – 43/3153 – 5 4 3 2 1 0

This Monograph is dedicated to all those who saw a potential in me and motivated me to strive hard in the education and career. They are many and difficult to isolate from the sea of well-wishers. I dedicate this volume to my parents (Shri Madan Lal Pathak and Mrs. Bhagwati Devi Pathak); brothers (Mr. Goverdhan Pathak and Mr. Giridhari Pathak) and sisters (Mrs. Vidya Mishra, Mrs. Lakshmi Mishra and Mrs. Binu lata Tiwari); parents of my wife (Mr. Kiriti Ranjan Das and Mrs. Minuprava Das); my late teachers (Dr. N.K.Sharma and Dr. S.M.Bijli); Dean of Odette School of Business, Dr. Roger Hussey; my students in India and Canada, Nupur, my wife; Joy, my son; and many unnamed others.

Preface

Information Systems (IS) auditing is a component in the domain of Modern Auditing as well as accounting information systems. This component has acquired pre-dominance with the extensive use of computer technology in the business information processing area. Modern computer-based highly integrated information systems are fast replacing the traditional centralized and distributed information systems. The audit methodologies developed and used by the auditors in the earlier information systems have acquired adequate soundness and if at all any problem exists, it is more to do with the application of these methodologies rather than these methodologies themselves. Information needs of all the levels of management is not only fast evolving but getting diversified dramatically during the last two decade as a result of the growth and diversification of business interests. Economies of some of biggest countries of the world are fast opening up their markets to seek global participation and remove the obsolescence from the technological scenario. A New World trade order has emerged to seek the barrier less market mechanism. The concept of protectionism is almost given a good bye by many of these economies to open the channels for the global market forces to interact and decide optimally. And, of course, one should not forget the aftermath of ENRON and other big name's meltdown in the history of business and corporate world. Auditing had always been a key point of discussion and decisions made under various provisions of Sarbanes-Oxley Act 2002.

New information processing and communication technologies are being applied to satisfy managements' information needs. In Response to this need, communication and digital electronic computer technologies have merged to provide the high-speed data communication capabilities (information super highways) used by many large business houses across the world. Multi-national business activities share the need for data communications capabilities, but also have other requirements that increase the complexities of management information needs. For instance, the need to accommodate currency conversion, regulatory reporting, and variations in accounting disclosure practices in developing information systems is felt more in case of multinational business entities.

Expansion in target markets and product lines has involved acquisitions for much business. This has led to consolidation of activities in some situations and diversification in others. Increased transaction volumes and an expansion of existing information systems often accompany consolidation. Diversification through acquisition has, in contrast, often required an information exchange between previously unrelated management information systems. In some cases, diversification has resulted in a significant expansion of data processing/ information processing capabilities in order to provide required management information on a con-solidated basis.

The monograph in your hand is the outcome of my researches in the realm of information technology auditing during the span of more than twenty years in on different generations of hardware and software. The embedded objective of com-piling these ten scholarly and applied essays in one book is to provide the deve-lopmental agenda at one place in this fast evolving field of specialty. The growth of EDP Auditing into a major force to reckon with in modern cyber environment is mostly due to the tireless efforts made by the Information Systems Audit & Controls Association (ISACA), many scholars of EDP Auditing, many professio-nal certified information systems auditors and various prominent accounting bo-dies of professionals and big auditing firms of international stature.

These ten essays have applied and scholarly flavor so as to make them useable by the professionals of all hue in this field of knowledge. The chapters carry many new developments and their potential impact on the auditors and their procedures. I have made my best efforts to provide synergy and integration of research and practice into this monograph.

This monograph is basically designed to provide the basis for serious study and application of various recent developments in the segment of information and communication technology auditing. Any typical text on information technology auditing talks about many more complex concepts, techniques and software and refers them without often explaining the impact of those on the information tech-nology auditing as many of these concepts, methods, applications are fast develo-ping into industry standards, like enterprise resources planning or enterprise appli-cation integration etc. An auditor would be able to identify, understand and comprehend various new and fast evolving technologies to face them professional-ly. I have integrated many of my past papers with several modifications to extend the continuum to these chapters.

I am indebted to many of my former and present colleagues who have contribu-ted directly or indirectly to this monograph and its development which include my self development in acquiring the capability to write this monograph. I would ex-tend my thanks to Professor Andrew Chambers, Former Dean & Professor, City University of London (UK); Professor (Dr.) Gerald Vinten, Head, European Busi-ness School, London (UK); Dr. Scott Summer, Brigham Young University, Utah (US); Professor (Dr.) Ram Sriram, Georgia State University, Atlanta, GA; Dr. Amelia Baldwin, University of Alabama, Tuscaloosa, AL; Professor (Dr.) Mary Lind, North Carolina A&T State University, Greensboro, NC; Professor (Dr.) Ramesh Chandra, Professor (Dr.) Jeffrey Kantor, Dr. Ben Chaouch, all of Univer-sity of Windsor, ON, Canada; Professor (Dr.) S.N. Maheshwari, Director at Delhi Institute of Advanced Studies, New Delhi, India, Late Professor (Dr.) N.K. Shar-ma, Visiting Professor at Birla Institute of Technology & Science, Pilani, India & Late Professor (Dr.) Shah Mohammad Bijli, Former Dean, Faculty of Business at University of Goa. The list is not complete as there are still many who are not in this list but their contribution has been tremendous. My thanks go to them as well.

I am also indebted to my wife Nupur and my son Joy who were always my source of joy and encouragement in this arduous task of putting my stray thoughts together in this monograph.

Finally, I am as usual responsible for any error in this monograph and would make my best efforts to correct those errors in the second edition of this text (if it ever happens!).

February 2005

Jagdish Pathak, PhD
Odette School of Business
University of Windsor
Canada

Table of Contents

1 IT Auditing: An Overview and Approach 1
   1.1 Evolution in Managements' Perceptions 1
   1.2 Evolution in Information Processing Capabilities 2
   1.3 Exposure to Loss 3
   1.4 Objectives of IT Auditing 5
   1.5 Internal Controls and IT Audit 5
      1.5.1 Various Internal Controls 7
   1.6 Growth and Genesis of IT Auditing 7
   1.7 IT Audit Approach 9
      1.7.1 Nature of IT Controls 9
      1.7.2 Controls and Loss 11
      1.7.3 Internal Controls and Auditing Approach 12
   1.8 Steps in an IT Audit 12
   1.9 Audit Decisions 15

2 Auditing and Complex Business Information Systems 21
   2.1 Complex Integrated Accounting Systems 22
   2.2 Distributed Data and its Effects on Organisations 24
      2.2.1 Networks 25
      2.2.2 Portability and Systems 31
      2.2.3 Integration of Applications 32
   2.3 Productivity Aspect of the Technology 32
   2.4 Business Process Re-engineering 33
   2.5 Intelligent Systems 34
   2.6 Auditors and Changing Technology 36
   2.7 Strategic Use of Technology and Audit Implications 37
   2.8 Internal Controls and Auditing 40

3 Generation-X Technologies and IT Auditing 45
   3.1 Generation-X Enterprise Technologies : 46
   3.2 Information Systems Integration: A Challenge 48
   3.3 Assured Information Emanates from Assured Systems 51
   3.4 Information Assurance: A Function of Strategic Importance 53
   3.5 Various Information Assurance and Control Measures 56
      3.5.1 Web-Level Assurance Measures 57
   3.6 Control Objectives and System Assurance 58

3.6.1 British Standards: BS7799 and BS 7799-2:2002 60
3.6.2 System Security Engineering Capability Maturity Model:
         SSE-CMM 60

4 Complex Information Systems, Auditing Standards and IT Auditors....... **63**
4.1 The Approach and Objectives 63
  4.1.1 The Scenario 65
4.2 Impact of Technology Complexity on the Auditor.................................... 65
  4.2.1 Complex Information Technologies and Audit Risks....................... 67
  4.2.2 SAS-94 and its Effect on the Audit Process.................................... 70

5 ERP and Information Integration Issues: Perspective for Auditors **75**
5.1 What is Enterprise Resource Planning?... 77
5.2 Implementation Cycle 79
5.3 Conceptual Models.. 80
  5.3.1 Successes and Disasters 81
5.4 Types of Implementation... 82
5.5 Social Integration.. 83
5.6 Resistance in Social Integration 84
5.7 Process Integration 84
  5.7.1 Communications in Process Integration... 85
  5.7.2 Alignment of Culture in Process Integration................................... 86
  5.7.3 Knowledge Integration... 86
  5.7.4 Workflow Integration... 89
  5.7.5 Best Practices in Functional Integration... 90
  5.7.6 Virtual Integration.. 91
5.8 Auditor and ERP... 92
  5.8.1 ERP Internal Control Procedures 92

6 Technology, Auditing and Cyber-Commerce **95**
6.1 Technology and Auditing 96
6.2 Risk Understanding in e-Commerce for IT Auditor 99
6.3 Information at Risk.. 101
6.4 Controls and Audit Evidences 105

7 IT Auditing and Security of Information Systems **107**
7.1 Information Security.. 108
  7.1.1 Computer Assets 109
7.2 Security Controls 110
7.3 Security Evaluation and Certification Criteria.. 112
  7.3.1 Networks Security.. 113
  7.3.2 OSI Architecture 115
  7.3.3 Security Mechanisms 118
  7.3.4 Integrity... 120
  7.3.5 Security Mechanisms Location... 122
7.4 Future Trends 123

7.5 Exemplary Case Laws Related to Security Needs and Breaches in USA 124
  7.5.1 Case Laws Related to Data Preservation.. 124
  7.5.2 Case Laws Pertaining to the Scope of Discovery............................. 125
  7.5.3 Case Laws Related to the Records Management 131
  7.5.4 Case Laws Pertaining to the Use of Experts 133
  7.5.5 Case Laws Related to the Costs and Allocation............................... 134
  7.5.6 Case Laws Related to the Spoliation and Sanctions........................ 136
  7.5.7 Case Laws Pertaining to Inadvertent Disclosure............................. 139
  7.5.8 Case Laws Related to the Method of Litigation............................... 140
  7.5.9 Case Laws Related to Criminal Issues of Security........................... 142
  7.5.10 Case Laws Related to the Reliability 142
  7.5.11 E-Sign Statute and Case Laws 143
  7.5.12 Case Laws on Privacy.. 144
7.6 Kind of Audits Called Security Audits.. 145
  7.6.1 Internet/Perimeter Audit.. 145
  7.6.2 Website Audit 145
  7.6.3 Penetration Audit (Ethical Hacking) 145
  7.6.4 Wireless Audit.. 146
  7.6.5 Network Audit.. 146
  7.6.6 Security Policies and Procedures Audit 146
  7.6.7 Facilities Audit (Physical)... 146
  7.6.8 Business Continuity Plan (BCP) and Disaster Recovery (DR)........ 147
  7.6.9 Regulatory Compliance Audits 147
7.7 How Can Security Audit Help the Enterprises? 148
  7.7.1 Protecting the Physical Safety of Your Employees, Vendors,
    and Visitors 148

8 Information Technology Governance and COBIT®..................................... 151
8.1 Why Do we Need IT Governance?... 152
8.2 Introduction to COBIT® 153
  8.2.1 COBIT and the Reality.. 154

9 Database Management Systems and Auditing... 157
9.1 Concepts of Database Technology for Auditors..................................... 157
  9.1.1 Data Independence... 158
  9.1.2 Database Management Systems and its Functions......................... 158
  9.1.3 Relational Database Management Systems (RDMS)....................... 162
  9.1.4 Database Security.. 167
  9.1.5 Distributed Database Systems.. 174
  9.1.6 Object Data Management Systems 175
  9.1.7 Relation and Object: A Comparison 175
  9.1.8 Data Warehouses... 177
9.2 Operational Systems Compared to Informational Systems 178

10 EAI: Auditors Should Know Potential Risks to Enterprise **181**
   10.1 The Promise of EAI 184
   10.2 Improvement in Productivity 184
      10.2.1 Data Flow Streamlined 185
   10.3 EAI Reaches Beyond Your Borders 185
      10.3.1 Lowered Costs 186

Bibliography and Further References **189**

Glossary of IT Auditing Terms **209**

1 IT Auditing: An Overview and Approach

Information Systems (IS) auditing is a major component in the domain of Modern Auditing. This component has acquired pre-dominance with the extensive use of information and communication technology in the business information processing area. Modern information systems (IS) are fast replacing the traditional information systems. The audit methodologies developed and used by the auditors in the manual information systems have acquired adequate soundness and if at all any problem exists, it is more to do with the application of these methodologies rather than these methodologies themselves. Information technology (IT) auditing is the process of collecting and evaluating evidence to determine whether an information system: (Pathak, 1999)

- safeguards assets
- maintains data integrity
- achieves organisational goals effectively and
- Consumes resources efficiently

Asset safeguarding consists of ensuring that the computer assets (both hardware and software) are protected from damage or destruction, unauthorized use, and being stolen. The state of data integrity means the data is accurate, complete, and consistent. These two aspects have always been the main concern of auditors. Nevertheless, the definition of IT auditing as proposed also integrated a concern for effectiveness with which the computer hardware and software systems (both system and application) fulfil their objectives and the efficiency with which data is processed. IT auditing function has been carved out of the conventional auditing function to ascertain whether computer systems are capable of safeguarding the assets, maintain data integrity, and obtain the goals of an organisation effectively and efficiently. Stakeholders of a business entity, both internal and external, are interested to know whether information technology fulfils these objectives.

1.1 Evolution in Managements' Perceptions

Information needs of all the levels of management is not only fast evolving but getting diversified dramatically during the last two decade as a result of the growth and diversification of business interests. Economies of some of biggest countries of the world are fast opening up their markets to seek global participation and remove the obsolescence from the technological scenario. A New World trade order has emerged to seek the barrier less market mechanism. The concept of protectionism is almost given a good bye by many of these economies to open the channels for the global market forces to interact and decide optimally.

State-of-art information processing and communication technologies are being applied to satisfy managements' information needs. In response to this need, communication and digital electronic computer technologies have merged to provide the high-speed data communication capabilities (information super highways) used by many large business houses across the world. Multi-national business activities share the need for data communications capabilities, but also have other requirements that increase the complexities of management information needs. For instance, the need to accommodate currency conversion, regulatory reporting, and variations in accounting disclosure practices in developing computer-based information system is felt more in case of multinational business entities.

Expansion in target markets and product lines has involved acquisitions for additional business. This has led to consolidation of activities in some situations and diversification in others. Increased transaction volumes and an expansion of existing information systems often accompany consolidation. Diversification through acquisition has, in contrast, often required an information exchange between previously unrelated management information systems. In some cases, diversification has resulted in a significant expansion of data processing/ information processing capabilities in order to provide required management information on a consolidated basis.

1.2 Evolution in Information Processing Capabilities

The changing information requirements of management brought changes in information technology capabilities. Many important advances are made in this vital area of technology and its application. Some of these advances relevant to the business organisations and their information processing needs include:

- increased computer usage
- increased use of data, communication and networking technologies
- new data processing areas
- distributed data processing
- data base management systems
- very large data bases
- enterprise-wide computing (client-server systems)
- end-user computing
- knowledge-based expert support systems
- decision support systems
- Graphic user interface (GUI)
- fuzzy logic based object oriented programming and

- Electronic fund transfer (EFT)
- E-Commerce technologies
- Data Warehouses and Data Marts
- Data Mining

The information needs of different levels of management and the information processing capabilities have both become more complex and have merged. As more business functions are computerised, business activities and management have become dependent upon electronic data processing and the internal controls that ensure accuracy and completeness. Traditional controls of manual systems have become outmoded with their audit methods, tools, and techniques, as a result of changes in the structure and form of computer application systems. The overarching impetus given to the reliability and robustness of internal controls under the Sarbanes-Oxley Act of 2002 in USA, after the great meltdown of large business entities in the annals of the global economic fiascos, have placed an auditor in a precarious position. Under the Section-404 of the said Act, an auditor is also expected to issue opinion on the reliability of the internal controls of the client. With greater reliance on computer - based processing have come new potentials for loss.

1.3 Exposure to Loss

The increase in the usage of information technology in business operations has increased the associated potential for loss in varied forms, as procedures once formed and established manually are entirely automated. Conventional systems and procedures relied on manual checks and verifications to ensure the accuracy and completeness of data and records. In such an environment, exceptions could be handled as they were encountered. Decisions could be made without much delay in processing. Manual control was maintained over most, if not all, phases of transaction processing and record keeping.

Manual controls are replaced by computer application control function with the expansion of information systems in the organisation. Applications are required that anticipate exceptions previously handled manually on an ad-hoc basis. Without such control routines, incomplete or incorrect transactions can be processed unnoticed. When information systems are linked (or networked) and integrated, an undetected error that is accepted by one application can result in errors in several others. Once accepted, an erroneous transaction can be processed against several files without any manual checking until the processing cycle is complete. The potential effects of a single error are much greater in this environment. When such errors are detected, their correction can require extensive manual analysis in order to determine what files and records have been affected, and to prepare proper correcting entries. Several internal audit and EDP managers too opine that the primary area of focus for a further reduction in loss exposure will be organisational information systems.

Majority of top executives of large business houses has shown their concern for the increasing dependence upon information systems and a continuing trend toward centralisation and concentration of data resources. Interruptions in the availability of either information or processing mechanism can be catastrophic consequences for organisations highly dependent upon complex information systems. Various layers of management as well as internal audit personnel are concerned that effective programmes be developed to protect information systems facilities and minimise this loss exposure.

Controls in Use

These controls are enumerated as follows:

- limited access to computer facility
- disaster recovery mechanism
- back up processing and data files
- off-site storage of important data files
- controls on authorized users or access controls
- intrusion detection and firewall
- encryption of data/information
- network controls

Need and Importance of IT Audit changes in the corporate governance scenario and the induction of latest information and communication technology hardware and software systems have made the audit and control of information systems almost mandatory. There are the factors also influencing the decision to opt for system audit as a function in an organisation. The examination of internal and external controls of information systems is needed for the following reasons:

- chances of incorrect decision making based on incorrect data
- abuse of hardware and software in organisation
- unpredictable cost of data loss, if any
- chances of loss of information processing capabilities
- denial of service attacks
- external hacking and virus/worms
- maintenance of individual privacy under the legislations

It is often said that the technology is neutral, neither good nor bad. It is the application of the technology that produces problems in the organisation. But, it is well accepted that the individual organisations should have a social conscience that includes the use of information and communication technology. Abuse of computer and its related technology has proved another stimulus for development of the information system audit function within organisations. It has been further defined as any incident associated with information and communication technology in which a victim suffered or could have suffered loss and a perpetrator by intention made or could have made gain. Nevertheless, information and communication abuse is a third most important problem after the most serious problems or errors and omissions causing losses and the second one is disruption to the information processing by natural calamities, viz., fire, water, earthquake, or power failure. It has been suggested that data provide the organisation with an image of itself, its environment, its history, and its future. If this image is accurate, the organisation increases its capabilities to adapt and remain afloat in this global evolving scenario.

A strategic planning decision made by the higher levels of management may withstand the onslaught of inaccurate data, but decisions pertaining to the operations cannot tolerate inaccuracies in data as it may cause costly and unnecessary inquiry to investigate the error. Similarly, shareholders of a company too need accurate financial data so is the case with the taxation people and many other regulatory authorities.

1.4 Objectives of IT Auditing

IT auditing function is basically a support function for the attainment of conventional audit objectives. As has been described earlier, that IT auditing is the process of collecting and evaluating evidence to determine if an information system safeguards assets, maintains data integrity, achieves organisational goals effectively, and consumes resources efficiently. The main objectives of IT auditing are as follows:

- review of soundness and adequacy of various operational controls, and promotion of these controls at a reasonable cost in the organisation
- ascertaining the extent of compliance with the policies, plans and procedures of the organisation
- ascertaining the extent to which the corporate information systems resources are accounted and safeguard for various loss exposures
- ascertaining the correctness and the completeness of the information processed through the information systems in the organisation
- recommending various internal controls for maintaining data integrity in the information systems
- ascertaining the effectiveness and the efficiency of various information and communication technology hardware and software in the organisation

1.5 Internal Controls and IT Audit

Internal controls are of increasing importance in the IT environment to ensure the accuracy and completeness of data provided to management for decision-making. Internal controls in information technology-based systems environment pertains to the processing and recording of an organisation's transactions and to resulting reports generated for managerial use. These are the procedures that ensure the accuracy and completeness of manual and computer generated records. They encompass source document origination, authorisation, proceeding, software record keeping, and the use of information processing records and reports in controlling an organisation's activities.

Internal control is recognised as a vital feature of modern management, with the extent and effectiveness of internal controls being just as important to the auditor. The use of information technology-based systems, no matter how small, large or sophisticated does not in any reduce the need for the auditor to evaluate the reliability of that system in determining the scope and character of the audit. The introduction of new controls (over such areas as system development and testing, i.e. authorisation of systems and applications, the use of applications and modern integrated databases, and the detection and correction of errors), and, on the other hand, the erosion of the basic element of internal control (i.e. separation of functional responsibilities and exercise of human judgement), are two aspects of information systems which must be considered in the evaluation of controls.

In a manual system the element of human judgement is present in the form of an employee using his common sense, experience, and knowledge of the organisation's transactions to assess the validity and/or reasonableness of a particular item and its accounting treatment, even after other persons have handled the transaction. The incorporation of information technology removes this element of control, as the information systems will process the item as instructed. Consequently fewer, if any, personnel shall process or check a transaction, especially in the more advanced systems. Unless detected by system checks (i.e. batch control or hash total technique), the computing system will accept wrong data and there is therefore, a greater possibility than in a manual system that an erroneous result will be produced.

Further to this, most information systems related departments suffer from control problems arising from the concentration of responsibility amongst few people. Concentration of controls and work in the single department reduces the extent to which responsibilities can be divided and independent checking can be performed. The evaluation of internal control is therefore probably more vital in the audit of an information system than in a manual system. It is generally accepted that the auditor is limited to determining whether the system is such that a relatively large number of people must be involved in order to circumvent the internal controls. While concentration of duties in an IS department makes internal control a sensitive audit problem, such problems can nevertheless, be overcome through some degree of control being vested in the user department and the control groups. The review of internal control by the auditor must, therefore, include both the computer and non-computer aspects of the system. Evaluation of internal control is important to any audit, and especially one involving information and communication technology supported information systems. In broad terms these controls can be classified as:

- organisational controls, encompassing administrative and systems development controls
- procedural controls, covering input, processing, networking, output and data base management systems (DBMS) controls

1.5.1 Various Internal Controls

As discussed earlier, the basic objectives of internal control do not change in information and communication technology supported information systems environment. For instance, complete and accurate operation of database requires a set of system-based controls. Also, the system development controls include procedures for testing applications that would not be found in the development of manual systems. Audit trail provides the records of all the events that take place within an application system. These trails are in-built in a well designed system and application software and do not disappear as was considered by many auditors in earlier days. Fortunately, modern day client-server systems have many built-in features for the creation and maintenance of audit trails for auditors' use.

Comparison of recorded assets and real assets also help to determine whether or not incompleteness or inaccuracies exist. Information and communication technology supported information systems have some programmes to sort the existing data files and even prepare the counts for various items of assets. If unauthorised modifications are found in the applications or data bases that the applications use, a fraud is possible. Therefore, internal controls must be implemented and their operations ensured if any irregularities are to be prevented or identified.

Errors in a manual system may not be comparatively that serious what one may find in information and communication technology supported information systems. As the tendency of error occurrence in a manual system is stochastic in nature whereas the occurrence of error in information and communication technology supported information systems is considered to be deterministic. This is considered so as a clerk may commit error periodically whereas a software system, irrespective whether it is system software or application software, if in error, shall always commit error as and when the system is run. Secondly, such deterministic errors are generated at high speed and expenses to correct and return the system may be very high. Thus, internal controls that ensure superior quality systems are critical to the overall benefit of the organisation.

1.6 Growth and Genesis of IT Auditing

People often carry a confused notion of considering IT auditing as and extension of traditional auditing. But, the truth is different as the recognition of IT auditing came from the auditors (of course conventional) as well as from corporate information systems management. Auditors realised that information and communication technology-based systems had influenced a great deal of their ability to perform the attestation function. Similarly managers recognised information technology assets as valuable resources requiring a thorough control like any other valuable resource in the organisation. IT auditing as a study is considered to be inter-disciplinary in nature borrowing its theory and methodologies from the diverse disciplines:

- traditional auditing
- computer science
- behavioural science and
- information management.

Internal control techniques of IT auditing find their genesis in the traditional auditing discipline. Basic principles of internal control as applied to the manual information processing systems are required to be applied to the information and communication technology supported information systems. These controls, if applied, lead information and communication technology supported information systems to maintain the data integrity. Different methodologies for evidence collection and evaluation used by IT auditors are rooted in the traditional auditing. Similarly, the long evolution and experience of traditional auditing highlight the critical importance of objective, verifiable evidence and independent evaluation of systems.

The technological complexity of computer science provides both benefits and difficulties for IT auditing. On the one hand, IT auditor is allowed a liberty about the reliability of certain hardware and software components in the information systems. But, if this knowledge is abused, it may become extremely difficult for the IT auditor to identify and detect the abuse. Fraud perpetrated by a skilled systems programmer may become almost impossible to be detected by an IT auditor who does not have a corresponding level of technical knowledge.

A study revealed a fact that the major reason of failure of information systems is through ignoring organisational behaviour and social engineering related problems in the design and implementation of information systems. The failure of a system can impact asset safe-guarding, data integrity, system effectiveness, and system efficiency. Therefore, the IT auditor must know those conditions that lead to behavioural problems and possible system failure. Some organisation theorists emphasise the need for system designers to concurrently consider the impact of a computer system on task achievement, the technical system, and the quality of work life of individuals within the organisation.

There had been some spectacular disasters while implementing computer-based systems in the early period of computerised data processing. Massive cost over-runs and failure to achieve the stated objectives were some of the difficult situations in that period to handle. Modern system designers are concerned with better ways of developing and implementing information and communication technology supported information systems. As a result, several advances have occurred. These advances impact IT auditing because they ultimately affect asset safeguarding, data integrity, system efficiency and effectiveness.

1.7 IT Audit Approach

This section of the chapter explains a general approach to carrying out IT audit in an entity. It describes some techniques in general for simplifying and extending orderliness to the complexity faced by an auditor while making evaluation judgments on information systems. Further, it discusses some of the major decision the auditors must make when planning and implementing an IT audit.

1.7.1 Nature of IT Controls

The evaluation of the internal control system is facilitated if the IT auditor conceptualises controls over IT in different ways. Generally speaking, two major bases are considered for classifying IT controls, viz. Applications systems and Management controls, and preventive, corrective and detective controls. The classification of IT controls on the basis of management controls and application systems controls is used for various reasons. Firstly, it is considered to be relatively efficient for an IT auditor to evaluate management controls before the evaluation of application systems controls. Secondly, within this basis, IT controls can be organized further to provide an orderly basis for conducting the IT audit. Thirdly, the following discussion shall make it apparently clear that a useful conceptualisation of controls within a computer installation is like the layers of onion skin constituting various levels of management as well as application controls. Various forces eroding the data integrity, efficiency and effectiveness of a system must penetrate through these layers of peel. The outer layers of control are intact then it is likely that the inner layers too are intact.

Management controls ensure the development, implementation and the execution of IT proceeds in a pre-planned and controlled manner. There are many levels of management controls corresponding to the hierarchy of organisation and the major functions performed within an information systems facility. Top management of the organisation must ensure the IT is well managed. It is responsible primarily for long-run policy decision on how information technology shall be used in the organisation. Information systems management has overall responsibility for the planning and control of all IT activities. It also provides inputs to top management's long-run policy decision making and translates long-run policies into short-run goals and objectives. Systems development management is responsible for the design, implementation, and maintenance of individual application systems. Programming management is responsible for programming new systems, maintaining old systems, and providing general systems support software. Data-base administration is responsible for the control and use of an organisation's database or the library of application systems. Operations management controls the day-to-day operations of information systems. It is also responsible for data preparation, the data flow through the installation, production running of systems, maintenance of hardware, and sometimes maintenance of programmes and file library facility and facility security. The absence of management controls is a serious concern for the IT auditor as these controls are basic in nature that applies across all the applications. In a situation where the weakness exists in the management controls, it may not be worthwhile to review and evaluate application systems controls.

The audit efficiency point of view too demands that it is useful to evaluate management controls first. For example, if the high quality documentation is an accepted control by the management after it is found by an IT auditor then it is unlikely for an auditor to review the documentation quality of each application.

The application system controls make sure that every application safeguards assets of the entity, maintain integrity, and process data efficiently. These controls are exercised at **different** stages in the flow of data through an information system. At data capture stage, controls ensure all transactions are recorded and that the transactions are authorized, complete, and accurate. They also ensure source data is transmitted to the point of data preparation for input to the computer, and that source data is returned and properly filed. Data preparation controls, ensure all data is converted to machine readable form, and is authorised, complete and accurate. They also ensure input data is transmitted to input device for input to the system and that input data is returned and properly filed. This explanation may sound a bit archaic as the modern data entry is no longer a replica of the earlier data entry systems. However, those who are familiar with this two decade old style of data entry would find this explanation a bit familiar one. Controls on the system access ensure only authorised personnel gain access to the computing resources such as application systems. Input controls ensure all data entered into the system is authorized, accurate, and complete. These also ensure errors identified are corrected and re-entered for processing. Transmission controls ensure data sent a network system is authorized, accurate and complete. Controls on processing ensure applications process all data entered into the system and that processing is authorized, accurate and complete. Output controls ensure that output produced by the computer is authorized, accurate and complete, distributed to the authorized personnel, and properly filed. Audit trail controls ensure data can be traced through a system from its source to its final destination, and vice-versa, and that the integrity of a corrupted audit trail can be restored. Back-up and recovery controls ensure that the physical existence of data can be restored if the data is lost or its integrity is corrupted.

Application controls are horizontal in nature. These controls cut across lines of organisational authority and follow the data flow through the organisation. Management controls are on the other hand considered to be vertical in nature as they follow the hierarchical lines of the organisational structure. Another basis of classifying controls in information system as preventive, corrective, and detective is useful for the IT auditor as it highlights when the controls are exercised during the flow of data through a computer system. Various controls, viz. good form design, separation of duties, etc. are called preventive or general controls and exercised at the early stage in the flow of data. Their generality often allows them to be robust to changes in the systems where they are used. However, preventive controls being general may allow many types of errors to occur. Detective controls identify errors after these have occurred. These controls include input validation controls also. Such controls are specific in nature. After error identification phase, corrective controls are exercised so as to correct the identified errors. For example, writing-up data mismatches to a suspense file should ensure errors are corrected and re-entered. However, corrective controls also must be subjected to detective controls since errors may also creep in while correcting an error. (Weber, 1988)

1.7.2 Controls and Loss

Systems of internal controls are set up by the management to reduce the potential for loss to the business entity. The value of such controls can be assessed in terms of its cost and the extent to which it reduces expected losses. The expected losses can be reduced by reducing the probability of the loss occurring, and by reducing the amount of loss if the loss at all occurs. Internal controls reduce the potential loss by removing the causes of losses. The IT auditor's task is to evaluate how well controls act on the causes of losses to reduce the potential losses. Nevertheless, the evaluation of controls is not an easy task for an auditor as it is a real complex task. Presently, Section-404 of Sarbanes-Oxley Act requires auditor to assess the effectiveness and efficiency of these internal controls and the management is expected to provide its assertion to an auditor who in turn is required to issue opinion on the reliability of asserted internal controls. Why an organisation may incur losses? Following list is identified to know the answer to this question:

- fraud and embezzlement
- lost revenue or excessive cost to the organisation
- destruction of loss to the assets.
- unacceptable accounting practices
- unacceptable recording and record-keeping
- business interruption
- faulty management decision
- regulatory and legal sanctions
- disadvantages from competition

These 'upper level' causes of loss can be further broken into 'lower level' causes. The concept of hierarchy of causes of losses is a useful way for the IT auditor to conceptualise the internal control system evaluation process. For instance, at a lower level in the hierarchy, good forms design reduces the number of data entry errors made. This affects the potential losses resulting from high-level causes in the hierarchy, because the likelihood of incomplete data arising during the data capture process is reduced. Hence, there is less probability of wrong or faulty management decision being made.

There is no simple direct and proportionate relationship between causes of loss and internal controls or in between high-level causes and the lower-level causes. Further, the effects of several high-level causes of losses are a function of the effects of incomplete and inaccurate data. Such data may also cause faulty management decision, legal adverse sanctions, and losses of organisational assets. The recent corporate breakdown has also made one aspect amply clear that management has and can carry a tendency to override internal controls for personal advantage or to deceive the stakeholders. Hence, assessment of losses needs to be made from this newly devised angle where management will have a tendency to keep mum on intentional abuse of or override of internal controls.

1.7.3 Internal Controls and Auditing Approach

The overall quality of various internal controls facilitates the auditing of applications to a great extent. IT audit can well be performed in small sized systems by auditing the end-products assuming that the internal controls are well placed. In large enterprise systems, IT auditors may still have to further collect the evidence of quality of systems (both operational and application) to vouch for the data integrity, system efficiency and effectiveness, asset safeguarding objectives of IT audit. If the internal control system is intact, the IT auditor can have more confidence in the quality of the application systems being evaluated.

1.8 Steps in an IT Audit

The discussion done so fare in the earlier sections of this chapter shows the methodology to approach an IT audit. Following algorithmic steps shall attempt to further clarify this approach:

```
START
1.      Review Controls of management and application
2.      Evaluate this preliminary review
DEITION NO: (1)
Do you rely on these controls?
IF YES THEN
1.      PERFORM detailed review of management controls
2.      PERFORM detailed review of application controls
3.      PERFORM evaluation of detailed review
ELSE GOTO10
DEITION NO: (2)
Do you still rely on controls?
IF YES THEN
1.      PERFORM compliance testing
2.      EVALUATE compliance test results.
ELSE GOTO 10
DEITION NO: (3)
Do you still rely on controls?
30. IF YES THEN
1.      PERFORM substantive testing
2.      PERFORM overall evaluation
3.      PERFORM audit report
STOP
```

ELSE GOTO 10
10.   DEITION NO. (4)
Do you want to withdraw from audit?
IF YES THEN
1.   Advise management accordingly
STOP
ELSE GOTO 20
20. DEITION NO. (5)
Do you want to rely on user controls?
IF YES THEN
1.   **PERFORM** testing and evaluation of user controls.
2.   GOTO 30
ELSE GOTO 30
END

The above mentioned algorithmic steps can further be grouped into different phases in IT audit.

- Preliminary Review Phase
- Detailed Review Phase
- Compliance Testing Phase
- Testing and Review of User Control Phase
- Substantive Testing Phase

The first step in IT audit is to review the system and its hardware and software including utilities, etc. This is preliminary in nature and the objective is to obtain the necessary details on how to go ahead in audit. At this stage, as has been depicted in algorithm an IT auditor may either:

- decide to continue with the audit or
- decide to withdraw from the audit or
- decide to rely on user's controls

The evidence collection during this preliminary phase is primarily done through observation, interviews, and the reviews of available documentation. Decision tables or flow charts can be constructed for evidence documentation purpose. The preliminary reviews carried out by the internal auditors are different from the external auditors. The detailed review phase is meant for thorough understanding of the system controls used in the information systems facility. At this stage too, IT auditor may either:

- decide to withdraw from audit or
- decide to proceed to compliance testing or
- decide the review user's controls

An IT auditor may decide for some applications to rely on the internal controls and for others, alternative procedure may be selected as appropriate. In this phase, too both management and application controls are reviewed. If management controls are found to be lacking or weak then an auditor may drop the review of application controls as unnecessary. In this phase, it is important for the auditor to identify the causes of loss existing within the facility and the controls established to reduce the effects of these causes of loss. At the end, an IT auditor must evaluate whether the controls established reduce the potential loss from these causes to a minimum level. Still at this stage, an auditor will have to assume that the controls function reliably unless there is evidence to the contrary.

The compliance testing phase determines the operating efficiency of the system. In other words, it establishes whether a system is performing effectively what it is expected to perform. An IT auditor determines whether they are liable or not. Computer-assisted evidence collection techniques may be put to use by an auditor to establish and determine the controls and their reliability. Test data generator may be used to evaluate the validation controls in an input programme. Test data generator is a one of the well known computer assisted audit techniques (CAAT). It is also a cost-effective way to obtain the validity of input programme. At the end of compliance testing, the IT auditor again must evaluate the internal controls in the light of the evidence collected on the reliability of individual controls.

Review and testing of user's controls are performed by the IT auditor only in some cases when the internal controls within the information system could not be relied upon by him. User's controls are also known as compensatory controls. End users exercise controls that compensate for any weaknesses in IT internal control system. For instance, event though weak controls may exist over the network from source of data to the processing facility, end-users may carefully reconcile their own control totals with those produced as output from application systems. The evaluations of end-user's control also prove to be cost-effective from an external auditor's point-of-view.

Substantive testing phase's objective is to acquire sufficient evidence so that the IT auditor can make a final decision on whether or not substantial losses have occurred or could occur in processing. This decision is expressed by IT external auditor in the form of an opinion as to whether a material mis-statement of the accounts exists.

Normally five different types of substantive tests are suggested for an IT auditor

- identification test of erroneous processing
- tests to assess the quality of data
- tests to compare data with the physical counts
- tests to identity inconsistent data
- confirmation of data with outside sources

Some of these tests need a good quantity of computer support. Generalised audit software (GAS) can be used to select and print confirmations. However, the basic processes involved are more or less same as those for manual systems.

1.9 Audit Decisions

Steps in IT audit made us aware though briefly about some of the difficulties involved in making some of the major decision needed while carrying out an IT audit. These audit decision can affect the audit approach for a system in substantial manner. Hence, in the succeeding section, these decisions are described with some of the considerations involved in finalising these decisions:

- evaluation decision
- decision on the timing of audit procedure and
- decision on the application system selection

Evaluation decision is perhaps the most difficult decision for IT auditors to make during an IT audit. This judgement should be made at the end of preliminary review phase, and also at the end of substantive testing phase, compliance testing phase, and detailed review phase. It pertains to the decision whether an IT auditor shall continue the audit or not, whether the internal controls can be relied upon, what controls are critical to the IT audit, how they should be tested for compliance, the extent of substantive testing required, and lastly, whether or not the system has satisfactorily safeguarded assets, maintained data integrity, and achieved system efficiency and effectiveness.

There is no single method of making this evaluation judgement. However, one can draw a matrix to conceptualise controls that reduce the expected losses during data capture. The elements of matrix might be some rating of the effectiveness of each internal control at reducing the potential loss from each cause, the reliability of the control with respect to reach cause in the light of compliance testing results. The IT auditor performs three types of evaluation in terms of the matrix. These are columnar evaluation, a row evaluation, and a global evaluation. The columnar evaluation involves asking the question: For a given cause of loss, do the controls exercised over the cause reduce the expected loss from the cause to an acceptable level? As explained, the IT auditor asks this question before and after testing the controls for reliability. The row evaluation means asking the similar question. The global evaluation involves finding out the optimal set of controls for the organisation. Such optimal set of internal controls needs somehow a joint evaluation of columns and rows to be made. With respect to the problem of optimal set of global evaluation, there are still two more complicating factors. Firstly, the marginal costs and benefits of a control often depend on what controls are being exercised, the marginal benefits of any one control exceed the marginal costs of that control.

The matrix conceptualisation of the evaluation decision also can be used to depict the varied functions of the external and internal auditor. The external auditor is primarily concerned with the columnar evaluation. Whether or not the choice of controls is optimal in a global sense is a secondary consideration, whereas, an internal auditor performs all the three evaluations. How these three evaluations are to be performed is, unfortunately, still an area in the need of research. Few professional bodies of auditors have so far come out with standards in this area.

The decision by an IT auditor on the timing of audit procedures is considered to be an important one and equally a controversial area. Many auditors opine that hardly any change is required in the traditional auditing schedule of interim, end-of-period, and post period-end work. Even when, they recognise that audit use of the compute for evidence collection purposes often requires substantial preparation in advance. Whereas, some auditors argue fundamental changes are required to the timing of audit procedures when information systems must be evaluated. They support the idea of audit participation in system design phase too. This particular view means audit shall be performed in three phases:

- audit during the system design phase
- audit during the operation phase
- evaluation during the post-audit phase

Design phase participating by IT auditors is needed for two major reasons. First, by changing the system to incorporate required controls after it has been implemented can be expansive. Second, it is often difficult, if not impossible, for the auditor on the basis of a periodic review to understand a system that has taken several thousand man-hours to design and implement. However, majority of IT auditors opine both external and internal auditors should at least, review and evaluate the design of information systems controls at various major checkpoints in the system development process.

There are three ways in which IT auditors decide on the audit use of computers to perform audit procedures:

- processing the auditor's test data on the client's system as a part of tests of internal controls
- testing the records maintained by the systems as a means of verifying the client's financial statements and
- using the computer to perform audit tasks independent of client's records and systems

These procedures are accomplished by the use of test data, GAS and microcomputer-aided auditing. The objective of test-data approach is to determine whether the client's computer programme can correctly handle valid and invalid transactions as they arise. To achieve this objective the auditor develops different types of transactions that are processed under his or her own control using the client's application on client's hardware. The IT auditor's test data must include both valid and invalid, transactions in order to determine whether the client's application will react properly to different kinds of data. Since the auditor has complete knowledge of the errors that exist in the test data, it is possible for the auditor to check whether the client's system has properly processed the input. The IT auditor does this by examining the error listing and the details of the output resulting from the test data. Test data are helpful in reviewing the client's system of processing data and its control over errors, but several difficulties must be overcome before this approach can be used. Some of these are as follows: Test data must include all relevant conditions the auditors desire to test.

Application tested by the auditor's test data must be the same as that used throughout the year by the client. In some cases, test data must be eliminated from the client's records. The test data should test the adequacy of all controls applicable to the client's application under review. Because, considerable competence is needed in developing data to test for all the relevant types of errors that could occur, the assistance of an IT expert is generally needed. One approach the auditor can take to ensure that this condition is met is to run of a master database such as the bills payable or accounts payable trial balance. It would not be proper to permit fictitious test transactions to remain permanently in a database. There are feasible methods of eliminating test data, but they generally require the assistance of an IT expert. It should be noted that in circumstances in which elimination of test data is not feasible, it is common practice for auditors to enter only invalid data. These tests are incomplete. However, they are useful for testing certain controls. Although, it is possible for auditors to write specific modules to perform the above mentioned functions, or to use organisation's own application system for that purpose, the most common approach is to use generalised audit software (GAS). Generalised audit software is normally designed and developed by the firms of chartered accountants or some independent software vendor and can be used on different audits. The GAS consists of a series of computer application system that together perform various information processing functions. GAS is considered to be relatively old thing in auditing by now that has greatly increased the potential use of a computer for auditing tasks. A more recent development than GAS is the use of microcomputer to perform audit tasks. It is now common for auditors to use lap-top personal computers (PC) as an audit tool. Many audit tasks such as analytical procedures and working paper preparations, can be performed by using microcomputers, hence sometimes called microcomputer-aided auditing. There is an important distinction between using the microcomputers as an audit tool and using generalised audit software. GAS is a method of verifying the entity's data recorded in lower level language. PC is often used even when the entity's data are not computerised or when the entity's application systems are not compatible with the auditor's. Typically, input is entered into the PC by the auditor and subsequently used by him for analysis and summarisation. A common example is to input the client's trial balance into the PC and use those data to calculate analytical procedures.

The last but equally important audit decision pertains to the selection of application system. As a general practice the IT auditor should select for audit of those application systems most critical to the continued existence of the organisation. Since budget constraints usually apply, the auditor wants to select those application systems where the highest pay-offs will be obtained. Some of the general guidelines for selecting application systems for audit are given below:

- User Audit
- Application System characteristics

The elimination of test data is necessary if the application being tested is for the updating the test data on a surprise basis, possibly at random times throughout the year. This approach is both costly and time consuming. A more realistic method is to rely on the client's internal control over making changes in the programme.

User audit is a useful way of finding out which application system is problematic. When application systems do not function correctly, users are affected because reports generated by these systems are either late or incorrect. Source data coding is difficult or error resubmission is onerous, etc. The control assistants in the user area are often in the know of an application system's weaknesses. User management can provide information on any problems experienced with the quality and timeliness of reports generated by the application system.

An IT auditor also needs to investigate carefully a further aspect of the user environment. Sometimes an application system has detrimental effects on the quality of work life of its users. This can produce a variety of problems that impact asset safeguarding, data integrity and system efficiency and effectiveness. At one extreme, users attempt to directly sabotage the system. At the other extreme, users simply show disinterest in the system. Ultimately the application system deteriorates through lack of active user support. Often these problems are difficult to identify being converted in nature. User audit can be either formal of informal in manner or conduct. If the user audit is part of the evaluation of an application system's effectiveness, user opinions may be solicited through various means, viz. questionnaires, or structured interviews. In case an IT auditor is simply carrying out a user audit to identify potential application system for further study, the approach may be more informal. However, even if the approach is informal, it still requires to be planned and the results documented in working papers. The auditor's problem always is to ask those questions that elicit a response enabling problems to be identified. Selection of application system can also be made on the following basis.

- systems pertaining to financial controls
- systems with high-risk potential
- systems with high potential for competitive damage
- technologically complex systems
- very high cost system

An IT auditor is expected to pay high attention to those systems providing financial control over the assets of the organisation, viz., cash receipts and payments, payroll, debtors and creditors, etc. Some applications are considered to be riskier than others because they are susceptible to various losses, e.g. fraud and embezzlement; their failure may cripple the organisation; they interfere with other applications, and errors generated in them permeate these other interfaced systems.

Some of the applications give an organisation a competitive edge in the market, viz. strategic planning system. Others through patents, copyrights, etc. are major sources of revenue for the organisation. Others through their loss would destroy the image of the organisation. Those applications utilising advanced technology, such as data base management system (DBMS), client-server system, etc., with which the facility has little or no experience, it is more likely that such applications will be a source of potential control problems. Those systems which are costly to develop are often complex systems and also a source of again potential control problems.

2 Auditing and Complex Business Information Systems

The migration from desk-top computing to web-enabled computing and its acceptance has altered the paradigm in IT systems deployment and strategies in most of the business entities. Various recent studies of top executives related to the technological aspects of the entities have consistently indicated that the Internet is a high priority among the currently planned initiatives. The rush to integrate the web technologies by the organisations has generated some legitimate concerns about the ability to identify and address the risks that accompany this technology. Web technologies offer the hope of providing cost-effective, interactive access to a customer population many times larger than previously would have been imaginable.

This Chapter contains mainly discussion around the web-based technology and trends, complex integrated accounting systems, distributed data management and its effect on organisations, networks, client-server systems, IT as an enabling technology, internet, portability of operating systems, and system productivity. The entire discourse veers around the general understanding without much of technical exposure assumed from the auditors. The complex systems and their impact on the auditors is discussed in the concluding section of this chapter.

A good number of web application service providers, web technological consultants, and out-sourced software services in retail and in packaged form are rapidly decentralizing the web and improving the accessibility of the technology to even the modest sized business organisations. Another year, if not another millennium, is upon us, and the pace of change shows no sign of abating. Keeping pace with this advance continues to stretch the abilities of most organisations.

The business units that are most directly involved and responsible for the implementation, administration, and oversight of information technology (IT) are certainly more challenged than ever before. Implementing and administering today's information technology would be an impressive challenge in a steady-state environment, with organisations that were well trained and fully staffed. However, that is far from the situation that most organisations and their IT units now face. Technology infrastructures are growing more complex, while many IT departments operate inadequately staffed.

However, like all privileges, the Internet comes with responsibilities and has implications for protecting the confidentiality, integrity, and availability of information and assets. While there may be no change in the potential impact of a failure in the confidentiality, integrity, or availability of a given application or set of information, it is clear that the Internet will allow the less cautious organisation to significantly increase the potential that such an event will occur. In opening up to the Internet, the organisation may be opening itself to unrecognized and un-addressed risks. Adequately controlling for these risks requires intentional efforts to ensure that networks and systems are adequately planned and designed, implemented, and monitored, and it requires skills beyond those of many of today's organisations. Organisations with significant Internet involvement must become familiar with entirely new technology and terminology.

The challenge and the effort required will be great, and the issues and efforts will likely bear little relationship to an individual organisation's size or to its IT budget. Given the fixed nature of some of the costs of adequately managing Internet-related risks, and the enthusiasm for establishing an Internet presence, it is likely that smaller, less technically competent organisations may be much more exposed as a result of Internet-related initiatives.

Having successfully met the Y2K challenge, most organisations have moved into a new round of technology initiatives. Many of these initiatives present potentially significant operational impact and have far-reaching implications for how the company will conduct and control its key business processes. At or near the top of the IT priorities for today's businesses are projects to provide further integration. These projects include developing and implementing strategies to integrate the Internet into business processes and enhancing business processes with more integrated systems.

The Internet and its underlying technology are opening a broad rage of new opportunities and risks. Today's "integrated" supply chain and general accounting systems are replacing the traditional batch controls and balancing procedures of our past experience. The introduction of these changes into business processes, systems, and controls, requires that control structures must be upgraded to remain relevant.

2.1 Complex Integrated Accounting Systems

Over the past several years, a significant advance in the acceptance of accounting systems has augured dramatic improvements in the time and cost over traditional systems and business processes. It has long been recognized that at the core of every ineffective system are ineffective business processes and that a major breakthrough in effectiveness normally requires more than a new set of accounting software.

Experience with business re-engineering techniques and improvements in the ability to integrate process and systems have fostered new interest in, and confidence toward, making more improvements to eliminate redundant tasks, reduce errors and costs, and be more responsive to customers by integrating processes and their respective systems. Accompanying this trend is the growing use of electronic techniques for ordering and payment transactions, which is further accelerated by the improving accessibility of these systems via the Internet and third-party network providers. These advances will influence how the new processes and systems ensure that objectives (e.g., accuracy, timeliness, and authorization of the transaction) are being achieved. Traditional batched processing and batch-based control procedures may no longer be adequate, or even relevant.

Distributing data over networks and client/server systems have become commonplace, in order to meet the increasing demand for more localized processing, albeit sometimes without an understanding of the need for localized control. In this type of computing, the client and server work with the data and its processing in a distributed manner. It is important to remember that client/server is not a particular technology or product, but rather a style, or an approach to computing. Normally, the "client" is a desktop PC or workstation. Depending upon whether it is a "thin" or "fat" client/server distribution, as a user makes a request for processing, the "server," which can be another PC, a workstation, midrange, or possibly a mainframe computer, usually does the processing, holds or updates the data in a repository, and sends the results back to the client. This example refers to a "thin" client. A "thin" client relies on most of the function of the system being in the server. Another example of a thin client is your web browser.

It connects to different applications of which it has no knowledge and still provides an acceptable user interface. If the client provides a lot of business logic, then it is referred as a "fat" client. A "fat" client will pass little data to the server because the client does most of the processing.

Even when there is a knowledge of the need, being able to provide good local and network control is another issue. As the various departments and/or line units have, in effect, developed their own operating centres to allow them to do their own processing within the network, they have not taken equal steps to ensure that what they do is controlled, and that the data is and remains complete, accurate, current, and all of the standard control objectives.

Although this idea is not new – distributed processing has been around in one form or another since the 1970s – the ways in which it is being done have changed, and the audit and control responses need to change as well. When confronted by the proliferation of end-user systems at the end of the 1980s, some experienced IT auditors likened end-user computing (EUC) to the older distributed processing concept, using new machines and user-maintained systems, rather than centrally developed software on a mainframe as in the past.

Now the same might be said for the distributed processing and client/server systems of today, which require networks and distributed data, may include end-user-developed systems, and quite often will have centrally developed software. As their use increases, appropriate control models should also develop. As this new style of computing takes shape, we will be able to learn more about how the actual implementations are done, and then how they are controlled and audited. In general, no matter how a system is designed or implemented, the audit concerns about distributed data – completeness, accuracy, integrity, currency, security, and such – remain the same.

2.2 Distributed Data and its Effects on Organisations

The trend toward client/server architecture is probably the most dramatic and wide-ranging change in data processing in recent years. Many client/server applications are being developed and are already in use in all sectors. However, there is still a need for full-blown development tools and really complete client/server solutions, which are still being created. At this point, some of the client/server systems that have been developed just do not work the way their users hoped, possibly due to many factors.

These might include the current limitations of the technology itself, or of the development tools used, the relative inexperience of developers, the use of inadequate development methodologies that did not result in quality systems, or the lack of an appropriate technology infrastructure. Nevertheless, this trend toward distribution of data and client/server power will continue for some time to come. As more tools to implement complete client/server systems come into the marketplace, this style of computing will continue to grow at an increased pace.

In some cases, large central mainframe computers will be used to house the corporate databases, in what is often referred to as a data repository or data warehouse, while in others, the databases will be distributed as well. Much of the information in those databases will result from processing at various sites throughout the company. Results will be communicated to the central machine, or to the other nodes over the network. In the case of distributed databases or repositories, they will have to be replicated appropriately to the nodes so that the data remains complete, accurate, and current throughout the organisation. As a result of client/server computing, many people are predicting the end of the mainframe as it is known today. In one organisation, the CFO has mandated that the mainframes be out of the environment by the year 2000, regardless of what applications are being run there currently.

This is, needless to say, causing some concern among the people who provide the IT support within that organisation today, since they are not certain that they can, or should, be able to accomplish this task on time. Other people in the industry feel that there will always be a need for the large mainframe-style machines to provide the additional computing power for massive "number crunching" when a site requires it. Another school of thought holds that the mainframe is the perfect server for client/server systems. Whichever is right, the need for the massive computing power required by many of the engineering and scientific applications will certainly continue. In business, the view is that for the most part, processing will continue to be localized. A large central computer will hold and provide the corporate accounting information in a large data repository, sometimes referred to as the enterprise data. Since many companies are still working with existing, or legacy, systems that already work in this manner, this model still makes sense.

Processing to develop the information will be performed at the most appropriate sites, where the data originates or resides and to which the computing power has been distributed. The size of computers at the sites will vary, based on local requirements. In some cases, client/server systems, developed and running on workstations or microcomputers, will be able to satisfy local needs completely. In others, midrange or minicomputers, and possibly mainframes, will be required for the servers to have enough storage capacity and processing power to accomplish the required tasks.

Like the largest companies, medium-size companies are also distributing data and computer power. The growing availability and use of powerful PCs, LANs, and packaged applications has allowed just about all organisations to take advantage of distributed processing. While the size of their databases and computers may be smaller and their sites fewer, small- and medium-sized companies will have many of the same requirements and resulting uses of the technology as large companies.

To those concerned with controls, client/server systems point out the need to ensure that local processing areas have the same understanding of controls and their value as the traditional data centres do. This can be hard to accomplish in day-to-day business: corporate policies will be needed to mandate that control be established and maintained at all local sites.

2.2.1 Networks

Networking, LANs, WANs, and internetworking provide the ability for ever-larger numbers of computer users to communicate, sharing data and processing, in both local and regional offices and in vast global networks. There are now thousands of daily interactions among various parties – suppliers to customers, customers to suppliers, suppliers and customers to banks and other financial institutions – linking LAN (local area network) to LAN, WAN (wide area network) to other WAN, and so on, in what has rapidly become a worldwide network. In some cases, users access their own system and make a request for information or processing.

The answer comes over the wires via telecommunications, or possibly through a wireless connection. Often the users do not know where the data they receive in reply actually originated. This transparency of access is usually seen as a useful feature to get the information needed to users, but can create real problems for the auditors of those systems. Global telecommunications networks that support the systems of huge banks and other financial organisations have become commonplace. Other types of organisations are developing new systems that extend these links even farther. Some of these networks are so vast and interconnected that the managements of companies that use them do not know all of the existing linkages, let alone all of the possible end users.

Even in some control-related diagrams that are supposed to depict how systems are structured, one can see a marked-off fuzzy area that is referred to as the "network cloud" where, admittedly, no one is positive of all the connections. To complicate the process further, many thousands of networks are also linked to the Internet, a relatively unsecured means of communication, rife with potential hackers and other access and control risks, and increasingly in use for business communications.

Networks and Organisations

The driving forces behind the explosive growth in networking have been the need for local, usually cost-effective, computing power provided by LANs, and the requirements for global communications provided by longer-range wide area networking needed by the large companies that network with their suppliers and customers through private and/or public carriers. For example, numerous hospitals and healthcare centres are connected through PCs or terminals with modems to the computers of their healthcare suppliers so that they can order their supplies quickly and easily through a direct link.

This was an early strategic – and very successful – use of networking, which changed the competitive nature of the healthcare supply industry and also changed forever how its suppliers and purchasers worked together. Networking and the use of LANs has already affected all U.S. businesses. Not only has networking itself had an impact, but it has made possible many of the newer styles of computing, such as client/server, which must have a local area network environment to provide the processing links between client workstations and the servers in order to function correctly. Similarly, many automobile dealerships are connected to their manufacturers to order parts.

The automobile manufacturers are now linked to their suppliers in the United States and Europe, supplying invoices and delivery schedules through an EDI (electronic data interchange) system. Here the overall trend toward globalization in the industry is reflected in the information systems that they use. In fact, many large manufacturers now require that their suppliers use EDI or they will not allow purchases to be made from them.

The obvious benefits of EDI have caused its use to spread rapidly. When implemented correctly, networked EDI systems help reduce errors on input, reduce slowdowns caused by using the mail, and eliminate hard copy. Another networking trend is the widespread use of EDI linked to EFT (electronic funds transfer) systems, to allow for immediate payments as well as immediate transactions. These rapid transaction processing applications have been so successful in business that there is a growing desire to transmit additional types of communications as well as the standard business documents that were the first EDI transactions sent over the networks.

The IT auditor at one organisation that was a heavy user of EDI speculated while contemplating their disaster recovery plan that the company would be unable to work without their computers, since many, if not all, of their workers had no idea how to process a transaction manually. The benefits to organisations obtained by the speed, accuracy, and relatively low cost of EDI are such that its use is continuing to grow faster than anyone predicted.

However, as a result, the need for adequate controls over the various telecommunications networks has become even more crucial to businesses. Loosely controlled networks can allow many control problems, such as letting trespassers enter and perform unauthorized activities, read confidential data, and other difficulties. One of the biggest trends for the future, being talked about almost as much as client/server is, and potentially connected to it, is the growing use of groupware and workflow technology for collaborative computing. Normally, this is accomplished by a suite of software tools which are specifically designed to be used by groups of people, rather than in a stand alone, one-user environment. In workflow technology, the data is massaged and changed as it flows through the system.

This is a new approach to using technology to promote teamwork. It is not merely the automation of standard business documents. Users, individually in sequence or working as teams, will each have different areas to act upon, or apply various aspects of processing, or provide input data to the business event in question. The input of each area or person is critical to the final output. Group members may be able to modify or act further on what others have already done, to provide a real teamwork concept in software terms.

Enabling Technologies

These enabling technologies are usually thought to include: the ability to provide communications throughout the group with some sort of real-time messaging or Email system, the ability to set up group appointments and meetings in common calendars, good project management and scheduling tools, group document handling systems, group decision support systems, the ability to hold audio and video conferencing, true shared data products, a common data repository, system utilities for maintenance, and full-blown workgroup development tools. Workgroup solutions are already becoming a daily part of business even though many of the groupware and workflow solutions are still in their infancy.

Many other technologies will have to come together in order for these concepts to work well in organisations. These systems depend heavily on shared data. Multiple servers on possibly several LANs with bandwidths that are sufficient to handle the traffic over the network will also be needed in order for this workflow technology to work well. Added to the list from an auditors' perspective are the control requirements, which must be applied for the workflow to provide meaningful, auditable results. The use of the Internetwork (INTERNET) has increased significantly in the last two years as corporations and consumers find more and more uses for the Internet.

Corporations are now routinely using it for commerce and communications with suppliers and customers. In many industries the ability to bypass traditional retail outlets and shop for goods and services has profoundly changed the way that business is conducted. For example, car buyers that use the Internet to plan the purchase of a vehicle have caused automobile dealers to significantly discount the price of cars due to the additional information buyers now have as a result of information available on the Internet.

This ability to, in many cases, bypass the traditional distribution channels will continue to impact all producers of goods and services in the future. This has happened even though most companies still do not allow employees unlimited use of the Internet. The Internet's expanding role, though, has caused virtually all companies to examine how they use the Internet and Internet- type systems (i.e., Intranets) to conduct business. In many cases, employees are connected to the Internet through their home computers and so understand how the technology can be used to help their company and its bottom line.

Many businesses expect the companies they do business with to be using the latest technology such as the Internet or EDI. This requirement has accelerated business use of the Internet, as companies need to stay competitive. These factors as well as low cost of entry have, therefore, rapidly increased business use of the Internet. Today, many organisations are utilizing an internal Internet referred to as an Intranet.

Intranets are simply an internal Internet that conveniently makes information and applications more accessible to an organisation without the expensive and time-consuming application rollouts. Corporations now have the ability with an Intranet to transparently access computing resources, applications, and information that may be located anywhere in the world (albeit still within their corporate purview).

There are several reasons why corporations are adopting an internal web:

- access to information: the web is an easy way to distribute corporate information such as policies or operating procedures
- platform independence: there are browsers on every major platform developers no longer need to worry about cross-platform client development
- multiple data types: easy access can be provided to multimedia as well as textual information

With this in mind, many corporations are migrating their applications to an internal web in order to be totally web-based. This change is causing the remaining corporations to follow in order to remain competitive. Another change presently occurring is the move toward the "virtual office." In the past, employees were located as needed to handle customers that may visit a location, or where information processes were performed. In the future, employees will be located where it is most cost beneficial to the company. Many employees will work from home or cars, depending on the product or service being offered. Offices will still exist but will be much smaller and will be used for specific purposes that require face-to-face or group contact.

The two biggest obstacles that currently exist are the cultural changes required of society and the ability of the networks to support large-scale data transmissions that will be required. Both issues can and will be overcome; however, it may take several years before these issues are fully addressed. The vision of the new services is a range of things enabled by technology, such as multimedia, videoconferencing, telephones with built-in screens, interactive television, and access to libraries, archives, and public databases, all speeding along high-speed fiber-optic pathways. A basic part of the plan is that they will be available to anyone who wants to use them, similar to today's regular telephone service. As anyone who is familiar with the state of today's industries that will support the information superhighway is aware, this is an area that will be fraught with difficulties in attaining the goals of "universal access."

Despite the fact that there is a shared vision of an all-around service, with an all-purpose cable of some sort that will bring computing, telephone, television, movies, data, and all manner of other services into every home and business, many people feel that there is little chance that all local marketplaces can realistically support the overhead of such a service in the near future.

Companies worldwide are merging and forming partnerships to make the vision of universal access available to all. Because of the variability and unpredictability of the marketplace, the final determination of how and who will carry this information into our homes and businesses remains to be seen; however it is certain to happen. If the information superhighway runs along a cable, then the real universality of access – many people cite schools and universities as a particular concern since now they are usually charged for usage the same way as businesses – just may not be economically viable.

This is just one of the concerns on the path toward the future of information technology and communications. For auditors, the idea will bring a new set of complexities to providing accuracy, completeness, data integrity, security and control, and "understanding the system", one of the most basic requirements to audit well. Open systems architecture is intended to allow application software to run seamlessly on different platforms and various computers without requiring reprogramming. This is an idea that has been discussed for some time, but is still far from being reality. As organisations are coming to expect that the same software and hardware will be able to run on all of their computers, the software and hardware manufacturers are responding, and have made many strides in that direction. They are working toward a more seamless style of computing, through open systems, where software will be completely portable from one machine to another.

The Open Systems Foundation, or OSI, had working members from many of the industry leaders to help accomplish these goals: Their model is still in use for future efforts. The most widely used current example of what is closest to the perceived goals of planned open systems architecture can be seen in applications developed under the mainstream versions of the UNIX operating system.

In fact, many people now refer to UNIX when they talk about open systems, although it is only one of several planned open systems operating systems. As one of the most currently "open" environments, in many cases, applications written in one type of UNIX can run fairly easily on other of the various UNIX-based platforms, from PCs to minicomputers to mainframes. However, with some people estimating that there are over 150 variants of the UNIX operating system, sometimes the portability is not that smooth; those totally seamless transitions that everyone hopes for in the ideal situation do not exist, as many applications still must be recompiled or otherwise manipulated.

Even as everyone works toward the idea of open systems, there is still a great deal of difficulty in implementing them in reality. Just getting everyone together and agreeing on one universal operating system seems totally unlikely. There are many reasons why open systems architecture appeals to the business world. As anyone who has tried to run an application designed for one type of hardware on another already knows, this is still a problem. There is now a growing agreement about the need to set standards for true open systems.

The ability to follow those standards grows, and hardware and software organisations are developing systems to meet those goals. Among the reasons for the need, true open systems will allow people to use different-size computers from different manufacturers more easily. As it is now, the use of different systems, or sizes of computer, often requires complete retraining. Many manufacturers are planning, or already have, this kind of transportability among their own systems of different sizes and types.

A related idea is often referred to as "connectivity" or the ability of devices from different manufacturers to talk to each other. In many cases, there is still a need for the use of interfaces and protocols to allow such different systems to communicate, even though there is a greater degree of connectivity among machines with the same operating system, lessening the difficulty in making different machines communicate, but thus far not eliminating it. In order to take maximum advantage of distributed processing, companies will expect their computer vendors to allow the same software and databases to be run at all of their various sites on different-size machines without reprogramming. This will ensure both uniformity and efficiency in the initial design and implementation of software, as well as its subsequent maintenance.

It will also bring an end to years of confusion over the various types of machines and overall applicability of software to different business situations. Today, despite the move to open, client/server systems, it is still common for an organisation to have numerous vendors, with completely different packages performing similar tasks on microcomputers, minicomputers, and mainframes, without any ability to share the software, or even the data in many cases.

The use of truly open systems will affect companies of all sizes as they link to each other through networks, as described previously. True connectivity will allow different devices to communicate with each other, as well as for the devices at each site to do multiple other processing tasks in addition to communicating with outside parties. Controls over access to and use of the system will become all the more important as systems are linked together. One of the most universal standards currently being used for open systems is the Internet Protocol or IP for short. Sometime this is referred to as TCP/IP. Because many companies can and are using the Internet both within and outside the company, the ability to use this IP format is considered a form of open system.

The IP format, through the Internet, has expanded into the consumer market which, like the VHS Tape format, won the battle as more and more consumers bought VCRs that would only read VHS tapes, despite the fact that other formats were often of better quality. As more and more consumers use the Internet, it is likely that consumers may dictate that the open system of the future will be the Internet Protocol (IP).

2.2.2 Portability and Systems

Operational systems have become an integral part of business. As systems' power and portability increase, and their physical size decreases, today it is common-place to see portable data entry devices with wireless communications in many in-dustries. As an everyday example, most of the package delivery systems include handheld devices which allow input of information, screens for people to sign for their packages, and many other features which would have seemed unlikely at best twenty years ago. Most of these are real-time systems, where transactions are exe-cuted as they occur, and necessary information is updated immediately; the exist-ing data on the file is changed as it is updated with the new transaction data.

This is the mode which will prevail as systems themselves are updated and cli-ent/server architectures are put in place. Provisions are usually made for an auto-matic record to be kept of the previous version of the data, to provide for recovery or start-up if need be. Having an appropriate audit trail built into these transactions is also critical.

Many people use the term real-time when they are actually talking about on-line systems. On-line systems provide immediate responses to queries for informa-tion, but do not normally change the data on file at that time. The distinction be-tween on-line systems and on-line real-time systems is still worth making, since many legacy systems are still in use where on-line entry takes place all day but the actual update takes place in batch, overnight or at another specified time.

A shadow or memo update to a copy of the file takes place immediately, to al-low for reference to the most current information during the day, before the actual update occurs. Despite the newer systems, the number of legacy systems still in use in corporations worldwide is quite large. New software packages called "wrappers" are being developed to try to use the legacy data in a more object-oriented fashion.

Miniaturization of Systems

The sight of business people carrying the black nylon briefcases which hold note-books and other very portable computers has become ubiquitous in airports throughout the world. The ever-decreasing size and lowering costs of systems have made it possible for the lightest notebooks to come in at around three pounds, with more functionality and huge hard drives as compared to their earlier "luggable" brethren.

This trend will only continue, as the miniaturization of components increases. The ability of smaller, portable systems – eventually to work with voice input and better handwriting recognition for pen-based input – to help in the day-to-day run-ning of businesses increases all the more as standard processes are automated fur-ther and linked together within the system.

In the delivery systems cited above, it is possible to find out where a package is physically by reference to its bar-coded tracking number in the system. In the past, finding something that quickly would not have been possible since the systems weren't linked appropriately enough to do so, and individual items were not tagged as clearly with as much information.

2.2.3 Integration of Applications

Many of the operational systems in use today, for example in manufacturing, include all of the processes from managing inventory and the shop floor to providing strategic information for planning a business's future, such as making informed decisions on product lines which are likely to succeed and which should be discontinued, based on trend analyses and other information these systems can provide.

Accounting information generally is a by-product of these systems, and its processing often takes place within them in real-time. Initially, business computing was used primarily for accounting or financial systems. When it was used for operational purposes, as in, for example governing a process flow on the shop floor, the system used was usually separate from the computer that processed the accounting data. Results of the operation were entered into the "accounting computer" separately so that the same data or information was often entered repeatedly.

Today, integration of operational systems and accounting systems is pretty much complete. One example of this is a just-in-time (JIT) inventory system. Another example is tying reservation systems with revenue systems, as in a large hotel, whose systems in turn feed the corporate headquarters systems, in order for the company as a whole to have accurate and complete financial data.

This effect has already been seen in the large and middle-size organisations. Smaller companies still use their computers initially for accounting purposes. As they grow larger, smaller companies follow in the large companies' tracks by using the computers for operational purposes. There are also a growing number of totally integrated packages available for businesses of all sizes.

2.3 Productivity Aspect of the Technology

The service sector alone is thought to have spent $ 800 billion on information technology, and the lack of increase in real productivity in this sector was thought by many to be among the worst in overall results. This, of course, reflected the economy itself, as there also seemed to be no real gains in the standard of living. The entire nation's productivity increased at only about one percent a year, not what an optimist would have hoped for, at any rate.

Now, in the 2000 onward, many companies are actually beginning to see some real returns on that information technology investment. However, there are still many economists in the United States who feel that the full realization of true productivity gains has still not begun to occur. Bill Gates, CEO of Microsoft, recently compared the computing industry today to the automobile industry of the 1920s.

Many companies thought that they could automate even further and eliminate staff, all the while making those who remained far more productive through the use of technology. A goal of much of this growing use of computers, robotics, and automation in general has been increased productivity.

It is estimated that during the 1980s, U.S. companies invested an incredible amount of money in information technology. Some put that number at one trillion dollars, a hard figure to comprehend, let along figure out what the return on the investment ought to be. Yet, in early years of this decade, many surveys showed that the expected productivity gains from all of this investment in technology seemed not to be what was hoped for.

While many improvements had been made to automobiles in the 1920s and many Americans could afford to buy one, there are still significant improvements to come. Automobiles, while seen on every street, were often limited to one per family, and many families did not own a car. Like cars in the 1920s, computers are often limited to one per household.

A computer for every person in the future is just as likely as the two, three, or four cars per family today. It is apparent that the productivity gains in the future will be as significant as the difference between a Model 'A' Ford and a new 2004 Ford. These gains in productivity will, however, produce a significant increase in the complexity of auditing and the control of the systems that produce those productivity gains.

2.4 Business Process Re-engineering

Now, through Executive Information Systems (EIS), for one example, the data is transmitted from the sales force or the monitoring systems on the manufacturing floor to an enterprise data repository which can be queried easily by executives without computer training using GUIs and mouse-driven point-and-click technology. They have a faster interface to the real information they need without the need for that middle layer of people.

They also have the ability to send out their own commands in record time. Through the efficient design of decision support systems, client/server tools, databases, and computer networks, the heads of a unit or an organisation can have almost immediate access to data that used to take weeks to assemble. With increasingly workable handwriting recognition, usable Personal Data Assistants (PDAs) with wireless links will be the new norm. As corporations continue to re-engineer their business processes and cut back on staff through downsizing, the theory is that re-engineered processes and workflow technology will make it possible to do more work with far fewer people. Many of those cut – most often from the ranks of middle management – used to form an important link between shop floor processes and executives who were far removed from the action. There will be a different workplace.

There is even a trend toward no workplace at all, as many become telecommuters, linked constantly through cellular PDAs and notebooks but without any "real" office to go to. We are already seeing how the use of information technology is eliminating entire layers of management, automating warehouses to the point where there are more robotics than workers, and changing the roles of managers dramatically.

Those who are retained despite downsizing will be expected to use technology to do more things faster, with increased responsibility, more current, better data at their fingertips, but far fewer workers. Even now, there are estimates that people who do the same jobs but without computers earn more than 10 percent less than the computer literate.

The availability of efficient computing power and communications, together with software packages, will allow all aspects of American business to benefit from gains caused by the more efficient and effective use of computer systems. Controls over who can enter data, audit trails to indicate who did what, and how it is reported will become critical as the systems update information immediately and people rely on that information to make critical decisions. Backup and recovery procedures must be provided and used.

2.5 Intelligent Systems

Other terms for these systems are expert systems, or decision support systems, which rely on the data and rules people have developed and employed within the software. As such, these systems can make seemingly intelligent choices, since they have been given the rules and data needed to make those choices. However, this is not true artificial intelligence, which would require that they be capable of original thought. As currently defined, the term "intelligent systems" has replaced the use of "artificial intelligence." It is the ability to use software that can bring the knowledge of experts to bear on a particular task, or to make some decisions about the data the systems are processing. There is not yet a computer that can really think, in the sense of imagining new concepts, although computer scientists are working on it.

Through the implementation of nonlinear approaches such as fuzzy logic, machines are coming closer to humanlike thought patterns. Intelligent system concepts are becoming commonplace, as many operational systems depend to some extent on modules which can take some other action or make decisions. The benefits of intelligent software have led to its use in many kinds of systems, found on the shop floor, in warehouses, and so forth.

These systems are embedded in many applications, whether purchased or developed in-house by formal management information systems (MIS), and have been accepted as part of the computing environment. Neural networks, which have the ability to "learn" from the examples and cases provided as they process data are also growing in use.

These allow for the transactions being processed to provide new information to the system itself, which then incorporates it into its processing in the future. There are neural nets, as they are more familiarly called, in place and functioning in some systems today, and some are in use by auditors to monitor huge on line transaction processing (OLTP) systems. Intelligent modules have become a major part of many operational systems. The ability to bring expertise to users through computer software has shown considerable advances over the last five years, to the extent that now these systems are rarely discussed as new or different.

They have had the most dramatic effect on large companies with many employees and high turnover, where the standard working procedures are embodied in the systems. The use of such systems allows retention of the knowledge pool, even when key employees leave the organisation. They are in use daily, doing such things as monitoring credit histories, reviewing user accounts, and the like. Medium-size companies will also make considerable use of such systems once they are within affordable range.

They are ideally suited for organisations that cannot attract experts to work for them. Through acquisition of expert systems, these companies will have access to experts. Smaller businesses, especially in professional areas, will make considerable use of these systems to maintain a high quality of work. Albeit with different motives, all segments of American business will take advantage of this technology. As noted previously, numerous areas of technology will have varying effects on organisations of different sizes. Adoption of the technology depends on particular driving forces. In some industries, such as financial services, there is little choice. An individual company in this segment can hardly afford to ignore technological advances.

Such a company must adapt to remain competitive. In other industries, implementation of a particular technology may be slower, but the advances made in technology have had an impact on most of the business world that cannot be ignored. A continuing assessment of the technology will become critical, both to survive and to position products and services better. To employ technology effectively, organisations need implementation skills.

While the equipment or other vendor provides tools (for example, currently, the telephone companies are often those to provide the network; hardware vendors provide the computers, hubs, and routers; and software houses provide the network management tools), it will be up to the organisation to implement those tools in a timely and cost-effective manner.

The lack of trained technologists is often a considerable risk factor in developing or implementing advanced systems. When considering the skill sets in relation to an organisation's needs, it is important to note that the competition for people with skills in many of these areas is already severe. As technology continues to trickle down to the middle-market and medium-size companies, the competition for skilled personnel may become even more acute. The impact of the Year 2000 has, as expected, contributed significantly to the demand for both skilled technology staff as well as staff trained in many of the older technologies due to the need to work with those technologies as part of either upgrading the existing systems or in many cases converting the older systems to the newer technology.

Current salaries are significantly higher for trained staff of two years ago. In addition, staff with specific skills can command salaries that are two to three times the amounts that would have been expected two years ago. Decisions about whether to use outside resources in certain of these areas may be coloured by the fact that an organisation is unable to get that particular kind of assistance. For example, in the area of advanced system design and implementation, many organisations need to change their requirements in order to fill their jobs.

As a result of resource constraints, there may be a decline in in-house design and programming of systems and a shift to packaged software selection and integration. In many places, this shift is already quite evident. Another logical result is that large computer manufacturers provide much-needed consulting services in networking, database, and system integration.

Clearly, organisations that can afford it will use outside resources to obtain skill sets not available internally. For some time, larger organisations have relied on training and growing skills internally. Owing to timing and today's competitive pressures this course of action may no longer work. Conceivably, these organisations will move toward the new technology using facility management by a third party for certain systems until they can "grow their own." Outsourcing of technology is another answer.

Medium-size organisations may have even fewer choices. They will be pursued by vendors offering combined software-hardware solutions. Manufacturers are increasing their efforts in their Independent Software Vendor (ISV) and Value Added Reseller (VAR) programs to meet those requirements and capture the market. A medium-size company may go to third parties for assistance in system selection, but does not, except in unusual situations, design and implement its own software. A small company is far less likely than the medium-size company to be able to attain its own internal technology skills.

Vendors offer software/hardware solutions that the small company will likely accept as is, as it has been doing for some time. Much of this will be done through retail computer stores, as well as through small consultants who are VARs. Their buyers need assistance in selection and implementation. Whatever happens in the various-size organisations, it is clear that an abundance of computer power will be available in intelligent workstations and that the distinction between microcomputers and midrange or minicomputers and mainframes will continue to blur. The availability of less-expensive computing power will have a profound effect on all hardware and software vendors in the products they will offer, and on consultants in the field.

2.6 Auditors and Changing Technology

In reviewing the effects of technology, it is apparent that it affects not only systems developers and line management but auditors as well. Auditors can no longer choose to ignore technology, because they simply cannot perform their function without understanding how their organisation is using technology to run the business. The business generates the numbers that appear on the financial statements. The financial audit will change significantly as business changes, because of the use of technologies such as networking, client/server, and real-time systems.

Use of these technologies, among other effects, minimizes or eliminates historical paper audit trails and, therefore, changes how audits are performed. The use of software to assist in the audit function will have to respond to changes in technology to maintain high-quality work. At the same time, equipment and software vendors have made advanced software available to query databases and generate reports. Generic tools used to query databases, such as SQL (Structured Query Language) are used increasingly by auditors, and seem to have begun to eliminate audit software as we know it. Tools used to fine-tune networks and LANs can also be used by auditors to ascertain who has permission to do what, and where they reside in the network. Vendors are also expanding their efforts to supply the necessary software, particularly in areas such as security and microcomputer-based audit retrieval and automated audit work paper tools.

2.7 Strategic Use of Technology and Audit Implications

From an attest viewpoint, there will no longer be the traditional paper trails that were needed when people used to audit around the computer. Indeed, many major vendors now consider paper an option, although many in the industry view the idea of the totally paperless office as one which will never occur.

Even now, one survey indicated that there are still more faxes sent than Email, despite the huge increase in electronic mail users. As industry trend moves toward a transaction-processing facility or real-time mode, screen displays will give up-to-the-minute status reports, and the audit trail will be an electronic one. In fact, well-designed electronic audit trails may provide more data than is available currently.

To retain data, it will be moved into archiving in a machine-sensible mode through imaging technology, probably for storage on optical disk. Companies must become technology companies in order to stay competitive in the marketplace. Companies' expert use of technology to deliver value to customers is what determines their success.

For example, geographic location may not be significant to consumers of companies that offer help desks and same-day delivery of goods by air, since consumers receive the same efficient service regardless of where the company is located. Increased mergers and partnerships may therefore result in order to provide full services to customers from only one or two vendors. This increased focus on technology also puts additional pressure on auditors to upgrade their skills to stay knowledgeable about the current marketplace.

The use of CD-ROM as a storage and distribution medium is growing daily as the costs come down. The auditor will have to understand access routines that give system entry, thereby governing authorization and division of duties, in addition to understanding how the system does computation. Understanding how the systems work and are linked together becomes especially important when they are heavily networked and new systems allow processing of data from anywhere in the network. Visualizing the network as a series of telephones that can call each other through a number of switches that can be just about anywhere, it is possible to gain an understanding of how a network operates, except that in this case the switches are governed by network managers. For example, the network software generally does the routing of requests for processing of transactions from a client or workstation on the network.

The actual processing may take place at the client, at the server, at another server or client in another system, or any variation thereof. The network manager often knows who can connect to whom by using the network operating system routings. What each of the nodes can do; can be defined in the system resource definitions. For external systems that may be linked in, this information is rarely available to the other organisation, a potential control issue.

When a transaction originates at a client PC, some editing of data takes place; the request is then forwarded to another processor, or server, that does additional edits and validations. It is then forwarded to another processor that updates a master file and prepares a response. The updated master database and responses are routed by the servers to local smaller processors.

At the originating PC or workstation, the user may not know which machine the transaction is processing on, or whether there is more than one processor involved, or whether appropriate controls exist over those processors. If one processor is busy, the system may move the transaction to another processor to do the work. This increasing complexity means that it can be very hard for the auditors of such systems to ascertain exactly how they work. The auditor must be able to follow the transaction flow from client to server, and eventually back again, as well as to identify the various resources and how they are controlled.

The auditor is concerned with the completeness, accuracy, and existence of transactions and related results. For example: Where should security be exercised? Where will there be a need to authorize the transaction? What kind of security should be exercised at each client and at each server? How does it all come together to form a controlled system?

The auditor will need an understanding of the network and the various resource definitions of what each server can do, and who can access each client. The auditor must also understand which of the applications are on each server and the controls to ensure accuracy and authorization.

When looking at networking and client/server computing, auditors are really examining a newer method of providing distributed processing. Distribution can occur in many different modes. What is important are the controls to ensure completeness, accuracy, and existence at each of the distributed nodes, or servers. In some areas only object code is distributed to the nodes, as is done by large companies concerned that uniform controls are applied at the various processing nodes.

Such distribution is typical of companies with uniform operations. In this case, auditors using the network facilities can compare the object code loaded at the distributed server facility to the Authorized Version maintained at the headquarters or development site. In a similar manner, access control software at the nodes can be tested by auditors electronically from those nodes, or remotely, and analysed for propriety at any given location. Very often, the central site retains summary records, or even detailed backup, of what is at the nodes. The auditor may do testing of the data centrally, or test the data at the node through the network. The auditor may download selected data to an audit workstation as a node on the network, for analytical review or other purposes.

Auditors will encounter a more difficult situation the more diverse the operations are on a network. When some programs are developed locally, and access control software is selected on a local basis, while the central computer on the network may still assemble summary data for consolidation and analytical purposes, the auditor will have to ensure that the locally developed software includes proper controls. Auditors can use the network to sample data and perform appropriate analytical reviews. As suggested previously, the ability of software to be processed on any node has significant advantages to organisations.

It also offers significant advantages to auditors. When they develop or use software that conforms to the standards, it can be used throughout the network with no change, limited only by machine capacity. Combined with SQL and databases, auditors can take maximum advantage of software for selection and analytical purposes.

Central to the architecture of advanced computing is the use of shared databases throughout the network. For example, relational databases usually have distributed versions to run on the various sizes of computers: mainframes, midrange or minicomputers, and microcomputers, PCs, or workstations. The use of SQL, which is now an ANSI (American National Standards Institute) standard for database query, makes it possible to do ad hoc queries of the database for information or data required by the auditor. The ability to have the same view of data throughout the network is critical and is part of most current strategies. Independent software vendors will have to provide their own proprietary databases for various-size machines to allow such transparency. What does this mean to the auditor?

The old-style audit software retrieval packages required "flattening" of the database and/or reformatting records to be able to foot files, select data, and so forth, usually freezing the files at a given point in time. With the expanded use of SQL, the auditor can perform many of these tasks dynamically across the entire network from a central point without special coding, and with only limited training. Standard SQL shells can be generated to perform routine audit tasks. The auditor can browse the databases and transfer data in the same format to the workstation to allow further analytical work. For many years, there has been discussion about the ability to record and process transactions as they occur, in real-time, and the ability to provide continuous transaction monitoring.

To trace the history of real-time systems, consider the earliest airline reservation systems. They processed a transaction (a seat request) against seating availability of a flight. Such a system cost many millions of dollars and had no effect on the financial records. It required massive computers and had limitations on the number of terminals that could access the system. In the same type of system today, thousands of terminals located at travel agencies, airports, and so forth have access, with many providing direct entry into the financial systems. Access is also available to consumers through on-line services. In order to track such huge and varied environments, the use of embedded intelligent modules to monitor transaction processing and other systems is becoming widespread.

2.8 Internal Controls and Auditing

As we have seen throughout this chapter, the changes in technology have been so fast and so dramatic that their effects on the auditor are truly significant. There may be elimination of some of the traditional controls, such as batch totaling, and more reliance on computer matching to ensure completeness. Authorization will be directed more than ever by the computer, with extremely heavy reliance on access controls for approval to proceed. Traditional paper that allowed an historical audit will disappear, and auditors will have to adopt a forward-looking, prospective way to audit. Auditors will do much of their auditing on a continuous basis from workstations.

Why is all of this so important? Given a lack of paper, auditors will be unable to re-perform programmed procedures over the entire period under review. Using an auditor's workstation on the system, auditors will monitor the flow of transactions and use such techniques as interactive test facilities. Monitoring controls used by management to run the business will also be reviewed by auditors to ascertain areas where controls may need improvement.

Relying so heavily on computer-based controls, auditors of all kinds will need to have at least a basic understanding of the various information technology or general controls, such as systems implementation and maintenance, and computer operations. Security – how it is exercised over the application systems and how security is applied to the network – will be critical to the audit, since the application controls will rely on the security to be able to ensure that application controls can function. Understanding controls over system changes will require testing of maintenance controls.

To ensure that changes are not made in an unauthorized manner will require understanding how the program and data security controls function as well. Recoverability will be key to these systems; thus auditors must also understand computer operations. Networking and client/server architectures increase the importance of understanding where and how transactions can be routed and which nodes on the network can do what. In batch systems, auditors tended to rely on manual controls and review of reports to determine whether a significant error or irregularity had occurred. Batch controls ensured completeness:

Although individual details could be changed in an unauthorized manner, the total could be controlled manually. For computer-generated transactions, major reliance was on the maintenance controls, computer operations, and program security. Now, with real-time systems, auditors must rely on the data file and program security controls as a primary method to enforce division of duties, to prevent irregularities, and, if irregularities occur, to detect them.

Preventive and access control are crucial in real-time systems. From an audit perspective, auditors will have to understand the system development life cycle to evaluate whether appropriate controls and quality are built into the system, maintenance controls to understand whether changes are made properly, computer operations for access and recoverability, and program and data file security for validity and integrity. Since most of the applications that formerly were written in-house are now acquired from software vendors, auditors will need an acquisition review model.

Software purchases range from large mainframe systems with elective options that change the way accounting transactions are recorded and controlled to the now-endemic spreadsheets. Auditors must have a detailed understanding of a package and of how it is implemented in the environment. The in-house IT people may have done extensive modifications that change the way the package really works. To understand more basic applications, often vendors offer courses in their packages and how to implement auditability. Many packages have report generators or other utilities that can help the auditor foot files and select items for further investigation or analytics.

The auditor must understand the use of packages and their controls. The effect of an operational system on audit procedures is dramatic, as can be seen by a JIT inventory system. The system affects audit work with respect to inventory valuation and existence; and in some cases, audit risk in those areas increases significantly. To understand whether the system is working or not, auditors must know the system and its terminology.

Newer client/server systems will be integrated, and as part of the process, accounting records updated automatically. For example, in an insurance company, claims are settled on-line between the adjustor and the claimant. In newer systems, imaging may even provide graphic details of the claim, such as a photograph of damage. The adjustor uses a terminal to query the system as to limits on a particular type of damage, and to find out whether the claimant is insured for the particular damage, and has a check cut on the terminal for the claim.

At the same time, the claim file, claim statistics, and other files are updated. In a manufacturing environment, the router is on a screen. As it passes each workstation, a function key is depressed, to remove the appropriate parts, inventory, and debit work in process for parts and appropriate labour.

The finished goods are debited and work in process credited. In retailing, the process begins with scanning the uniform product code. The SKU inventory is updated and entered into the buyer's records for automatic reordering. The open-to-buy books are updated, as are the sales plans for the sites. Accounting records are by-products of this system. The point here is that the business process results in the accounting records automatically. To understand how this is done by an operational system is crucial to auditing those systems appropriately.

The growth of expert systems or AI to help accomplish work has become a reality. Such systems for accountants, for example, are found in specialized areas such as Financial Accounting Standards Board (FASB) interpretations and income taxes and are gradually expanding into wider areas such as internal control evaluations for complex computer systems.

The whole idea behind expert systems is to bring the knowledge of experts to people's fingertips – not always to make decisions, but to help make decisions. These expert systems will be extremely useful in staff training. At PricewaterhouseCoopers (PwC), these techniques are being used now. For example, the ExperTAX package assists in tax planning and calculating tax accruals. This system is used by general practice and tax personnel, not computer-oriented people.

It holds the tax expertise of many leading tax practitioners and helps the engagement team do its work. Combined with making use of networking, connectivity, transparent databases, and an audit workstation or node, access to data can be combined with intelligent systems to help auditors do their work. The advent of powerful microcomputers and intelligent workstations offers the auditor an unparalleled opportunity to bring yesterday's mainframe power into the auditor's office. Desktop, notebook, or workstation, today it is easy to buy powerful multi-tasking machines with 4 to 16 gigabyte disk, and CD-ROM storage, since optical disks can store large amounts of data at low rates.

Data ranging from 40 to 60 gigabytes are available on personal computers. Costs are coming way down for all end users. Such a system for auditors might work as follows:

- data is written from tape (print image or other) to write-once, read many CD-ROMS, off-line from the computer
- the system builds indexes to find the data required
- next, the system searches the data on the CD-ROM and processes it using various software packages: analytics, spreadsheets, charting graphics and so forth.
- last, the system displays, prints, or does further processing of results

Such a process obviates requiring access to the mainframe for audit work, avoiding downloading and connect time. It would bring greater masses of data to PCs for detailed audit or analytical work. The increasing availability of databases on optical disks allows greater use of analytics. (Time-sharing networks used to be the only way to gain access to such data.)

The ability to provide massive storage on disk used in this way combines mainframe power on a microcomputer with tremendous availability of data, which may revolutionize auditing through microcomputers, using the technology in a network or standalone environment. When looking at how technology will affect audits, it is important to consider how management will run business using technology. What sort of monitoring and reports will they have to control the business?

The quality of the information will govern the ability to detect material error or irregularity from numbers being generated by the system. It is critical that these reports contain the appropriate data to allow such detection to take place. This top-down approach will be important to understand. Auditors must view such management reports in terms of audit objectives: completeness, accuracy, existence, and valuation.

To the extent that management provides the necessary controls in these systems, the more auditors can rely on them and their consistent application. The risk is that errors or irregularities will not be discovered on a timely basis. With all this system complexity, how rapidly would an error or irregularity be discovered? Audit teams will require technology skills to assess that risk. Knowledge of microcomputers alone does not qualify an individual to audit complex computer-based systems. In the auditing world of the year 2000 and beyond, all will feel the impact of technology changes, from the smallest company to the largest worldwide organisation. Small companies will use technology in order to become part of a large network of customers or suppliers, potentially driving along the information superhighway along with other businesses of all sizes.

Large companies will continue to be the leaders and set the pace for technology to help provide strategic advantage. Auditors will use their own on-line, real-time client/server systems, developed in-house or using purchased software packages, on PDAs, notebooks, PCs and workstations linked in LANs with gateways to larger networks. Auditors in companies of all sizes will need a basic level of knowledge in understanding and using computers, as their colleagues in IT audit will need to become even more technical and have special skills to perform their functions effectively and efficiently.

The use of analytical tools to help detect and report on control weaknesses or areas that need audit attention, and knowledge-based or expert systems to help assess risks, plan engagements, will be possible throughout the profession. Auditors of all areas must be able to use them to be successful in this century.

3 Generation-X Technologies and IT Auditing

As businesses increasingly use information and communication technology to process their accounting systems, auditors need to gather critical information more efficiently and effectively. The tools and techniques of modern generation-X enterprise technology signal the end of the traditional manual and centralized systems audit methodologies and procedures. Technology has made input of information for transactions and events simpler - and evaluating the related controls and results more critical. Accumulating sufficient evidence needed to construct an informed decision means understanding where to look for that evidence, what control procedures to consider and how to evaluate those procedures. Today's enterprise systems extend beyond the traditional corporate data centre (Marlin 1999, Pravica 1999, Robinson 1999) to include customers, suppliers, partners, and electronic marketplaces. Because the adoption of e-business transaction models has significantly outpaced the development of tools and technologies to deal with the information explosion (Saracevic, 1999; Lesser et al, 2000), many businesses find their systems breaking under the sheer volume and diversity of their data. Enterprises that can quickly extract critical nuggets of information from the sea of accessible data and transform them into valuable business assets are in a strong position to dominate their markets. Such an undertaking is no small task.

This Chapter addresses the enrichment of basic information systems assurance measures and models. In addition, recent developments in enterprise technology are addressed and probable assurance measures are identified. The focus of this chapter is on the following questions.

- What are the state-of-art technologies in the integrated enterprise-based information systems arena?
- Why the information systems integration is considered such a challenge?
- Why does assured information emanate from assured systems?
- Is information assurance a function of strategic importance?
- What are the existing information assurance and control measures available to the professionals from the cross sectional fields?

The information integration challenge to the next generation enterprises are characterized by reviewing the next generation technologies and platforms with their components and describing the process of integration in terms of internal controls and assurance. Then, the impact of information integration on audit processes and procedures, both external and internal, is discussed. Next, the information assurance is addressed as a function of strategic importance for the information systems-centric organisations' well-being in the eyes of its stakeholders. In the end, it describes various measures of information assurance and controls devised by the enterprising entities, including the professional bodies of internal, external and the information systems security auditors. Finally, future needs and directions for both basic and applied researches are briefly described.

3.1 Generation-X Enterprise Technologies

For the past three decades, data management systems have been at the core of enterprise software infrastructure (Petreley 2002). The introduction of the relational data model and the concept of data independence (Stephen, 1986) revolutionized the data management industry and quickly overtook network and hierarchical systems for large-scale data management. Over the next two decades, the relational database is expected to be transformed into a high-performance, high-volume query processing engine (Ling et al. 2001) mainly through innovations in storage and retrieval techniques, concurrency control and recovery, and query processing technology such as cost-based optimization, etc.

Distributed systems and parallel processing techniques enabled global enterprises to manage large volumes of distributed data. Extensible database architectures (Blake et al. 2002) have allowed data types, access strategies, and indexing schemes to be easily introduced as new business needs arise. Federated database technology (Saran et al. 1996) provided a powerful and flexible means for transparent access to heterogeneous, distributed data sources. As database management system [DBMS] technology evolved to manage business data, other important technologies evolved in parallel to make the tasks of managing business logic and business processes easier. Data warehouses, data mining, and on-line analytical processing technology (Cody et al. 2002) added business intelligence, providing a means for discovery- driven and hypothesis-driven analysis over business data to identify trends and patterns and play out "what-if" scenarios. Workflow systems helped to automate business processes, providing the infrastructure to manage processes such as order fulfilment from step to step, assign tasks in the process to the right resources, and invoke automated steps at the appropriate times.

Business applications evolved alongside data management and enterprise management systems, exploiting the best features of both to create sophisticated software packages that form the foundation of nearly all of today's businesses. Significant development and computing resources are devoted to transporting the data from one system to another, and transforming the data from one format to another. Likewise, data federation has a solid research foundation and several commercial implementations.

Databases deal quite naturally and robustly with the storage, retrieval, and reliability requirements for traditional business data, and can easily accommodate a variety of data and access patterns. A platform that exploits and enhances the DBMS architecture at all levels is in the best position to provide robust end-to-end information integration. In a business environment, this translates into automatic cooperation between enterprises. Any enterprise requiring business interaction with another enterprise can automatically discover and select the appropriate optimal web services relying on selection policies (Bussler et al, 2002).

Web services can be invoked automatically and payment processes can be initiated. Any necessary mediation is applied based on data and process ontology and the automatic translation of their concepts into each other. An example is supply chain relationships where an enterprise manufacturing short-lived goods has to frequently seek suppliers as well as buyers dynamically. Instead of employees constantly searching for suppliers and buyers, the web service infrastructure does it automatically within the defined constraints. Still, more work needs to be done before the web service infrastructure can make this vision come true.

The explosion of the internet and e-business in recent years has caused a secondary explosion in the amounts and types of information available to enterprise applications. This abundance of information presents an exciting cross-industry business opportunity (Simpson 2001, Dykstra 2002, Bansal 2002). The prime challenge facing today's businesses is information integration (Liu et al, 2002; and Anderson et al, 2002). Enterprise applications of today must interact with databases, application servers, content management systems, data warehouses, workflow systems, search engines, message queues, Web crawlers, mining and analysis packages, and other enterprise integration applications. Similarly, these enterprise applications must use a variety of programming interfaces (Waddington and Hutchison 1999) and understand a variety of languages and formats. They should be enabled to extract and combine data in multiple formats generated by multiple delivery mechanisms.

Clearly, the boundaries that have traditionally existed between database management systems, content management systems, data warehouses, and other data management systems are blurring, and a great need has arisen for a platform that provides a unified view of all of these services and the data they deliver. More data will be generated in this decade, if this trend continues, than in all of recorded history. The widespread adoption of the Internet has made nearly all of it just a URL (uniform resource locator) away. These enterprise-wide systems might interact with databases, application servers, content management systems, data warehouses, workflow systems, search engines, message queues, WebCrawler's, mining and analysis packages, and other applications. Therefore, the challenge for enterprise applications today is information integration (Liu et al. 2002).

Information integration is a technology approach that combines core elements from data management systems (Hennel 2002, Heidorn 2002), content management systems (Anonymous 2001), data warehouses (Merher 2001, Arlinghaus 2001), and other enterprise applications into a common platform. These systems combine data with different time properties, such as real time stock tickers (Anonymous 2000), news wires (McGuire 1999)), databases, slightly out-of-date midtier caches, database replicas (Kemme and Alonso 2000), and data warehouses. Stieren (1999) indicates that such data are generated by multiple delivery mechanisms in a variety of formats e.g. relational tables, XML documents, images, video, and sound.

3.2 Information Systems Integration: A Challenge

Clearly, the world is becoming more wired. While all countries have become more connected over the last few decades, network proliferation has been concentrated in the most developed countries, especially in the US and Canada. These countries continue to computerize the public and private infrastructures, which now run everything from telecommunications and banking services to electric power generation and distribution. The still-accelerating development, proliferation, and adoption of information and communications technologies have benefited the world enormously. The nations of North America have made huge strides in science and medicine, and have greatly increased productivity.

However, as computers and networks become more ubiquitous, we grow more dependent on them. Thus, we become more vulnerable to criminals and terrorists who would use these systems against us. Just as technology has improved the efficiency and effectiveness of business operations, it has also increased terrorists' abilities to launch sophisticated attacks against our increasingly interdependent infrastructures. Information today is worth more than ever. Whereas in the past, attackers could only collect information while it was being transmitted from place to place, today our data is vulnerable 24 hours a day, wherever it is located. Systems to handle the various disaster scenarios must rely on data management systems and enterprise applications that come with their own set of application programming interfaces (APIs) and tools, and an enterprise must develop complex inhouse integration and administration software to maintain them. Although these different scenarios come from a diverse set of industries, they indicate that the boundaries that have traditionally existed between DBMSs, data warehouses, content management systems, and other data transformation and integration services are blurring. Various similarities between these scenarios illustrate a common set of requirements for robust information integration platform.

Enterprise applications require support for XML as a first-class data model. Although the relational data model has driven business applications over the past three decades, XML has become the lingua franca for portable data. Businesses rely heavily on it for enterprise integration. XML is more suitable for representing both semi-structured and unstructured data, and, unlike the relational model, it also provides a standard representation of the meta-data to describe those data. This flexibility allows financial services company to receive reports from multiple publishers, provides a common language for a freight broker to negotiate bids with multiple carriers, and enables a telecommunications company to integrate the various customer support systems acquired through its mergers.

Clearly, businesses rely on multiple, diverse sources of data in their enterprise applications. A financial services company relies on real-time data feeds, databases, spreadsheets, and media servers. A freight broker depends on real-time access to external flight scheduling systems and carriers. A telecommunications application requires access to multiple autonomous vertical applications. These scenarios make use of information consolidation, where data are both collected from multiple sources and consolidated in a central repository, and federation, in which data from multiple autonomous sources are accessed as part of a search but are not moved from their original sources. Some sources of data conform to a schema, whereas other sources, such as information portals do not.

Because an enterprise receives information from so many sources, meta-data to describe the data available from a source are as important as the data. Today's enterprise systems require sophisticated search and data transformation services with increasingly demanding performance requirements. Such scenarios require parametric search, full-text search, mining, and digital asset management services over data stored in a variety of systems and in a variety of formats. Although specialized systems with different APIs exist today to handle each kind of search, a single system that provides access to all data and services through a unified interface would simplify application development and provide better performance.

One scenario also demonstrates that business processes are inherently asynchronous. Customers reporting problems are satisfied with a confirmation number and do not need to remain on the phone while the problem is repaired. Busy stock traders may not want to poll for information, but instead prefer to be notified when events of interest occur. Furthermore, continuous availability requirements mean that applications must continue running in the face of failures. Data sources and applications come up and go down on a regular basis, and data feeds may be interrupted by hardware or network failures. If the telecommunications customer service system goes down, field technicians should continue to work on repairs assigned to them. If a particular carrier is not available, the freight broker should negotiate bids from the carriers that are available. A single system that provides access to all data and services through a unified interface would simplify development and provide better performance.

Finally, the complexity of the applications in these scenarios illustrates an essential requirement for open standards. Such applications weave together a host of data sources, management systems, and applications. Without standards governing their interfaces and a consistent programming model, the effort to integrate and administer new sources in this dynamic environment could be astronomical, and the cost to recruit and retain staff with the skills necessary to develop the integration software might quickly overtake the value of the system itself.

A layered architecture for a robust technology platform that addresses the information integration challenge is depicted in the figure 1. The base layer supports storage, retrieval, and transformation of data in different formats from different sources. A second layer of integration built on top of the base layer draws from enterprise integration applications to provide the infrastructure to transparently embed data access services into enterprise applications and business processes. The layer at the top provides standards-based programming models and flexible query language support to access the rich set of services and data provided by the base and integration layers.

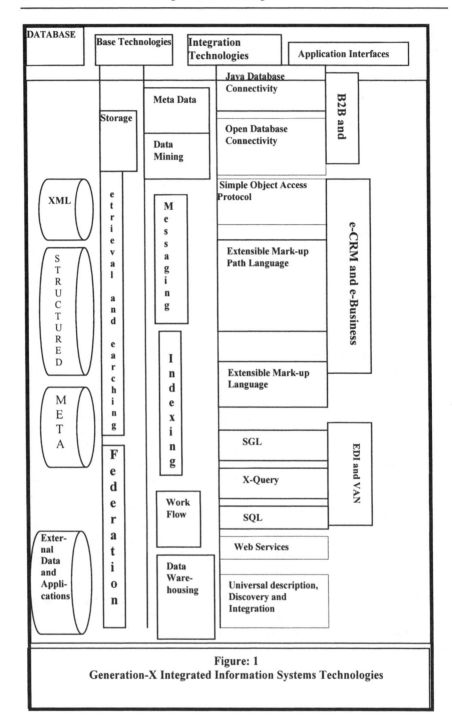

Figure: 1
Generation-X Integrated Information Systems Technologies

As shown in the figure 1, the base layer is at the heart of the information integration platform, and provides a core set of services to store and retrieve heterogeneous data. The base layer is dependent on a high-performance DBMS engine extended at all levels with data integration functionality. These extensions include support for XML as a native data store, XQuery as a native data interrogation language, and a federated data access component that provides access to external data and applications as though the data and applications were natively managed by the engine. The convergence of communications networks with the systems, however, also increases business susceptibility to cyber attacks. Indeed, by the end of the twentieth century, businesses had become more vulnerable than any other segment of the society to cyber attacks aiming to interrupt, degrade, or destroy vital services such as electrical power, banking, or stock trading. Current trends indicate that information integration is a cross-industry challenge. Industries from financial services to manufacturing have all been touched by the volumes and diversity of data and continual demands introduced by a web-based business model. Securing the business networks is a huge task, though the discussion on security is not within the scope of this paper. However, the basic understanding of security shall be the mainstay of identifying the assurance provided by the information systems. Such assured systems in turn will be essential for obtaining assured information for decision making by all levels including the stakeholders.

3.3 Assured Information Emanates from Assured Systems

Strickland and Willard (2002) stated that it is the assured and trusted information systems that carry the integrity element in the information provided for decision making. What matters most is the quality of information and data retrieved from the databases whose integrity is neither assured nor trustworthy. The assurance starts from the data gathering stage. They further boost their point by citing the case of the issuance of a US visa to a known terrorist, who ultimately masterminded the World Trade Centre (WTC) garage bombing in 1993 or the issue of student visa after his death to the terrorist who took active part in the 9/11 plane crash. This viewpoint reiterates that assured information can only emanate from an assured information system. The assurance aspect of complex information technology should not be limited to the IT knowledgeable people but should percolate down to the level of end users, particularly the external and internal auditors -- who are the users in the form of verifiers of internal controls to determine their opinions for statutory or operational purposes. And, to other stakeholders who must trust the systems providing information and data for policy and decision making.

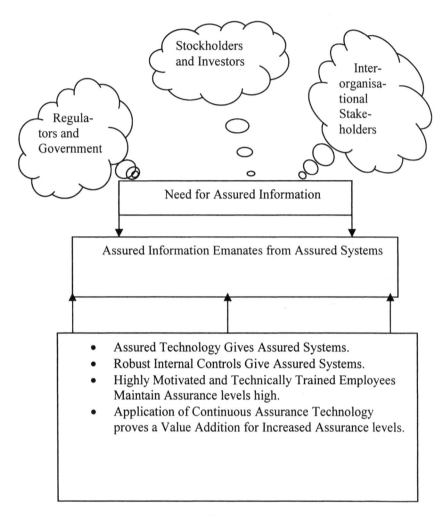

Figure: 2
Need for Information Assurance ← Assured Systems ← Gen-X
Technologies

Electronic dependencies and interconnections create vulnerabilities that are rapidly exploited by criminals. A substantial growth has been reported in the number of known electronic breaches of information security over the past few years. The business community has, however, begun recognizing the potentially catastrophic costs related to information infrastructure vulnerabilities. The level of private sector motivation and resources devoted to information assurance is increasing, and stakeholders have begun to understand the strategic importance of the information assurance function.

The time is right for government, industry, and academia to engage in a strong, long-term collaborative effort to create the methods, technologies and means for generating information assurance. Progress requires careful consideration of the equities of all the parties involved and focused efforts to transcend cultural and national boundaries and minimize or eliminate legal boundaries on cooperation (Berg 2001).

3.4 Information Assurance: A Function of Strategic Importance

The IT resources in the entity and the optimal utilization of these scarce resources have become an issue for devising a competitive strategy in globalised businesses. In the present dynamic and competitive markets, management is placing increasing demands on IT resources to operate as a major component of market strategy. Thus, increased quality standards, decreased through-put time and continuously evolving service levels on both the hardware and software fronts are being demanded.

Several factors point to an expanding IT universe and are placing greater demands on the IT control environment: increasing system complexity due to increasing use of web technologies, constantly decreasing cost of hardware and effective and efficient end-user computing due to graphic user interfaces (GUIs) in applications, and also a trend toward open and decentralizes architecture in computing. The greater emphasis on applications and system resources outsourcing, demand for reduced system development time and the tendency of entities toward the enterprise-wide computing adoption are some other factors in the same direction. Therefore, the importance of maintaining and monitoring controls over this expanding universe must also be treated as a strategic issue.

Strategy for any entity is knowledge-driven which in turn is information-dependent. Data generates information if presented in cohesive and coherent format to the right person at right time. Data is of paramount importance and the quality of data impacts the ultimate quality of strategy formulated by the entity. Internal control systems in place in organisations affect the quality of data. Poor internal controls have serious ramifications on the end product, and, in this case, poor quality data (low integrity and reliability) will result in equally poor strategy for the entity. In a similar vain, the failure to optimally implement strategic initiatives into operational modules can also have equally serious impact on the organisational results. It is at this point that management utilizes IT/IS auditing as a tool for ensuring: the reliability and integrity of information, compliance with IT policies and procedures, the safeguarding of IT assets, the economical and efficient use of the IT resources, and the accomplishment of established IT objectives and goals (IIA 1978).

Information technology is also used to facilitate the shrinkage and collapsing of the organisational structures and enterprise-wide resource planning (ERP) applications are the coincidentally handy to all the strategic managers in fulfilling this desire. Services are being demanded under the increasing cost constraints. These cost constraints not only involve the deployment of cost effective strategic information technologies but also often involve the smart sizing or de-layering of organisations. Many of these layers had been part of organisational internal control systems' infrastructure in origin. The control functions performed by these layers are either overlooked or not replaced by suitable alternatives during and after the de-layering process.

The above cited deficiencies are indicative of an inadequate internal control environment and imply that, with respect to end-user computing, we may still be in the Nolan's (1979) contagion phase of IT assimilation. Therefore, not only do the IT resources need to respond to increased functional demands, they also need to respond to the need to replace or enhance internal controls, which stem from changes in the organisational structure and objectives. In order to ensure that the business requirements for information are met, adequate control measures need to be defined, implemented and monitored to ensure the stakeholders that controls exist, that they are working, and that they are adequate given the risk involved.

Ratliff et al. (1996) indicate that activities within the management structure are subject to established policies, standards, and procedures which can be thought of as a pervasive network of system controls, generally called internal controls. These controls are employed to maintain effective vigil over activities and operations. Auditors (both IT/IS and internal) are used by the management and stakeholders to assist in monitoring the control environment, including testing compliance with management directives and evaluating the efficiency, effectiveness, and economy of internal controls and operations.

As demands on IT resources mount and their complexity increases exponentially, the need for IS/IT audit expertise should increase correspondingly. In this context, we can easily define the IS/IT audit's basic or primary mission as providing stakeholders with a level of assurance that the entity's IT resources are being efficiently, effectively and economically deployed to support the organisation's strategic objectives. Therefore, a major dilemma faced by many organisations is how to adequately, efficiently, effectively and economically control IT resources, while at the same time allocating and balancing audit activities under existing constraints in a way that maximises the added value of internal audit resources. While a good amount of empirical research has been done in the area of management information systems (MIS) and in auditing, no such body of knowledge or theory addresses the unique needs of the IT/IS audit community.

Internal controls constitute the policies and procedures adopted by management to assist in achieving the entity's objective of ensuring the orderly and efficient conduct of its operations, including adherence to management policies, safeguarding of assets, the prevention and detection of fraud and error, the accuracy and completeness of records, and the timely preparation of information (AICPA, 1996). The primary objective of internal auditing is to provide an appraisal of the entity's controls to ensure that business risk or uncertainty – variety – is addressed and that the entity's goals and objectives are achieved efficiently, effectively and economically. Internal controls provide a road map to navigate the organisation's anastomotic reticulum. This assertion is better explained in visual schema as shown in Figure 4. Management enacts internal controls to reduce variety, ambiguity, risk and uncertainty in the decision making process. Management employs internal auditors to evaluate the existence, functioning and adequacy of these internal controls.

What is the role of internal auditing in such reticulum? Internal auditing has an important role to perform in the form of patrolling this reticulum and act as a constable-at-the-beat by directing those who have strayed back onto the course. Here the role implies issuing tickets to the defaulters in the form of audit reports to the most serious kind of offenders. The relative variety, uncertainty, or risk of various activities is the single most critical factor in directing the activities of the internal audit function (Ratliff et al. 1996). It is important to note, that Beer (1995) mistakenly identifies management auditors, whose primary responsibility is evaluating the state of internal controls, as variety reducers, when in fact it is the internal controls created by management and imposed on the organisation that reduces variety.

On the other hand, the role of the external auditor is to attest to the fair presentation of the financial statements. As such, the external auditor's role can be described as attesting to the state of the organisation at a given point of time. The external auditor is not directly part of the internal organisation's feedback loop, but sets as part of larger feedback loop that includes stakeholders, governmental agencies, and other external parties, who are often more concerned with states and outcomes than with the processes that generate those states and outcomes. Internal auditors, including IT/IS auditors act as a part of the internal feedback control system of an organisation. A historical role for auditors was to act as detectors in first order feedback systems.

This traditional role of an auditor was to detect deviations from goals and to provide negative feedback in the form of audit reports. The auditee or the client management was expected to correct the deviation restoring the equilibrium, irrespective of changes in the environment and/or the materiality of the events. As intelligent entities evolve, memories of prior experiences are maintained and used for the best alternative course of action. The ability to store and recall information, allowing the system to choose alternative courses of action is called learning (Schoderbek et al. 1990). In second order feedback systems, the entities have the ability to change its goals by changing the behaviour of the system. Thus, goal changing becomes the part of the feedback process.

Simultaneously, auditors also evolved from solely being both detectors and comparators. Auditors began weighing the significance of departures in the context of the auditee's environment (significance and materiality) rather than merely reporting departures from the established norms. Auditors in the 1980s and 1990s have also become part of the third order feedback systems by participation in the early stages of system development, participating in information systems planning functions, and developing applications which are utilized to better control the entities' activities, i.e. continuous and self audits. Third order systems not only have the ability to learn from the previous errors, but also incorporate a feedforward system, which provides information on the projected future environment.

As a player in the third order feedback systems, auditors play a significant role in the implementation of anticipatory controls, i.e. controls that anticipate future problems and make adjustments before departures from normality occur. Auditors intelligently scan the environment to detect conditions that could lead to future departures. Auditors often embed modules within information systems that log specified transactions into a system control audit review file. Most of the large systems manufacturers have started embedding such audit modules in their application systems in today's system application scenario. However, auditors; may wish to monitor a particular type of transaction not the part of generalized audit module; may embed it and announce it that auditors are 'watching'. The mere fact that the auditors are publicly known to be monitoring a specific situation may be adequate in itself to deter some from inappropriate behaviour. Today's auditors are being utilized to provide guidance early in the system development life cycle. Their participation in the life cycle and IT planning activities provide a higher level of assurance that future system control problems are actively anticipated and that changes are designed into systems early along in the development process in order to avoid expensive mistakes, repairs, and interruptions once the system has gone into operations.

3.5 Various Information Assurance and Control Measures

These measures are the measures to be implemented at the web-level and the measures to be followed in their entirety. The first type of measures is developed by enterprising entities, including two most prominent accounting bodies, to extend the assurance of the web-based information to the end users. Similarly, the second type, that is, the measures to be followed in their entirety, are in fact, frameworks designed and developed by another set of professional bodies, viz. Information Systems Audit and Control Association (ISACA), the Institute of Internal Auditors (IIA), British Standards (Directorate of Trade and Industry), and one of the international systems security engineering association (ISSEA). These measures are described in brief in that order in this paper and the related web addresses are also given for further information.

3.5.1 Web-Level Assurance Measures

The area of extending information assurance to the end users in the last 10 years has seen development at various levels. Professional accountants' bodies of the USA and Canada have made a good beginning by introducing SysTrust and Web-Trust seals of assurance. These seals of assurance have their inherent limitations as they can not extend a blanket assurance but certainly if followed in letter and spirit, these seals of assurance can help extend the horizon of e-Commerce. Even though research has shown that WebTrust may influence consumer's behaviour (Kovar et al. 2000), it has had very limited success in the marketplace for B2C assurance seals (Craig 2000) with less than 30 implementations since its inception. On the other hand, competitor seals such as Better Business Bureau On-Line (BBB On-Line), TrustE, and VeriSign have been much more successful while providing a more limited scope of assurance.

The cause for lesser implementations of WebTrust seal might lie in its cost aspect and also its scope. First, because of the scope of assurance, the cost to acquire a WebTrust seal is significantly higher than alternative seals. Second, most consumers are likely to be unable to differentiate between the information content of alternative seals (CPA Journal, 1999). Most probably, a combination of these two factors and perhaps other factors has contributed to the lack of success of Web-Trust assurance. Of particular interest in this study, however, is the second issue in terms of the impact of varying levels of information quality (i.e., information content and reliability) on Internet consumers' purchasing choices.

The focus on information quality is particularly important; if consumers cannot differentiate among different seals' quality, then acquiring WebTrust assurance with its greater expense would not be an economically prudent decision. On the other hand, if consumers can differentiate among seals and are influenced by the assurance provided by a CPA/CA, acquiring a WebTrust seal may be a sound investment for some companies. WebTrust is a different type of venture for CPAs/CAs in that it is a CPA service that is sold to a company's marketing department rather than its finance department.

WebTrust provides assurance in four areas:

- business practices and disclosures
- transaction integrity
- information protection and
- information privacy (CICA, 2001)

As Primoff (1998) noted, WebTrust was proposed as a potential solution to consumers' concerns with regard to the risk of transacting business over the Internet. Other assurance seals focus on a subset of these dimensions. For instance, VeriSign focuses on transaction integrity and information protection, while TrustE focuses on information privacy. The assurance offered by BBB On-Line is even more limited. An organisation pays a relatively small fee to register with the BBB and acquire seal usage rights based on documentation of practices; the organisation continues to display the seal unless a certain number of complaints are lodged

with the Better Business Bureau by consumers regarding the actual business practices. Nonetheless, if consumers tend to focus simply on the presence or the absence of a seal, then assurance seals that offer low information quality may be
equally desirable and cost may be the most significant differentiator in assurance
seal acquisition decisions.

3.6 Control Objectives and System Assurance

IT resources are critical to management's successful accomplishment of the objectives of creating value through effective, efficient and economical use of resources
(Lainhart 1996). The American Institute of Certified Public Accountants (AICPA)
Statement on Auditing Standards No. 1 provides guidance to external auditors,
whose primary responsibility is the fair presentation of the financial statements,
states that an internal control should have four fundamental control objectives:
(AICPA 1973)

- to encourage adherence to management's prescribed policies and procedures
- to promote efficiency in all of the firm's operations
- to safeguard the assets of the firm
- to ensure the accuracy and reliability of the accounting data and information

The Institute of Internal Auditors (IIA) in their General Standard 300 provide
guidance to internal auditors, whose primary responsibility is the efficient, effective and economic utilization of organisational resources, expand upon the
AICPA's definition and define a set of five control objectives including: (IIA,
1978)

- the reliability and integrity of information
- compliance with policies, plans, procedures, laws and regulations
- the safeguarding of assets
- the economical and efficient use of resources
- the accomplishment of objectives and goals for operations and programs

In 1991(revised in 1994), the IIA issued the Systems Auditability and Control
(eSAC) (IIA 1991,1994) report which provided one of the first attempts to codify
control in the IT context. SAC stressed the need to assess risk, weigh the cost and
benefits of controls and economic benefits of building controls into systems rather
than add them after implementation. SAC identified risks including fraud, errors,
business interruptions and inefficient and ineffective use of IT resources. It further
set forth a set of control objectives to mitigate these risks and assure information
integrity, security, and compliance. The report concluded that the system of internal control consisted of three components: the control environment, manual and
automated systems, and control procedures. The control environment includes the
organisational structure, control frame work, policies and procedures and external

influences. Automated systems consist of system application software. Control procedures consist of general, application and compensating controls. Within these controls, SAC provided five classifications of controls: (1) preventative, detective and corrective, (2) discretionary and non- discretionary, (3) voluntary and mandated, (4) manual and automated, and (5) application and general controls.

In 1996, in order to provide a comprehensive and detailed framework for establishing and refining control objectives in an IT context, the Information Systems Audit and Control Foundation (ISACA/F) issued its Control Objectives for Information and Related Technology(COBIT)(ISACA/F,1996). Starting the analysis from broad quality, fiduciary and security requirements, seven distinct, control categories were extracted. COBIT defines the IT control objectives as:

- effectiveness deals with information being relevant and pertinent to the business process as well being delivered in a timely, correct, consistent and usable manner
- efficiency concerns the provision of information through the optimal (most productive and economical) use of resources
- confidentiality concerns the protection of sensitive information from unauthorized disclosure
- integrity relates to the accuracy and completeness of information as well as to its validity in accordance with business values and expectations
- availability relates to information being available when required by the business process now and in the future, it also concerns the safeguarding of necessary resources and associated capabilities
- compliance deals with complying with those laws, regulations and contractual arrangements to which the business process is subject, i.e. externally imposed business criteria
- reliability of Information relates to the provision of appropriate information for management to operate the entity and for management to exercise its financial and compliance reporting responsibilities

COBIT (ISACA/F, 1996), Parker and Benson (1988), and others have emphasized the importance of linking IT strategy with business objectives. A busy IT manager working in isolation from the business environment will have difficulty identifying the relationships between investments in technology and improved results. Decisions to invest in technologies solely for the sake of the technology itself tend not to support improved business performance. In the same regard, a business manager working in isolation from the technology environment will also have difficulty making this same link. The optimum solution is as a partnership between strategy and IT investments. In this perspective and armed with the COBIT framework, IS Audit plays a crucial role in establishing and reinforcing the link between business and technology by ensuring stakeholders that the organisation is making the most effective, and economical use of the organisation's IT resources in the context of the organisation's business strategy.

3.6.1 British Standards: BS7799 and BS 7799-2:2002

BS7799 is the most widely recognized systems security standard in the world. Although it was originally published in the mid-nineties, it was the revision of May 1999 which really put it on to the world stage. Ultimately, it evolved into BS EN ISO17799 in December 2000. BS 7799 (ISO17799) is comprehensive in its coverage of security issues, containing a significant number of control requirements. Compliance with it is consequently a far from trivial task, even for the most security conscious of organisations. British standard 7799: Part 2: 1998 Specification for Information Security Management Systems provides a series of mandatory controls that a company must successfully implement before obtaining certification.

The controls cover the following areas in a significant level of detail:

- information security policy
- security organisation
- assets classification and control
- personnel security
- physical and environmental security
- computer and network management
- system access control
- business continuity planning
- compliance

The development of BS 7799-2:2002 is now complete. This new edition has been produced to harmonize it with other management system standards such as BS EN ISO 9001:2000 and BS EN ISO 14001:1996 to provide consistent and integrated implementation and operation of management systems. It also introduces a **Plan-Do-Check-Act** (PDCA) model as part of a management system approach to developing, implementing, and improving the effectiveness of an organisations information security management system. The implementation of the PDCA model will also reflect the principles as set out in the OECD guidance (OECD Guidelines for the Security of Information Systems and Networks 2002) governing the security of information systems and networks. In particular, this new edition gives a robust model for implementing the principles in those guidelines governing risk assessment, security design and implementation, security management and reassessment.

3.6.2 System Security Engineering Capability Maturity Model: SSE-CMM

The SSE-CMM is a tool for making analysis of security needs of an entity. This tool is both a model and a process. This model is owned by a community of 50 companies and agencies led by the U.S. National Security Agency (NSA) and the

Canadian Communication Security Establishment (CSE). The model presents security engineering as defined, mature, and measurable discipline. The model and appraisal method enable capability based assurance, focused investment in security engineering tools and qualifying vendors, suppliers and organisations connecting to a system (for a brief overview, visit *www.theiia.org*).

This particular model has five maturity levels defined from lowest to highest levels. It also includes 22 separate process areas. According to the approach advocated by the international systems security engineering association (ISSEA), the maturity level for each of these process areas is a separate decision (for detailed discussion, please visit *www.issea.org*).

The recent and the ongoing developments in the field of information technology with a focus on enterprise technology and its convergence with communication technology has a tendency to put often many of our age old auditing practices in jeopardy, particularly in relation to the electronic evidences and its acceptability by the stakeholders and especially the regulators. The complexity of enterprise information technology based systems makes all of us to sit up and make efforts to update the auditing techniques, methods, and auditing processes as the technology oriented people may not be able to appreciate the importance of internal control mechanisms put in place by accounting people.

Secondly, the assurance providers are also expected to update their relevant methodologies with the increase in the complexity of the systems assured by them not only from the accounting and auditing practices point-of-view but also from the infrastructure security view point. The assurance area researchers must find out the best practices from the established practitioners and also involve those who design such complicated systems. In the end, a synergistic view will only be a holistic view of the situation by the assurance services providers. And, it is shown in Figure 3 that Information Assurance is intertwined with Assurances of all the Segments pertaining to the operation, maintenance and governance of the information systems.

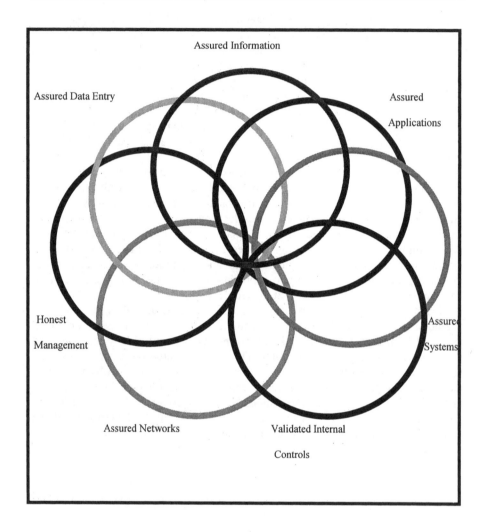

Figure 3

4 Complex Information Systems, Auditing Standards and IT Auditors

In a business environment increasingly driven by information technology (IT), mechanisms to monitor IT and business operations controlled by IT are needed as well as information systems that are properly planned and work effectively (Epelle, 2002). In the 1990's the emphasis was on "doing business on the Internet" with a firm's customers and suppliers (Cronin, 1994). In this context existing business practices were imported into the Internet environment. Now new business models, developed for the Internet environment, are emerging such as the auction model of product pricing. These models move beyond merely performing usual business practices on the Internet to "changing how the business is conducted on the Internet" resulting in new ways of conducting business in a world of electronic, paperless transactions (Viehland, 1999). Risk happens particularly as firms embrace more complex systems to monitor their firm's operations. While growing organisations often embrace risk, these risks should not be taken blindly (Ratcliffe and Munter, 2002). These firms should have a clear understanding of the potential consequences of increased risk, positive or negative, and how to insure positive outcomes. As firms are increasingly experiencing "virtualization" in their relationships with suppliers, partners and consumers, there is an increasing need for trust and assurance in these relationships (Pace, 1999).

4.1 The Approach and Objectives

The purpose of this Chapter is to discuss the new SAS 94 audit standards (AICPA, 2001) for organisations making extensive use of IT for electronic transactions (Figure: 1) This Chapter is divided into four major parts: (1) a review of the electronic transaction literature on the major issues, (2) a discussion of the impact of technology on auditors, (3) an examination of complex information technologies in terms of audit risk, and (4) the effect of SAS-94 on the audit processes.

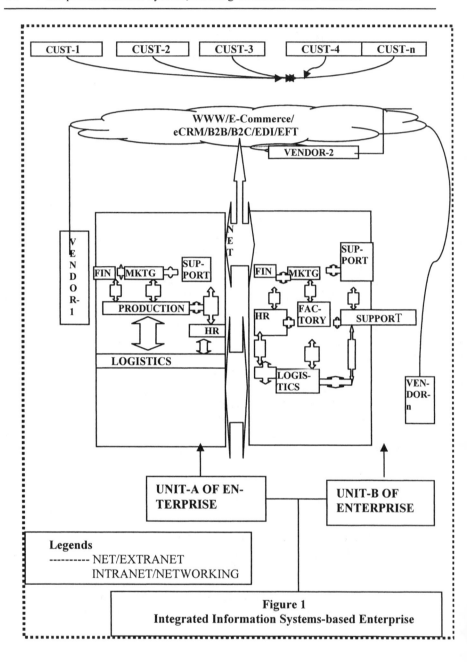

Figure 1
Integrated Information Systems-based Enterprise

4.1.1 The Scenario

There is greater pressure on independent auditors to attest to this trust and assurance (Harmanson et al, 2002). Ronen and Cherny (2002) indicated that independent auditors are expected to be trust providers to the level of being 'insurers'. Auditors have talked of 'reasonable assurance' and 'true and fair presentation' but now their stakeholders expect these auditors to be insurers of their investment! While bizarre, this is a reality for auditors (Barrier, 2002; Walsh, 2002; Green, 1999). The usage of IT in various business processes is becoming an increasingly complex affair particularly in this era of e-commerce. The landscape if how IT is run in organisations is changing with the increasing use of outsourcing. It is possible that the auditor in 2007 may not find any internal personnel in the firm running IT.

In this outsourced scenario, the American Institute of Certified Public Accountants (AICPA) promulgated a new statement of auditing standards (SAS) No. 94, replacing the SAS-55; however, it keeps the definition of 'internal controls' unchanged. With the emergence of e-commerce technologies, public key infrastructure, and secured digitally signed transaction technologies (Yu et al, 2000), the inherent reliability of information systems for transaction processing has increased tremendously. Controls over transactions are embedded in the software (Minghua and Leung, 2002) and extensive data on non-financial dimensions of business performance are becoming readily available for the auditor. However, as the swift transactions enabled by e-commerce increase, the financial statements become less reliable predictors of the future and those transactions themselves become more difficult to audit.

4.2 Impact of Technology Complexity on the Auditor

Auditors should consider focusing on the e-commerce strategies for their clients, the e-commerce risk that must be managed to achieve these strategies, and the ensuing audit risks from this e-commerce (Morgan and Stocken, 1998). Since auditors will have to make more serious attempts to do a formal analysis of an organisation's e-commerce strategy with SAS-94, the auditor needs to understand the IT-based/dependent internal controls. To work with the IT specialists, auditors need reasonable IT capabilities for conducting their detailed audit. (Martinov and Robuck, 1998). This IT understanding becomes more crucial as auditors are faced with accounting transactions entirely in electronic form without supporting paper documentation. Technologies such as electronic data interchange (Pathak, 2001), image processing and electronic funds transfers (Deshmukh and Romine, 2002; Scott, 2002) use little, if any, paper. These information technologies greatly change the nature of audits, which have so long relied on paper documents. Auditors performing attest services for such clients will need to be both financially and technically competent regarding IT.

They will also need to revise their traditional (annual) audit approach by focusing on an organisation's e-commerce strategy (Good and Schultz, 2002; Natraj and

Lee, 2002) and the associated e-commerce risks that may occur. E-commerce allows direct links to customers, anywhere, anytime so that the companies are building interactive relationships with their customers, partners and suppliers, delivering new products and services at a much lower cost than under the current "traditional" methods. Also the global reach of the Internet provides access to new markets and customers. It removes competitive barriers and erodes margins, subjecting unprepared companies to the mercy of constantly increasing competition and customer expectations by redefining customer (Robert, 1999), supplier and partner relationships (Issabella, 2002; Mirani et al, 2001; Brock-smith and Barclay, 1999; Dale et al, 1999). E-commerce mandates rethinking, repositioning and retooling a company's entire value proposition (Anonymous, 2001; Anonymous, 1999; Belisle, 1999). It is about attracting, retaining and building on long-term customer relationships (Morrison, 2002; Deshmukh and Romine, 2002; Peak, 2002; Weber, 2002; Crafton, 2002), revolutionizing supply networks, manufacturing practices (Carroll, 2002), and procurement systems (Dias et al, 2002; Wolf, 2001; Ageshin, 2001) to deliver the right products and services to customers in the shortest time possible, automating interactive business processes (Reimer, 2003; Seewald, 2002; Frigo, 2002; Bagranoff et al, 2002), capturing, analyzing and sharing business intelligence (Kampmeier, 2002; Marshall, 2002; Conhaim, 2002; Fordham et al, 2002), and making better business decisions.. Thus, we define e-commerce as a new way for companies to improve the exchange of goods, services, information and knowledge through network-enabled technologies (Long et al, 2002; Madden and Coble-Neal, 2002; Li and Johnson, 2002; Liebmann, 2002). There are roughly thirteen (13) application areas shown in Table 1 using e-commerce; and a well trained auditor must carry reasonable skills to comprehend the descriptions and assertions from IT specialists.

Information Security remains the number one issue for the IT, according to the results of the "2003 Top Technologies" survey by the American Institute of Certified Public Accountants (*www.accountingeducation.com*). This year's list exemplified exceptional change as six new items made their way into the final listing, including: business information management, application integration, wireless technologies, intrusion detection, customer relationship management, and privacy. The e-commerce evolution is taking place either in new companies, which started with e-commerce at their inception ("dot.com" company) or in existing "conventional" entities, which have converted to a combination of e-commerce and "bricks and mortar".

Table 1. E-commerce Application in Firms

Enterprise architecture	Levi and Arsanjani, 2002; Huang, 2001; Herman, 2001; Fruitman, 2001
Customer Relationship Management	Deshmukh and Romine, 2002; Lipsey, 2002; Ingram et al, 2002; Davis, 2002
Supply Chain Integration and Management	Halley and Nollet, 2002; Fawcett and Magnan, 2002; Schroder and McEachern, 2002; Heikkila, 2002
B2B and XML.	Chakraborty et al, 2002; Dehanayake et al, 2002; Hucklesby and Macdonald, 2002; Graziano, 2002
Enterprise resource planning	Kudyba and Vitaliano, 2003; Paper, 2003; Seewald, 2002; Osheroff, 2002
Enterprise applications integration	IDC, 2002; Bertheaud, 2002; Opie, 2002a; Irani, 2002
Knowledge Management	Manville and Ober, 2003; Kresner, 2003; Pagano, 2002; Knight and Liesch, 2002
Peer-to-peer computing (P2P) and Networking	Kushner, 2002; Kini, 2002; Chiasson et al, 2002; Millard, 2002
Security technologies	Suh, 2002; McCollum, 2002; Lee et al,2002; Hondo et al, 2002
Web Services	Landry, 2003; Levi and Arsanjani, 2002; Freemantle et al, 2002; Stal, 2002; Opie, 2002b
Wireless technology	Malladi and Agarwal, 2002; Poliski, 2002; Li and Johnson, 2002; Tarasevich and Warkentin, 2002
Business-to-customer Technology	Jahng et al, 2002; Devraj et al, 2002; Coltman et al, 2002, Ranganathan, 2002
Storage technologies	Geppert, 2002; Vice, 2001; Anderberg et al, 2001; Chadha, 2001

4.2.1 Complex Information Technologies and Audit Risks

E-commerce and its related technologies are still a new phenomenon, making it difficult for corporate executives to manage the ensuing risks. Like most IT, it is extremely difficult to estimate accurately the returns on an e-commerce investment in terms of a cost/benefit analysis (Mullin, 2002; O'Connor, 2002). Accurately estimating the future benefits of a large investment as e-commerce (Corbitt,

2002; Khan and Motiwala, 2002; Martinsons, 2002; Chatterjee et al, 2002) can be a daunting and imprecise job. Thus identifying risks associated with e-commerce (Koldzinski, 2002; Chapman, 2002; Helms et al, 2002; Adobor and McMullen, 2002) becomes increasingly important given the difficulty of estimating future benefits (Subramani et al., 2001). While e-commerce financial statement risks are similar to those traditionally considered, these risks may be exacerbated by the e-commerce environment. While integrated ecommerce- centric enterprise information system shows a diversity and multitude of risks, primary audit risks include: security (Koldzinsky, 2002), privacy (Peeples, 2002; Matherne and Mackler, 2002), and transaction integrity (Anonymous, 2000). As an alternative to a company managed Internet connection, a firm's transactions may take place electronically through an intermediary service provider or a virtual private network (Yusuf et al, 2002; Angeles et al, 2001; Angeles, 2000). Accordingly, the auditors need to be concerned that these transactions are authorized, not duplicated or modified, and then received by the appropriate party. The external auditor may feel it necessary to obtain policies and procedures manuals and transaction log files from the network service provider to better understand the manipulation and to track the flow of material (financial) statement assertions. Dynamic audit trails (Helms, 2002; Kanter, 2001; Gallegos, 1999) generated in real time have become a major concern of auditors. In the pre-IT business world, auditors had stacks of invoices and shipping records to vouch and examine. Today, these documents may never exist in paper form, only electronically for only short periods in electronic trails. For an auditor to offer an opinion on the material correctness of a corporation's financial statements, the auditor must rely more heavily on the company's business practices and internal controls in order to gain comfort in the reported numbers.

Auditors are also concerned that only authorized transactions are transmitted and received. Further, they test to ensure that transactions are not duplicated, altered or lost during processing. Since there are fewer tangible pre-numbered documents to examine as in manual and legacy systems, auditors must instead examine the computer based system that has replaced the paper documents with electronic transactions. Therefore, organisations have to place more emphasis on internal controls in information integration processes to ensure their operations are efficient and to obtain an unqualified audit opinion. These IT based audits will have to be performed more frequently (monthly or quarterly instead of annually) given the dynamic IT environment. It is also a possible that such an audit will be performed by another soft application, either stand alone or embedded intelligently (Kang and Han, 2003; Guan and Yang, 2002; Wagner and Turban, 2002) within the transaction processes. While it is premature to claim this as an alternative to the human auditor, there certainly is the possibility of providing continuous monitoring of the firm's transactions with ready 'red-flags' and 'exception reporting'. This kind of continuous monitoring is also known as continuous auditing (Vasarhelyi et al, 2002; Rezaee et al, 2002; Wright, 2002; Figg, 1999; Helms and Mancino, 1999). Security is an obvious candidate for testing in e-commerce. In 1998, the Computer Auditing Subcommittee of the AICPA (Helms and Mancino, 1998) identified the main issues that auditors should consider in planning an audit: (1) security, (2) e-commerce, and (3) continuous auditing. E-commerce systems must use the latest encryption technology, digital signatures and certificates (Helms et al, 2002; Hillison, 2001), and secure server technology and authentication (Busta, 2002; Garceau, 2000) to ensure that all information exchanged is secure. Thus independent verification must be used to ensure that all security controls adequately protect the organisation, its suppliers, partners and customers from the risk of (main) security breaches. To help alleviate some of the security and integrity risks, the accounting profession has attempted to offer some e-commerce assurance (Elifoglu, 2002; Helms and Mancino, 1999). In 1997 the AICPA/CICA created the "CPA/CA WebTrust" seal (Kent and Acton, 2001; Pugliese and Halse, 2000; Cashell and Aldhizer, 1999). Under this program, independent accountants or auditors examine three areas related to a website every 90 days:

- information protection
- business practices disclosures and
- transaction integrity

The WebTrust approach has enhanced customers' feeling of security with online purchasing. Also the Web Trust provides the auditors better information on the organisation's eBusiness controls. However, the AICPA/CICA Web of Trust is done in a highly litigious risk environment (Pacini and Sinason, 1999). People want to know how a site will handle confidential information. Without the assurance from independent third parties that confidential information will be protected, some individuals or organisations will never make online purchases. E-commerce entities must explain how they collect and handle information and post easy-to-read confidentiality statements.

Finally, the ultimate goal in providing trust and assurance for e-commerce entities is through the execution of the continuous audit process as described earlier. A continuous audit usually requires that the auditor be involved in the original design and implementation of the integrated enterprise information systems controls. Needless to say, such online / real-time auditing will have an enormous impact on the audit profession and its professionals. The accounting firms either have or are in the process of redesigning their audit process to deal with the evolution to integrated enterprise information systems. In redesigning the audit, the auditors place a much heavier emphasis on the business processes. Moreover, all auditors realize that besides financial auditing skills, technological auditing skills are vitally required competencies to be successful in a modern scenario of technological complexities. SAS-94 is a framework standard that resulted from the growth and influence of IT on business systems. Auditors must prove equal in comprehending these IT developments.

4.2.2 SAS-94 and its Effect on the Audit Process

The ASB issued SAS-80, in December 1996, entitled Amendment to Statement on Auditing Standards No. 31, Evidential Matter, in order to address questions about the validity, completeness, and integrity of electronic evidence. When entities transmit, process, maintain, or access information electronically, it may be impractical or even impossible to reduce detection risk to an acceptably low level by performing only substantive tests for one or more financial statements. Furthermore, SAS 80 concluded that tests of controls, in conjunction with substantive tests, should be sufficient to support an audit opinion (Helms and Lilly, 2000).

The AICPA also published an Auditing Procedures Study (APS) entitled "The Information Technology Age: Evidential Matter in the Electronic Environment" (1997). The APS describes electronic evidence and associated evaluation issues. Prior to the release of SAS 94, although some guidance had addressed audit considerations in an IT environment, there had not been an update to the evaluation of controls and assessment of control risk since SAS 78. SAS 94 filled this gap. SAS 94 is intended to fulfill the following objectives:

- incorporate the SAS 80 concepts and expand them to emphasize that an auditor may be compelled in certain circumstances to obtain evidential matter about the effectiveness of the design and operation of electronic data controls
- provide the auditors descriptions of how IT may affect internal controls, evidential matters, the understanding of internal controls, and the assessment of control risk
- describe for the auditor the internal control benefits and risks of IT and how IT affects the components of internal control, particularly control activities, information, and communication components
- provide guidance for deciding whether specialized skills are needed to consider the effect of computer processing on the audit, to understand the controls, or to design and perform audit procedures
- clarify the need to understand how standard, recurring entries and nonstandard, nonrecurring entries are initiated and recorded, including the controls to assure that they are authorized, complete, and correctly recorded

Recognizing the importance of IT, SAS-94 amended SAS-55, "Consideration of Internal Control in a Financial Statement Audit." SAS-94 does not change the basics of SAS-55, and its importance in the audit-risk model, but it addresses the effects of IT on the professional standards process. When significant evidence of an entity's initiation, recording, or processing of financial data exists only in electronic form, the ability of the auditor to obtain the desired assurance only from substantive tests is significantly reduced. SAS-94 still requires the performance of substantive tests for significant account balances and transaction classes. Basically the ASB took SAS-55 and modified it to include the effect of IT on internal control, the auditor's understanding of internal control, and the auditor's assessment of control risk. SAS-94 specifically requires that when obtaining this understanding of internal control, the auditor should consider how an entity's use of IT and manual procedures may affect controls relevant to the audit. The extent and nature of these risks will vary, depending on the nature and characteristics of an entity's information system and the extent to which the information system affects the entity's internal control.

SAS-94 guides auditors in determining if a professional possessing IT skills will be needed for an assignment. This person may be on the auditor's staff or may be an outside professional. To determine if a technology professional is needed, an audit planner is expected to consider the following factors:

- complexity and usage of the firm's systems
- significance of changes to existing systems
- extent of data sharing
- extent of the entity's participation in electronic commerce
- audit evidence available in digital form.

Many accounting firms, internal and external auditors, state and federal agencies already are using various types of software in the audit process. However, there are some groups who do not fully use or understand the available software, or fully understand the tools' underlying principles - such as digit analysis – and how to use this in an auditing environment. With SAS 94, a new era of auditing has arrived; and the accounting profession must keep up with technology advances or bear the consequences. Once an accountant uses, understands, and employs advanced IT techniques – such as data mining, digit analysis, and Benford testing – in the audit process, he or she often asks why such techniques were not used before. When it comes to advice on technology-driven audit tools and/or procedures, the ASB and the Public Oversight Board (POB) are not specific in their recommendations or requirements. The organisations do not want to restrict a professional's creativity or judgment. Many tools – especially software tools – have been available to the profession for some time. Other options are new or are in the process of development. Auditing can be influenced by technology in limitless ways, and how it eventually will be changed is subject to much conjecture. Imagine just one instance:

Instead of waiting to start an annual audit of financial statements weeks after the year's end using typical audit substantive procedures, what if we had the ability to use continuous auditing to examine and report on various data sets immediately. The potential benefits include reduced overall audit risk, increased audit confidence, and a timeliness that has never been achievable before. These examples show where auditing will go as the profession embraces technology. SAS 94 notes that assessing control risk at the maximum and performing a substantive audit may not result in an effective audit because the audit evidence does not exist outside the IT environment. Furthermore, even when evidential matter allows an assessment of control risk below the maximum, there remains a need to perform substantive tests on significant amounts. Stated differently, an audit involves the assessment of control risk and the design, performance, and evaluation of substantive tests to reduce audit risk to an acceptably low level. The evolution of auditing and technology is an exciting change for auditors. Since the Auditing Standards

Board (ASB) recognized that it is increasingly difficult for auditors to rely on traditional (paper) audit evidence to acquire sufficient competent evidence, they issued SAS-94. When the ASB issued SAS 78, it incorporated a "COSO model" approach to the definition of internal controls. Internal controls are affected by an entity's board of directors, management, and other personnel in order to provide reasonable assurance of achieving three objectives: reliable financial reporting, effective and efficient operations, and compliance with applicable laws and regulations. In addition, internal controls over the safeguarding of assets against unauthorized acquisition, use, or disposition will often include controls relating to financial reporting and operations objectives.

Internal control consists of five interrelated components: the control environment, risk assessment, control activities, information and communication, and monitoring. Because an auditor focuses on controls pertinent to financial statement assertions-how the transactions are authorized, recorded, aggregated, and displayed in the financial statements – when planning and performing an audit, it may not be necessary to obtain an understanding of the controls of operating units and business functions. The following controls might not be relevant to the audit:

- controls for compliance with health and safety regulations (although the auditor would need to consider potential indirect consequences in evaluating contingencies)
- effectiveness and efficiency of management decision-making processes, such as product pricing or research and development expenditures

Because of the extensive use of IT in today's businesses, SAS 94 cautions that its implications may need to be considered in evaluating any of the five components of internal control. As Enterprise Resource Planning (ERP) systems have become more comprehensive and more widely used, even small entities may have complex, highly integrated IT systems that share data and support all aspects of financial reporting, operations, and compliance.

IT may fundamentally change the initiating, recording, processing, and reporting of transactions. Controls in such IT systems consist of a combination of automated (e.g., those embedded in computer programs) and manual controls. Manual controls may function independently of the IT system or use information produced by the IT system to monitor the automated controls. The appropriate mix of manual and automated controls varies with the nature and complexity of the IT system. IT internal controls can provide only reasonable assurance regarding the achievement of an entity's control objectives. All internal control systems, regardless of their design, face certain inherent limitations that make absolute assurance impossible. In an IT system, errors can occur in designing, maintaining, or monitoring automated controls. For example, IT personnel may not understand how an IT system processes sales transactions, resulting in incorrect changes to the system for processing sales for a new product line. SAS 94 repeats the requirement to obtain a sufficient understanding of each of the five components of internal control in order to plan the audit. An auditor could still determine that performing substantive tests alone would be effective and more efficient than performing tests of controls for assertions in some circumstances. For example, in an audit of fixed assets and long-term debt, where there is a limited number of readily corroborated transactions, the auditor could perform substantive tests alone.

In more complex situations with a large volume of transactions processed in a complex IT environment, performing tests of controls to assess control risk below the maximum level for certain assertions would be effective and more efficient than performing only substantive tests. Alternatively, it may be impractical or impossible to restrict detection risk to an acceptable level by performing only substantive tests. In such cases, SAS-94 requires tests of both the design and operation of controls in order to reduce the assessed level of control risk. Not performing such control tests would likely result in a scope limitation and preclude the auditor from issuing an opinion on the financial statements.

The knowledge gained from an understanding of internal controls should be used to identify the types of potential misstatements that could occur in financial statement assertions. The controls that are likely to prevent or detect material misstatements in specific financial statement assertions may relate directly to one or more of them, but their continued effective operation usually depends on general controls that are indirectly related to the assertions. Indirect general controls usually include controls that restrict access to programs and related data. Techniques for testing automated controls may differ from those for manual controls. For example, computer assisted audit techniques may be used to test automated controls or data related to assertions.

In addition, other automated tools could test the operating effectiveness of indirect controls, such as access controls. Specialized computer skills may be needed to design and perform the tests of controls. Ultimately, these situations call for an assessment of the level of control risk for specific financial statement assertions. The assessed level of control risk (along with the assessed level of inherent risk) should determine the acceptable level of detection risk for the financial statement assertions.

As the acceptable level of detection risk decreases, the assurance provided from substantive tests should increase. SAS-94 changes the documentation requirements for understanding and evaluating internal control. Consistent with the previous guidance of SAS-55 (as amended by SAS-78), the form and extent of this documentation depends upon the nature and complexity of the entity's controls. For example, understanding the internal controls of a complex IT system in which a large volume of transactions is electronically initiated, recorded, processed, and reported might be documented by flowcharts, questionnaires, and decision tables.

Generally, the more complex the internal control and the more extensive the procedures performed, the more extensive the documentation should be. The basis for the conclusions about the assessed level of control risk also requires documentation. Conclusions about the assessed level of control risk may differ by account balances or classes of transactions. For those financial statement assertions where control risk is assessed at the maximum level, the level should be documented but there is no need to document the basis for that conclusion. For those assertions where the assessed level of control risk is below the maximum, the basis for the conclusion that the effectiveness of the design and operation of controls supports the assessed level should be documented.

5 ERP and Information Integration Issues: Perspective for Auditors

The use of enterprise resources Planning (ERP) application is growing among large multinational companies in Americas, Europe, Asia, and Australia. These organisations' aim is to integrate its global operations through the use of the ERP software. However, these implementation objectives are often found to be difficult and complicated. These implementations are often found to be challenged by many social and organisational issues. Hence, it results in failure of the implementations. Enterprise Resource Planning (ERP) has been coined as the "killer application" that is capable of integrating different information systems and business processes into a complete solution. A five process integration is shown to understand the ERP integration phenomenon by an IT auditor. The 5 processes are (1) social integration, (2) workflow integration, (3) process integration, (4) knowledge integration and (5) virtual integration.

My attempt in this chapter is directed to elaborate enterprise resources planning and information integration from its conceptual aspect and the segments necessary for an IT auditor to understand so as to be effective in the potential audit opportunity. This chapter is therefore, focused on the ERP, its conceptual models, implementation cycles, successes and disasters, ERP as a knowledge integrator and manager. The expectations from this chapter is to obtain a highly scholastic top-view about these various segments of ERP and information integration and at the same time assimilate the knowledge thus, obtained while planning an audit engagement keeping the impact of ERP implementation on the organisation and on its internal controls, in mind.

The impact of e-commerce in changing the way business operates is huge. The network effects of the Internet and the increase in electronic transactions have brought about a complete change in all types of communication and a growing need for inter-operable technology (Davenport, 2000). The need for a new information infrastructure that will support this new market has created a desire for a fully integrated system. Researchers (e.g. Boudreau and Robey, 1999, Davenport, 2000) have warned prophetically that those who do not implement ERP will be threatened with extinction by being left behind in the future. ERP is involved in the implementation of common IT infrastructures and business processes (Cooper and Kaplan, 1998; Davenport, 1998), allowing organisations to develop a fully integrated and homogeneous enterprise-wide information system infrastructure. And the goal of an ERP system is to integrate the core activities of an organisation so that these activities are easier to manage globally (Glover, Prawitt and Romney, 1999).

Therefore, it is appropriate to say that organisations adopting ERP aim to integrate as well as to extend the "Enterprise". For the past three years, the growing number of multinational firms adopting ERP systems has been phenomenal (Bancroft, Seip and Spriegel, 1998; Caldwell and Stein, 1998; Kirschmer, 1999). In most cases, organisations have adopted ERP systems in the hope of increasing productivity and efficiency as a means to raising organisational competitiveness (Davenport, 1998; Waglem, 1998). One obvious and early conclusion that can be drawn from most of these studies is that the ERP system software is not a standard package which we can purchase off-the-shelf. The profound complexity of the software package can be shown by the large investment of time, money and expertise in its implementation (Davenport, 1998).

ERP implementation involves significant changes across the organisation, for example, in the areas of business structure (Al-Mashari and Zairi, 2000), culture (Soh, Sia and Tay-Yap, 2000), information strategy (Rizzi and Zamboni, 1999), and information systems integration (Markus Tanis, and Fenema, 2000). These studies reveal that ERP implementation is a highly complex process and conclude that further research is needed to investigate issues that influence the success and failure of ERP implementation. Markus et al., (2000) and Ross (1999) caution that major problems in most implementations can arise from social or cultural barriers, and user resistance, especially in multi-site organisations where significant levels of integration and coordination are required among business strategy, software configuration, technical platform and management execution.

While existing studies have taken very different views on ERP implementation and have even made a variety of suggestions for improving the implementation process and result (Scheer and Habermann, 2000; Sprott, 2000; Kremers and Van Dissel, 2000; Markus, Petrie and Axline, 2000; Everdingen, Hillegersberg and Waarts, 2000; Kumar and Hillegersberg, 2000), almost none highlighted the processes and barriers in the implementation process from the viewpoint of integration.

In other words, the researcher wishes to argue that with the decisive change from employing a decentralized to a centralized information system strategy, the complexity of integration is more evident in ERP implementations than of any other kind of system.

Although integration is found to be a critical part of the implementation process, little research had look at how integration takes place within the ERP implementations. In the thesis, the researcher aims to understand:

- about ERP integration and also defining the process of integration within the ERP implementation
- how integration is a problem within the implementation process. Reveal problems through an in-depth case study research within a multi-national enterprise implementing its strategic ERP system

In the past, many IT departments have managed the IT services and resources within the organisation. Centralization and building a centralized management strategy has become a growing management trend when organisations are moving towards streamlining. It is also believed that ERP is a critical system which organisations must adopt to remain competitive and to streamline (Evans and Wurster 1999). As a result, organisations are beginning to adopt a centralization management concept when they implement ERP systems. The ERP systems are often seen as among the largest Information System implementation in most organisations. They are also known to require extensive resources in managing these systems (Kremer and Van Dissel 2000). However, there are arguments that such resources are frequently not managed effectively. In addition, many ERP failures were often due to negligence of the tacit factors (Ross, 1999b). These factors include user resistance and social issues.

5.1 What is Enterprise Resource Planning?

The ERP as these systems are popularly called, evolved from Europe and moved into the rest of the world (e.g. US and Asia). The software package, in technical terms, is seen as application software. It is different from a database solution, middleware and the operating system. It comprises modules which integrates organisational functional areas within the "Information System." The main ERP vendors are SAP, Baan, J.D. Edwards, Oracle and People Soft. These vendors make up a large portion of the ERP vendor market, which the Gartner group described to be a multi-billion dollar industry (Gartner, 2001). Until off-the-shelf ERP solution software has been developed, the only way to achieve the functionality that author find in many other ERP solutions today is to custom design.

The ERP packages are highly customizable and allow modules to be configured to fit into the organisational function by providing its own proprietary development language. Such a highly customizable package comes at an exorbitant price. In fact, ERP packages usually need customization so that a compatible integration would result in the implementation cost exceeding the cost of purchasing the shrink-wrapped software (Sawyer, 2000).

Researchers have also recognized ERP as an entirely different kind of package software which was previously available off-the-shelves (Davenport 2000a; Davis 2000; Ferrando 2000). These packages are not one that can be plugged into a server and ready for use. Corporations very often had to invest large amount of funds to customise the package. These corporations often make use of ERP to either solve existing problems or explore new opportunities in the Internet and e-commerce era using these packages. As it provides integration to business processes and practices for both industry specific and business specific processes, the ERP packages have become a strong industry-based solutions and business process-specific solution.

The comprehensiveness of the solution made it attractive to organisations. The use of an ERP package is now seen significantly as an essential package for business by the large multi-national organisations for many industries (Kumar, 2000). The ERP system is appropriate when an organisation is seeking the benefits of integration and contemporary best practices in its information system. The system also provides a full range of functionalities from the back office through operations and sales, to cover all aspects of the organisational implementation needs and reduce ongoing support cost. Currently, ERP systems are evolving into extended-ERP systems, embedding and providing support for inter-organisational processes such as e-commerce, and customer relationship management (CRM) (Kumar and Van Hillegersberg, 2000). Such added functionalities are now considered part of the ERP system. However, the reader should note that the issues about integration in ERP often mismatch of existing organisational processes and process knowledge when processes become more significant and more complex. As a result, the system fails when this mismatch cannot be resolved.

ERP made the humble beginning when it was built on the concept of Material Requirement Planning (MRP) and Manufacturing Resource Planning (Holland and Light 1999a). The readers can better understand the maturity of the ERP concept by looking at the ERP of the 1990s starting from the MRP era (Chung and Charles 2000). The success of MRPII was quickly seen as the next big step for organisation to manage other resources. With this concept, a German company, SAP AG, started to develop its first product of the R2 system running on the mainframe. It saw it as a business concept that would assist the building of an Enterprise (Klaus, Rosemann and Gable 2000). This made ERP grow to become a new software industry with Oracle, SAP, Baan and Peoplesoft competing within this niche market (Holland and Light 1999a).

These ERP soon grew to be infrastructures for business (Klaus, Rosemann and Gable 2000). As the industry grew highly competitive, ERP vendors went on to develop solutions for Small and Medium sized Enterprise (Avarini, Tagliavini and Sciuto, 2000). When ERP grew in popularity in the 1990s, these vendors also started to integrate other application areas such as Supply Chain Management, Customer Relationship Management and Manufacturing Planning components into their ERP programs. For example, SAP AG which developed the R3 began to focus on an extended system which includes CRM and Supply Management Solutions.

In addition, studies have shown that these packages which were previously designed for European organisations (Van Everdingen, Hillegersberg and Waarts 2000), are being implemented in a global context and are integrating organisation across the globe (Markus, Petrie and Axline 2000). This leads to organisational problems in the new cross-cultural and functional social environment which the ERP have created. And good examples of cross-cultural issues include different business practices, the mindset, and the ability to adapt to change. And functional complication in the ERP implementations includes getting business units to use common functional processes and functional departments to use common ERP systems. In recognising these issues, growing numbers of ERP researchers are trying to address these issues (Soliman and Youssef 1998; Soh, Sia and Tay-Yap 2000; Gupta 2000). In the studies on ERP, it was found that ERP systems brought about not only technological changes but also organisational and social changes (Riper and Durham, 1999; Caldwell and Stein 1998; Willcocks and Sykes, 2000; Holland and Light, 1999b; Harris 1999; Jacob and Wagner 1999).

Such problems (e.g. user resistance and change) are not new and are found existing in many historical information system implementations. In addition, these issues are seen in many information systems failures. Often these changes associated with implementing ERP are equated to significant amount of time and effort needed for ERP to be implemented. Various researchers have found that the understanding of ERP implementation is important to many organisations to increase the success in their ERP implementations (e.g. Chung and Charles, 2000; Ferrando, 2000).

5.2 Implementation Cycle

In many case studies, it has been found that phase models are used to segment the study of ERP into stages of which the ERP system gets implemented. In Parr and shanks' (2000) study of the process model, Integration Issues of Enterprise Resource Planning Implementation it is argued that ERP implementation is different from most of the legacy systems implementation. The ERP implementations are more focused on building standard business processes within the enterprise. ERP implementations can be based on several implementation models. These models are developed to categorize ERP implementation activities into periodic phases which will aid comparisons. These phases have isolated the stages into pre-implementation, implementation and post-implementation. As noted, these models include and emphasize the importance to look and evaluate ERP implementation during the pre-implementation and also focus on post-implementation for auditors to understand the full ERP implementation.

Bancraft et al.'s (1998) five-phase model evaluates the pre-implementation and implementation, but it does not model the phases to cover the post-implementation of ERP. Markus and Tanis (1999) and Ross (1998) models focus on the development of the ERP system and up to the post-implementation. In the Bancraft et al. (1998) model, the paper focus is on the post implementation phases of the ERP system. Research evolving around ERP implementation does focus on the use of these process models. Many other researchers (e.g. Parr and Shanks, 2000) are now attempting to understand how these ERP implementation functions and evaluate the critical success factors for successful implementation.

In developing the ERP implementation model, most of the researchers developed these models by using business cases. In deploying this development model, researchers have built necessary tools to assist them to roll out (Parr and Shanks, 2000). In Parr and Shanks' (2000) work, it is found that the success of these implementations is based on social aspects of the project within the phases. The phases, however, do not focus on the implementation throughout the entire phase of the implementation cycle. Most models segmented the implementation into phases and define individual critical success factors within each phase. As the research discusses how to break down the implementation phase, researchers are trying to integrate the issues with the phases of implementation.

5.3 Conceptual Models

Another type of model in ERP studies are conceptual models. The conceptual models are different from the ERP implementation phase models in understanding an organisational ERP implementation. These models look at different ERP management approaches. It aids the conceptual understanding about how ERP implementation takes place from strategic and knowledge management school of thoughts. The development of these models can allow building significant insights into the ERP phenomenon. As literature suggests these ERP systems are primarily strategic and directed at the goal-attainment of the organisation (Davenport, 2000b; Ferrando, 2000; Koch, 2001a).

Francalanci (2000) for example, developed a predictive model to predict ERP implementation cost. The author encounters researches developing ERP implementation models to formulate and develop a theoretical explanation for effective ERP implementation (e.g. Rosemann and Wiese, 1999). These models are often used to measure the effectiveness of ERP in attaining the organisation's formulated goals and other performance criteria. In the context of ERP process and workflow implementation, successful implementation is often defined as "best fit" to measure success factors (Soh, Sia and Tay-Yap 2000; Scott 1999; Aladwani 2001)

Numerous studies with focus on defining models for organisational ERP have tried to develop a conceptual framework to understand how ERP impacts the work environment (Rosemann, 2000; Al-Mashari and Zairi, 2000; Parr and Shanks, 2000; Kim, 2000). Among the models, the researcher found that Rosemann (2000) and Kim (2000) models mentioned about knowledge being a critical part of successful ERP implementations. The Kim (2000) model attempts to provide a framework where knowledge can be shared through sharing business process models across different organisation functions. The idea of sharing knowledge is also seen in the Holland (2001) model, where he focuses on social and people issue in the adoption of ERP. He focused on modelling how organisations will make use of the ERP system. This model explained about the problems which evolved from ERP implementation through to its post-implementation life cycle shows significant amount of issues that pertain to changes and people (e.g. "people feeling comfortable with decisions", people information handling skills).

Most models which evolved around the ERP system agree that ERP is a sophisticated system to implement. The success of an ERP implementation lies in integrating change management and creating support for information and people within the organisation. The author suggests that no research reference model in the literature integrates the different stages of implementation. To understand the problems in ERP, the author evaluates the success and failures in ERP implementation.

5.3.1 Successes and Disasters

According to a recent survey, almost two-thirds of all ERP implementations failed to live up to expectations (McCann, 2000). If this was true for the large companies that first adopted ERP, it could prove even worse for the many mid-size companies that are now beginning to install ERP. The new tools and pre-configured solutions that vendors are offering to midsize customers for quick implementation are highly useful. Yet they come without the customized optimization features that add much of the value promised by ERP. Unless the company identifies its specific operational needs and adopt a clear plan to extract them from the one-size-fits-all package, there may be added risk of additional cost. Current ERP researches have primarily focused on how to improve the ERP implementation duration.

This period is being seen as an 'obstacle' that needs to be overcome. Some researches discuss about the implementation process itself. For instance, Ross (1998) provides a process model that describes how organisations should execute an ERP implementation. Other researchers identify factors which contribute to successful and unsuccessful ERP implementations (e.g. Holland and light, 1999; Scott, 1999; Soh, Sia and Tay-Yap, 2000; Van Everdingen, Hillegersberg and Waarts, 2000; Barbara, 2001). These critical success factors include top management commitment, strategic vision, and users' training. None of these approaches explicitly recognize the need to identify the extent of the integration takes place across different organisational constructs. Further, the implications of failure to integrate the organisation using ERP system are numerous (e.g. user resistance, organisational culture, Knowledge transfer).

Prior researches on ERP performance measurements (Rosemann and Wiese, 1999) were mostly conducted by practitioners, e.g. Deloitte Consulting (Deloitte, 2001). Furthermore, the researcher found that the implementation success is often measured in terms of cost and duration of the implementation (Bingi, Sharma and Godla, 1999). The objectives associated with implementing ERP systems are to realize the promised benefits of enterprise systems (Davenport, 2000). Typically, these benefits are in the form of reduced cycle times, reduced inventory costs, increased agility, or improvements in the availability of strategic decision information (Bingi, Sharma and Godla, 1999; Davenport, 2000). These benefits can clearly be assessed only during the in-use stage.

Various studies on ERP systems in use concentrates on ERP performance evaluation and on identification of usage stage activities and problems. ERP performance may, for example, be evaluated based upon the Balanced Scorecard method (Rosemann and Wiese, 1999), which measure the degree to which the intended goals are actually obtained. An ERP performance evaluation helps to identify problems and opportunities for further development of the enterprise system. It is important to note that such goals are dynamic and thus require that the performance measures evolve over time as well. Potential activities, problems and errors that may occur after the system has gone live have also been identified (Davenport, 2000; Markus and Tanis, 2000). As seen by Davenport (2000), ERP implementation results in the formal representation of linking organisational strategy, knowledge, structure, processes and workflow together. Thus, ERP packages may be seen as contributors both to the capture and management of knowledge. There is a need to determine the success with which such resources is actually captured and integrated within the system (Wan and Pan, 2000). However, a word of caution is necessary here since knowledge may be refined, expanded and sometimes discarded during the implementation phase. Therefore, there is a need to assess the extent to which actual pre-existing resources are appropriately represented in the ERP system. As with many information technologies (Boudreau and Robey, 1999), results of the ERP implementation efforts range from extreme failures to extreme successes. Some projects are abandoned before the actual go-live date, or are assumed to have played an important role in the bankruptcy of a company, such as FoxMeyer (Scott, 1999). Other companies proudly report their successes, often through their software vendors and consultants, such as SAP AG, Baans, Oracle, etc. For Instance, the company used to require two weeks on average to ship to customers, 98 percent of products are now shipped within 24 hours. Financial closing times were cut in half, from 12 days to six. It has saved more on reduced inventory alone than its SAP system installation cost.

There is a danger here that improved performance in the short term may not be the result of improved process knowledge. There is a need for significantly more research into the location, nature and extent of how organisations can function effectively using the ERP system. Care must be taken to investigate how knowledge and relationships are constructed on different social constructs (e.g. Communities, Groups and Individuals). It is also worth observing that organisations are likely to have both formal and information processes for maintaining and enhancing organisational processes and workflows. These processes must be identified and reconstituted in the post-ERP organisation.

5.4 Types of Implementation

Prior studies have identified that in order to implement ERP system in the organisation, a significant amount of commitment to resources and the management of these changes within the IT infrastructure is needed (e.g. Soh, Sia and Tay-Yap 2000). Author found that theoretically, ERP is often seen in three dimensions as reported by Markus *et al.* (2000). For the implementations of ERP packages within organisations, scholars have found that migrating to the ERP system makes a negative impact on the users of the organisation (Davenport, 2000b; Markus, Tanis and Fenema, 2000; Markus and Tanis, 1999). These problems found to be prevailing even before ERP is implemented. Markus (2000) pointed out that the different ERP problems can be linked to even pre-implementation set-up of the organisation and user culture. This makes it necessary for researchers to identify these problems from pre-implementation to post-implementation. Author could closely link these problems through the different ERP integration issues revealed by prior research.

Prior research discusses social, process, workflow, knowledge and virtual integration in general but little has been done to evaluate a model that would integrate these factors. Although ERPs implementations use different approaches and possess different architecture, researches found similar issues prevailed across these implementations (e.g. Bingi, Sharma and Godla, 1999; Parr and Shanks 2000; Ross and Vitale, 2000). In particular, Ferrando (2000) and Hayman (2000) research in particular found that ERP have played a significant integrative role in the organisation. The integration nature has been evident in different implementations. In particular, in this thesis the researcher likes to look at the integration perspective of ERP implementation.

5.5 Social Integration

The computational ERP has little relevance to knowledge work, but the communication and storage capabilities of ERP systems make them knowledge enablers. Computers and networks can point to people with knowledge and connect people who need to share knowledge over a distance. These forms social networks of knowledge allow organisations to leverage expertise from within the organisation. ERP like any other computer system, it is only the pipeline and storage system for social exchanges. It does not create knowledge nor can it guarantee or even promote knowledge generation or knowledge sharing in a corporate culture that does not favour those activities.

Therefore, we need to look at how these systems can support social integration. Previous studies indicated that ERP implementation involves significant change. For example, the ERP implementation has triggered fundamental changes in the areas of structure (Al-Mashari and Zairi, 2000), culture (Soh, Sia and Tay-Yap, 2000), information strategy (Rizzi and Zamboni, 1999), and ERP distribution (Markus, Tanis and Fenema, 2000). These studies had revealed that ERP implementation is a highly complex process and concluded that further research is needed to investigate issues that influence the success and failure of ERP implementation. Markus *et al.* (2000) and Ross (1999) cautioned that major problems can arise from social, cultural barriers and user resistance in most implementations, especially in multi-site organisations where significant levels of integration and coordination are required between business strategy, software configuration, technical platform and management execution. As a result, the researcher must not neglect the existence of the working social environment.

Management politics and social settings in organisation have been studied in research (Grint 1995; Buchanan and Bobby, 1992). He noted that studies revealed significant resistance in the implementation of ERP (Koch, 2001b). It has implicated that politics and social environment is a process of building a social coalition between management and organisational life (Koch, 2001b). The literatures revealed strong insights which allow other researches in the social areas of the ERP implementation (Koch 2001b; Soh, Sia and Tay-Yap 2000; Markus and Tanis 1999). In the development of social integration, the researcher identified the importance of building a context for integration to take place. In the implementation of ERP, the prevailing social context for social integration is often the implementation team.

5.6 Resistance in Social Integration

ERP often fails when social resistance occurs in the organisation (Ross, 1999a). This was evidently found in previous studies that ERP involved a magnitude of user involvement and change (e.g. Laughlin, 1999). These researchers are concerned about how user resistance is seen as a critical factor in managing the ERP system change (e.g. Ross 1999b). They found that ERP impacts the people through changing their work environment and organisational practices. Social feelings and awareness is highlighted in Aladwani (2001) study. In developing the awareness of ERP, he emphasized that opinions, communication and involvement are three variables to focus in an actual ERP adoption. Communication is essential as feedback and workers' anxiety need to be evaluated since anxiety may have a positive impact on recorded ERP acceptance performance counters or negative impact on its use. The study also emphasized on involving the users where it makes acceptably fit for the users and the management. Fuchs's (2000) study, in particular, attempts to propose radical change to a centralized administration as a competitive strategic approach when ERP is implemented.

It is often found that while trying to change from a one system to another processing system through ERP implementation, many social resistant occurs. In short, the literatures argued about the importance of user problems within the ERP implementation as one of the major cause of ERP failures (Krumbholz, Galliers, Coulianos and Maiden, 2000; Ross, 1999b). Lacking, however, is any considerable understanding of the context of these problems and they are not able to identify the cause of these problems. Many of these literatures have addressed about the social issues during the implementation phase but they did not address the post implementation needs of the ERP support.

5.7 Process Integration

Process is a series of activities that is done collectively to generate a particular output that is of value to the organisation (Ng, Ip and Lee, 1999). Business practices, rule information and knowledge found in processes are often irregular and difficult to model. Organisations have been found to create hard to imitate processes which researchers call core competence. These processes often position the organisation strategically against its competitors through making their business core competence difficult to model. The quest for better work practices may even trigger a search for new resources, or the appearance of new resources (ERP technologies) may motivate individuals and groups to take advantage of them through new work practices. Recognition of potential work practices by individuals or work-groups may or may not be transferred across an ERP implementation. Recognition of these work practices and their transfer should be promoted to ensure common practice across an organisation. To be able to promote these consistently, the researcher need to understand these processes.

Hence, process integration is about understanding the processes and using these processes to develop effective workflows. The researcher needs to look at Process integration in ERP. Process integration differs from Business Process Reengineering in that it focuses on fitting the ERP and the people (Koch, 2001a). It can, however, be seen that process integration is a process of organisational change in the way people work in organisations (Koch, 2001a). In many studies, processes are often perceived in terms of individuals and departments (Wood and MCaldas, 2001). Wood found problems in managing the processes within ERP through reductionism or through being IT-focused.

This reduces efficiency when ERP processes are developed from these approaches. As a business comprise of a nested series of business practices which dependently on each other like in a system (Checkland, 1981). Hence like checkland (1981) suggest that the researcher needs to look at the process culture and social organisation environment which the business function takes place (Wood and MCaldas, 2001). In the study conducted by Themistocleous and Irani (2001), the system application is seen as a system which needs to be supported by process which is also dependant on the environment and the people. Process integration involves sharing information and collaboration. It means that processes are not isolated from the social environment. To integrate these processes, the researcher defines the organisational environment where processes can co-exist and work effectively across functional unit.

5.7.1 Communications in Process Integration

Communication is often defined as a fundamental issue in developing effective organisations (Senge 1990). This is further elaborated by Vosburg and Kumar (2001) who defined the effectiveness of ERP implementation is in the effectiveness to provide a mean to understand what each other is doing, and the value of ERP is in the process in the business function to allow people to work closely with each other. At a organisational level, it includes the involvement of everyone at all levels (Nah and Lee- Shang, 2001). From the perception of Levitt and March (1988), communication is defined as a process of information and knowledge diffusion. They view that communication must be effectively diffused and it takes place if only when people focus on communicate across the organisation. Vosburg and Kumar's (2001) defined process integration as an effective setup of communications, sharing culture, building complex information sharing and knowledge sharing within the ERP implementation. They found that if these factors are not managed well by the organisation, ERP will fail. By keeping them informed of the company business, it would allow them to support necessary modification to the reports and data input processes, and subsequently changing the ERP configuration.

The ability to update the ERP implementation ensures that the updates create continuous support. The need of continuous support ensures that new practices are constantly detected and updated into the ERP implementation. They view communication as a channel to detect changes in the process which needs to be embedded into the system.

5.7.2 Alignment of Culture in Process Integration

Kotter (1996) emphasizes the need for organisations to change in today's rapidly changing business environment. In his book 'Leading Change', he asserted that firms should be adaptive and flexible to stay competitive. In his words, "truly adaptive firmswith adaptive cultures are awesome competitive machines. They produce superb products and services faster and better." Hence, the researcher needs to focus on the culture In many discussions of process integration, team culture is seen as a critical factor(Sumner 1999; Nah and Lee-Shang, 2001).

It is important that work do not perform on just individual processes and the nature is very much team based. Culture has often been seen as a habit, attitude or idiosyncrasy of the organisation or users to perform a process(Aladwani, 2001). If working together is not a present culture, the alignment of such a culture in particular is emphasized in ERP implementation. Nah and Lau (2001) further explores that organisational culture governs the business vision and business plan of the organisation from a team-working environment. With the aligning of culture, people can develop a common vision and culture to share as a team. And in ERP implementation, the organisations are often seen to be working together and because they share a similar ERP system, the users need to share information. The alignment of culture, in particular the acceptance of ERP, is greater if only the users are comfortable with the ERP system functions (Huang, 2001). In particular, Huang had been interested in looking at the maturity of IT usage and the dependency of computers in the organisation. The dependency of the computers in organisation is an assurance that organisation culturally incline to accepting technological solutions. The culture component of the ERP can help us understand the acceptability of having ERP aligning the processes.

5.7.3 Knowledge Integration

ERP is a technologically enable knowledge to be shared and transferred. Knowledge integration allows the use of knowledge to be effectively used across the organisation. The researcher found knowledge integration evolves around two type of knowledge. The concept of knowledge type here consists of tacit and explicit. Tacit is nonverbal, intuitive, highly context specific and has a personal quality that makes it difficult to formalize and communicate (Nonaka, Takeuchi and Umemoto, 1996). While explicit knowledge is verbal in formal or systematic language, it can be easily codified or articulated in manual, computer programs, tools, etc. These two types of knowledge will not be separated here since it cannot be done easily, and there is no such thing as pure tacit knowledge or pure explicit knowledge. Being tacit is something difficult to share and maintain.

Sharing knowledge sometimes is difficult, since Davenport (2000) defines knowledge "as being originated" and is applied in the minds of the knowers. It can alsobe considered as giving away the competitive knowledge to other people, especially in a company where the competition among employees are high and personal knowledge is believed as their bargaining power towards the company. Hence, knowledge is often seen as a commodity of exchange. And it is not always easy to manage such a commodity and is often lose in the process of transfer. Of course the consultant is not the only source of knowledge for the implementing organisation. ERP knowledge is also obtained from other sources such as documentation, the vendor, generally available literature, other organisations and associates, and from experienced employees within the company.

In some cases the consultant is the major facilitator of knowledge transfer during the implementation period. This means that the consultant has a large control over the knowledge management dynamics of that transfer. It could, for example, not transfer specific knowledge about its implementation methodology. As such, knowledge in itself has many limitations in the process of exchange and utilization in the ERP implementation. By examining knowledge sourcing, explication and transfer events one can track the management of knowledge throughout the ERP systems lifecycle. One aspect of interest is the knowledge sourcing interplay between the implementing organisation, the consultant and the users throughout the lifecycle. Each of these parties is of vital interest in a successful implementation outcome.

Knowledge in Organisation

In the development of ERP, knowledge is a critical part of the management of organisational asset. Knowledge has often been seen as a necessary resource which provides the organisation with its competitive advantage. Drucker (1988) believes that the organisation of the future is one that is knowledge-based, and knowledge will be one of the most important and meaningful resources of an organisation for wealth creation (Marquardt and Reynolds, 1994). Learning creates knowledge, and thus the learning organisation fulfils Drucker's criteria of being the organisation of the future as it supports (and) provides a context for individuals to create knowledge (Nonaka, 1994).

Knowledge that is created through learning usually includes meanings, interpretations, experiences (Nevis et at., 1995) and other personalized qualities of the learner, and may not be formalized and communicated (Nonaka, 1994). This knowledge is considered as tacit and needs to be made explicit by interacting it with others (Nonaka, 1994; Spender, 1996) where it will also be amplified, as explained by Nonaka (1994). In Nonaka's (1994) model of organisational knowledge creation, he argues that it is through interactions between individuals will lead to the amplification and development of new knowledge. Through these interactions, tacit and explicit knowledge that are produced by one part of the organisation creates a stream of related information and knowledge which may in turn trigger changes in the organisation's wider knowledge systems (Nonaka, 1994).

In fact, it is this amplified knowledge that is meaningful as it increases the cognitive and behavioural repertoires of members to steer the organisation in the right direction (DeGeus, 1988; Richards, 1991; Schein, 1993). Therefore, it is important for knowledge created by individuals to be transferred throughout the system, in order to be made explicit and generate more knowledge. However, Nonaka cautions that knowledge created must be screened for relevance and quality (Nonaka, 1994). Thus, the researcher argues that the critical challenge of integrating knowledge in the case of ERP implementation lays in the ability to bringing key parties together vendors, key users and IS personnel (Soh, Sia and Tay-Yap, 2000). Deriving from this argument, knowledge integration in the implementation process applies not only to multiple sources of knowledge (Pisano, 1994) but also to solving conflicts of knowledge capabilities, cultural and social impact (Teece, Pisano and Shuen, 1997) brought forward by different parties to the implementation process.

This integration process is often met with obstacles, as knowledge is frequently tacit and embedded within routines of which few are stand-alone. Tacit knowledge within the system makes knowledge integration in these implementations slow and painful (Nonaka, 1994; Grant, 1996). Therefore, in striving to understand the barriers of knowledge integration encountered during the ERP implementation, the researcher adopted a view that sees knowledge per se as socially embedded and these knowledge sources are participants of these social systems (Wenger, 2000; Huber, 1991). In other words, this study examines the dynamic nature of the barriers that are found during the ERP implementation, and a particular focus will be on the relational, structural and knowledge-based barriers. The use of ERP software packages has grown at a phenomenal rate since it first started three decades ago (Hayman, 2000).

With the growth of organisation and globalization, the ERP systems began to grow and occupied a critical part of the IT infrastructure in many organisations since people are not confined to their work locations (Davenport, 2000b). Hence, knowledge has been highly decentralized as people begin to be distributed across many different locations. Developing new management concepts is an objective which the organisation must do to support the new evolving nature of the business world in going mobile.

Auditors must look at how ERP within the organisational structures has the ability to integrate new management concepts into the organisation (Venkatraman and Henderson, 1998; Ng, IP and Lee 1999) Prior research has emphasized on the significance of knowledge development in organisation. Practitioners and management academics have acknowledged that the old bureaucratic command-and-control model, even in its lean and decentralized mode is not up to the challenges ahead. They have accepted the concept of IT as a necessity for survival and foundation for a sustainable competitive advantage (Davenport, 2000b).

As it is recognized by Davenport (2000), current circumstances tell us that ERP is no longer a choice but a necessity; the most urgent priority is learning how to learn – and learning faster and that in an economy where the only certainty is un-certainty, the one source of lasting competitive advantage is knowledge and within successful companies are those that consistently create new knowledge, dissemi-nate it widely throughout the organisation and quickly embody it in new technolo-gies and products (Nonaka and Konno, 1998). ERP systems can be viewed as part of the organisational memory in an organisation, with contents relating to a di-verse range of organisational memory contents that is located in organisational processes, structure, and culture (Van Stijin and Wensley, 2001).

As such, it can be conceptualized in ways in which the knowledge embedded in the ERP system can be in conflict with other organisational knowledge, in particu-lar process knowledge (Jan, 2001). Organisational memory mismatches are dis-crepancies between organisational memory contents located in the ERP system and related contents that are stored at other organisational memory media (Van Stijin and Wensley 2001). For example, organisational structures and databases, such memory mismatches causes under-performance of the ERP system which leads to a need for coping. Coping strategies varies and may involve further en-hancements to the ERP system or to a variety of other strategies. As knowledge is critical, organisation must also not neglect the workflow efficiency from legacy to the ERP workflow.

5.7.4 Workflow Integration

Workflow integration has been an important topic in ERP implementation. The re-search has significant interest in bringing the enterprise physical work space into an ERP workspace where workflow can be integrated through the ERP system across organisations (Hayman, 2000). And for the organisation to be successful, Ng *et al.* (1999) suggested that ERP workflow has to evolve from a high perform-ance team structure to function as an integrated business workflow. Markus *et al.* (2000) noted that current ERP has often faced lack of functionality to support the existing workflow and tailoring the package to the organisational workflow.

They found a big problem in it where the workflow is complex and ERP does not precisely define the processes that appropriately fit the organisation. Ross (1999a) and Willcocks (2000) in their articles have emphasised on the change of the role of the IT function for fitting into the ERP environment. In which Will-cocks noted that the changes that went on within the ERP implementation created very different IT support needs which existing IT infrastructure is not adequate for managing the ERP system.

The role of the Chief Information Officer and the IT department shifted from a technical support to manage organisational capabilities, culture and organisational practices. Other existing literatures did not, however, explore any aspects of the IT services (e.g. IT department) issues. Researchers have found ERP workflow inte-gration problem are primarily cross-functional in nature (Markus, Petrie and Ax-line, 2000). These workflows apparently failed in building appropriate communi-cations across different organisational functions (e.g. marketing and logistic).

It is often due to the lack of resources that made organisation integrate internal legacy system to ERP instead of building effective ERP base workflows. This resulted in discontinuity in the ERP implementation of the workflow (Markus, Petrie and Axline, 2000). With the integration of workflows, ERP practitioners are thinking of developing and using ERP's best practice processes within the workflow.

5.7.5 Best Practices in Functional Integration

Although ERP has often been seen as a leader for adopting organisational best practices, but embodying best practices in their reference models are not without problems (Davenport, 1998; Kumar and Van Hillegersberg, 2000). Reference models supposedly reflect the preferred business models which include underlying data and process models as well as organisational structures (Kumar and Van Hillegersberg, 2000, p. 25).

Reference models are process models (often in broad sense, including function, data, and organisation models (Scheer, 1998)) that are available from third parties; for example, they may be supplied by SAP or ERP consultants. It is assumed that such reference models are based on theoretical and practical assumptions with regards to the best practices for a given process. There are growing agendas about how organisations are to be modelled within an ERP system. The process model has often been debated as a vital problem. Many cases found that ERP has been a misfit within an organisation.

This is due to the way the processes are being modelled. Similarly, as pointed out by Soh et al., (2000), a common challenge in adopting package software (such as an ERP system) successfully has been on the issue of "misfits" – the gap between the pre-written functionality offered and that which is required by the adopting organisation. Specifically, in their study of Singaporean hospitals, Soh et al. (2000) found different types of misfits, resolution strategies employed and the related impact on organisations adopting the ERP systems. According to their analysis, it was the knowledge gap between the three parties (key users, IS department personnel, and the ERP vendor) and the ERP implementation process as the cause.

While Soh et al. (2000) cautioned about the difficulties and importance of integrating the knowledge of all parties involved in the implementation process, Soh et al. (2000) failed to outline the barriers which prevent people from integrating their knowledge successfully. The development of best practices is an area which is quite clearly argued on how those closely best practices can be transferred into organisation. The question of building a business around the software needs has not been addressed (Ross 1999b). Practitioners are focusing on the use of a centralized service centre to allow functional financial controlling to be done through ERP.

With the increasing need to centralize brought about by the ERP systems, there is a significant interest in how the Shared Service Centre (SSC) can be leverage to increase value (e.g. Miller 1999; Goold, Pettifer and Young 2001). The concept of the SSC implementation was not a new concept and was used in the early 1980s by Ford (Ann, Rice, Mahhotra and Ba, 2000). It was noted that the SSC provides IT services (Institute of Internal Auditors1998). However, the literatures did not discuss about the issues of having a SSC and the role of the IT department. With regards to the organisation implementing ERP, there is a need to know how organisations with a diverse social and cultures context, such as multi-nationals, actually implement ERP and seek the match between the organisations' culture and their ERP implementations. This would happen only when there is a match with its operating environment whereby the organisation is able to produce competitive advantages. As such, it is important to fit the organisation to the ERP environment which it operates in. Willcocks and Sykes (2000) evaluate how the IT function impacted the way in which business processes are modelled. The IT function has long played a significant role in developing Information System for organisations.

5.7.6 Virtual Integration

E-commerce is said to leverage the organisational competence in many areas of the organisation. E-commerce is the final phase for organisations in its process of going into e-business. It can be described as disruptive technological change which impact mainstream activities (Christensen, 1997; Dhillon, *et al.*, 2001). Disruptive technology allows building and identification of integration areas which can be automated or delivered using a virtual environment. Virtual integration is often used to integrate technological advancement with the business to meet future challenges. With globalization, communication has been identified as the biggest challenge (Christensen, 1997). The vast areas coverage for potential customers and suppliers make traditional methods of communication expensive and slow. Hence, virtual communication is the best viable means since it is very fast, cheap and not limited geographically. According to Anderson (2000), globalization also results in large flow of knowledge and administration of such knowledge. It is through virtual internet based products and services adoption, organisations are now becoming part of the virtual integration approaches. By making use of these virtual integration tools to allow knowledge base distribution and sharing within the organisation. As products are growing to become more customised, local knowledge of the customer is needed to build the product (Sunny, 1999). These products are designed by global engineers but cater for local needs. Often a good virtual integration tool is one that allows people to draw on first-hand knowledge of each other to seek support (Kanter, 1998). It will also need to link people across multiple locations or transfer ideas across different location. For example, in Kanter's (1998) case where physical separation allows innovation to take place away from operating environment. It reduced the functional overseas of testing new and innovative ideas. Hence, it reduced the need on location dependencies of building and testing ideas and problem solving.

5.8 Auditor and ERP

The ERP solution also has implications related to the audit function and the role of the IT auditor. Effective and efficient internal control systems contribute significantly to the decision-making needs of management in then form of assured systems and equally assured business processes. An effectively monitored and audited system of internal control is capable of assets safeguarding, accuracy and reliability of accounting information, efficiency of business operations and the adherence to environmental and legislative policies by the organisation.

The ERP solution with its integrated built-in controls becomes an enabling technology for IT auditors. While the objectives of the internal control function remain the same, the mechanism of controls and control procedures change. Traditional controls, such as segregation of responsibilities, will not be cost-effective in the ERP solution and may not be able to deliver the required level of control (Chapman, 1998b).

The design of an efficient and effective internal control system in an ERP solution is an important issue. The involvement and the commitment of IT auditors before, during and after the implementation is essential so as to ensure that controls are designed, implement and tested for theirs efficiency and effectiveness. The American Institute of Certified Public Accountants (AICPA) and the Committee of Sponsoring Organisations (COSO) consider the internal controls with the following objectives (Ratliff et. al., 1996):

1. the reliability and integrity of information
2. compliance with policies, plans, procedures, laws, and regulations
3. the safeguarding of assets
4. the economical and efficient use of resources
5. the accomplishment of established objectives and goals for operations and programmes

These internal control objectives are established to maintain effective control over activities and operations. IT auditors have been concerned with accounting and financial issues with the operational auditors of the enterprises.

5.8.1 ERP Internal Control Procedures

The strategic and tactical business requirement of an organisation must be the driving force for implementing an ERP solution. An ERP solution replaces the huge number of databases in a company with one powerful system capable of integrating, analyzing, and reporting on information from the enterprise. Programs and data files are fully integrated into one virtual system. There are no subsystems, partitions, or non-interfacing legacy systems that need to be reconciled.

It also includes advanced control and audit features, such as security profile administration tools, logging capabilities, Business Workflow, and the fully traceable transaction capabilities. Financial closing entries can be accomplished quickly, in a matter of hours, not weeks, as in the case of the traditional environment. There is no need to do reconciliation activities or journal voucher adjusting entries because the sub-modules are fully integrated. However, the re-engineering associated with the ERP implementation may lead to inadequate or reduced business internal controls.

The IT auditor is now open to a broad range of activities that have not been considered before (Chapman, 1998a).The control focus is classified according to implementation and post-implementation phases. During implementation, the IT auditor roles include the following, in order of execution:

1. *Strategist*: is involved in the strategic planning and decision making of the organisation. Develops an understanding of the business process reengineering with users and facilitates the consultants' work.
2. *ERP Expert*: evaluates the control features of an ERP solution and assesses current and future risk exposure. Highlights the importance of soft controls and delegates the accountability of control.
3. *Communicator*: maintains relationships throughout the organisation and facilitates the adoption of audit controls with users, as well as with consultants from outside the company.
4. *IT Manager*: updates and unifies terminology to take advantage of the integrated nature of the ERP solution. Shares expertise, knowledge, and ideas with IS/IT management.

Internal controls are established to achieve management objectives and to maintain effective control over activities and operations. An ERP solution drives the organisation strategically upward and presents changes and challenges to the audit environment. It replaces the huge number of databases in a company with one powerful system capable of integrating, analyzing, and reporting on information from all of the company's business functions. An ERP solution brings about changes in the business processes, changes in hardware, and changes in the ERP software version, which affect the audit function.

This chapter has made a variety of suggestions for improving the implementation process and result (Scheer and Habermann, 2000; Sprott, 2000; Kremers and van Dissel, 2000; Kumar and Hillegersberg, 2000). Almost none of them look at the problem of ERP from pre-implementation to post-implementation. In Wan and Pan (2001) paper, they highlighted the barriers in ERP implementation. The research developed as part of the thesis to conceptually isolate the barriers in ERP implementation.

Thus, together with the importance of understanding the barriers and finding solutions to overcome them, the theoretical under-development of ERP integration has aroused the researchers' curiosity to explore the increasingly popular ERP phenomenon further. Instead of providing prescriptions on how knowledge can be integrated in the process, no research has fully understood the dynamic nature of the barriers of integration that are hindering ERP integration as well as the implementation process. In Pan, Newell, Huang and Wan (2001) paper, it is argued that the literature review did not focus on how integration impacted the organisations' social infrastructure.

The researchers found issues and complications in ERP implementation. In conclusion, it can be said that little is known about integration barriers throughout the ERP implementation cycle. However, future studies of the ERP phenomenon would certainly high light these issues in greater detail so as to enable IT auditors to plan ERP-based information systems audit engagement.

6 Technology, Auditing and Cyber-Commerce

Exponential growth in internet and the transmission bandwidth of the communication carrier is transforming the way businesses operate and communicate. In this technology-centric world, customers, partners, suppliers and employees are demanding unparalleled levels of service, collaboration and communications. Organisations must adopt a purposeful e-commerce strategy (Doherty and Ellis-Chadwick, 2003; Good and Schultz, 2002) to compete in the emerging marketplace.

The goal of this chapter is to examine the current state-of-art technology scenario in the business enterprises and the risk understanding by an auditor in the cyber environment. There is substantial discussion on the risk understanding and monitoring schema to be followed by an auditor while auditing in cyber commerce environment and various possible fraudulent acts and risks related thereof. In the concluding section, I present a model structure of audit in e-commerce as well as a model audit report structure to be followed by a prospective auditor.

The American Institute of CPAs (AICPA) and Canadian Institute of Chartered Accountants (CICA) have developed specific criteria that an entity must comply with to obtain and maintain the CPA WebTrust seal (Williams, 1997; Anonymous, 1997). The seal of approval indicates that the particular online business has been subject to an evaluation by a CPA firm. The seal also provides assurance regarding the following:

- Business practices and information privacy. The business must disclose how orders are processed and how returns and warranties are handled. The business must also disclose its policy on the maintenance of customer information (e.g., the selling of mailing lists)
- Transaction integrity. The business must report how transactions are validated and processed, as well as how the billing process is controlled. Disclosures of billing and settlement terms are also required
- Information protection. The business must protect the privacy of sensitive information, such as credit card numbers, through the use of encryption

E-Commerce as a technology is not very simple. It gets further complicated with the changes in communication technologies, database and other related information technologies. E-Commerce is not adopted by businesses simply to reduce their operating costs and increase their revenue. One should be very clear that if any business initiates e-commerce with the objective of reducing operational costs may not get the resultant effect without clearly chalking out the strategy and opting for the right model. It is a well-known fact that e-commerce is risk-based due to the technologies involved (Sutton and Hampton, 2003), which may expose a business's data and systems to unknown outsiders. Not everyone always has a genuine desire to conduct business; some may intrude into an organisation's systems with specific intent or out of sheer curiosity.

The intrusion may be facilitated either by malicious hacking techniques or by sheer chance (Gingler 2002; Biermann et al, 2001). Thus, any e-business is a sitting duck with regard to the illicit and illegal objectives of a malicious hacker or intruder who may wreak havoc on system resources and data.

6.1 Technology and Auditing

However, e-commerce increasingly appears to be essential for an organisation's survival and growth. In an e-commerce environment (Wei et al, 2002; Bette and Gilbert, 2001), the internal systems and processes of an entity are no longer operated in isolation. An organisation exchanges information via transactions that link entities together in ways unanticipated in the traditional environment.

Today, the term electronic commerce (e-commerce) includes all commercial activities performed through information technology and communication engineering such as the Internet, virtual private networks (VPN) (Walid and Kerivin, 2003; Harding, 2003) , automated teller machines (ATMs), electronic fund transfers (EFT), electronic data interchange (EDI) (Sangjae and Lim, 2003), e-supply chain management (e-SCM) (Williams et al, 2002) and also e-customer relationship management (e-CRM) (Pan and Lee, 2003).

Most e-commerce implementations concentrate on optimizing the Internet as a tool to facilitate transactions – on providing networked computers which allow end-users to create and transform business relationships (O'Toole, 2003). New enterprise applications and various applications integration technologies provide technology driven business solutions which improve the quality of dealing with the customers and vendors of goods and services, increase the speed of service delivery and reduce the cost of business operations.

This revamping also contributes to better, improved and standardized internal business processes (Barness et al, 2002) through business process re-engineering (BPE) (Wu, 2003). Enterprise-wide application integration (Fan et al, 1999) and complex systems integration processes (Pathak and Lind, 2003) though highly technical plays a vital role in holistic improvement of the business processes of any business entity planning to take a jump in the arena of e-commerce.

Figure 1 shown here depicts the e-commerce technologies on a graphical matrix in relation to structured and unstructured formats and also on high and low level of technology complexity.

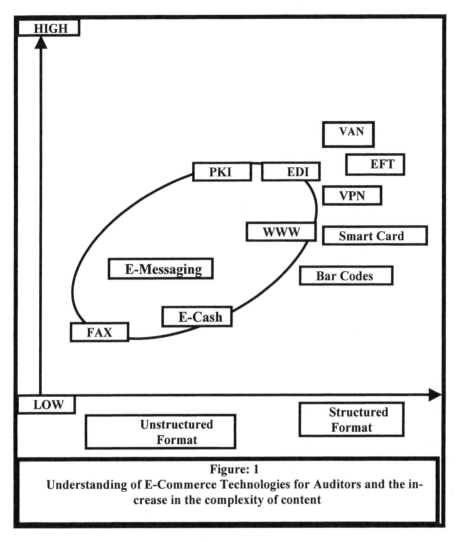

Figure: 1
Understanding of E-Commerce Technologies for Auditors and the increase in the complexity of content

A decade ago, this type of functionality was limited to EDI transactions. EDI, the precursor of e-commerce category called business-to-business (B2B), is a method of electronic data and information transfers which businesses used to complete transactions. This method saved time and effort over detailed paperwork, but it is relatively an expensive system to install and maintain. Also, it is a closed and proprietary system which is available to and used among only the relatively larger corporations. In contrast, the electronic data transfers (Litsikas, 1997) allowed by new forms of e-commerce are fluid and easy to use. Though the World Wide Web (WWW) is still in its growth phase and the processing of transactions in such open domain has its own drawbacks and the issues related to the integrity and reliability. But, it allows a free flow of information across an open, widely available network of WWW. E-commerce allows a variety of interactions, from business-to-consumer (B2C) transactions such as buying and selling information, products and services using the Internet, to transferring and sharing information within organisations through intranets. The another category which has truly picked up of late is business to business (B2B) e-commerce dealing with the vendors', dealers' and suppliers' network. It grants such benefits as improved decision-making, increased efficiency, less paperwork and greater empowerment. As a business paradigm, e-business supports and complements business process re-engineering and integration. A successful e-commerce implementation in an organisation should have goals defined. These goals may include:

- reduced transaction costs
- greater productivity Service availability 24 hours a day / 7 days a week
- opportunities for fundamental reform in how organisations and their supply chains communicate and work with other businesses and
- opportunities for local businesses to grow and compete in the global marketplace

Perhaps the most important facet of e-commerce is the way customers become empowered through the routes that companies use to reach and interact with them. These changes affect four areas which shape customer relationships:

- advertising
- order taking
- customer service and
- customised products/services

Whatever the competitive strategy (Gill, 2003) chosen, it is important to decide the extent to which the investment should be deployed, and the time frame for such investments. Such investments can include personnel and equipment needed to develop a web presence, communicate with customers, monitor the competitive environment (Avishalom and Bazerman, 2003), develop new products or a niche, and expand the supplier base.

Prior to the installation or shifting over to e-commerce, an organisation deserves to ascertain the level of risk exposure on two counts: the number of people involved and the value of the transaction (payment or contract). As a general rule, more the parties involved, the greater the risk. Similarly, a higher value transaction will generate greater risk. Because e-commerce allows international trading, the number and location of parties that can attempt to access the systems create new challenges related to protecting critical applications and activities. Streamlining approvals through electronic processes (Louise Scott et al, 2002) may remove existing internal controls and potentially increase risk a step further.

6.2 Risk Understanding in e-Commerce for IT Auditor

An organisation's IT auditors are in a unique position to ensure that changes, whether they are new business models and processes or new systems, support the organisation's mission and objectives and that adequate control procedures are an integral component from the beginning of the systems development process. In many organisations, in order to mitigate the risks associated with information systems, the IT audit function is assigned the responsibility of implementing a system of internal controls. Because of additional risks associated with e-commerce systems and the resulting need for strong control procedures, it is important that management appreciates the significance of having IT auditors participate in the systems development process. These internal controls are activities performed to eliminate risks or minimize them to an acceptable level. In most cases, it is cost-prohibitive to implement every type of control in an effort to eliminate all elements of risk. Thus, IT auditors must be aware of an organisation's objectives and must weigh the costs of implementing a control against the potential benefits of that control. Maximizing organisational benefits through the judicious use of controls in e-commerce systems can enhance control over the systems and reduce the costs of implementing these controls. Accounting professionals refer to rules, policies, and procedures involved in managing an organisation's risks as the "system of internal controls." The way accountants view internal controls changed in the early 1990s as a result of the landmark study, Internal Control – Integrated Framework by the Committee of Sponsoring Organisations of the Treadway Commission (COSO) (Vinten, 2001). Figure 2 is an attempt by me to provide a schema of the framework to be followed by IT auditors of e-commerce entities under review. This schema has a characteristic of obtaining information assurance at each level of hierarchy of operations and management.

Fraud is a highly publicized risk in an e-commerce environment. E-commerce fraud can either be perpetrated by an employee within the firewall or an anonymous party in a foreign country. All companies are vulnerable to sabotage and espionage from the inside and the outside, a risk heightened but not created by the Internet. Not all of it is malicious, and software companies in particular are prone to in-house high jinks by employees. Do you know how safe your company's secrets are? Perhaps you have measures in place to prevent large-scale corporate espionage, but do you have protection against the disgruntled employee who is fired or resigns? How can you prevent an employee in accounting from stealing trade secrets and using them personally or selling them to a competitor? Unfortunately, a company probably can not easily prevent a disgruntled employee from damaging its business. But companies can make it more difficult for an internal saboteur from a legal, physical and technical point of view. Protective measures are also advisable if someone leaves on amicable terms.

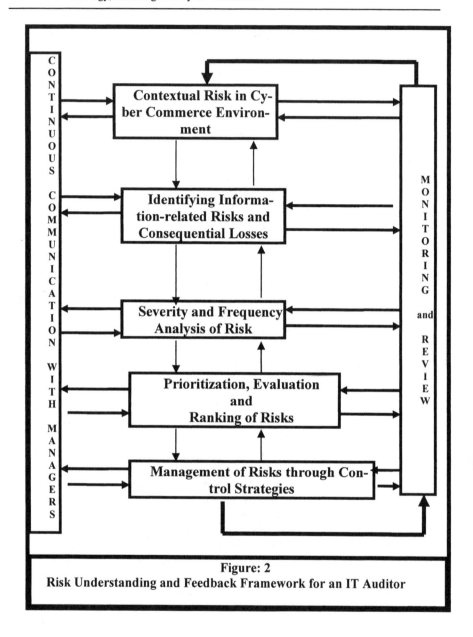

Figure: 2
Risk Understanding and Feedback Framework for an IT Auditor

Possible Fraudulent Activities

These activities may include some or all of the following:

- unauthorised movement of money such as payments to fictitious suppliers located in jurisdictions where recovery of money will be difficult

- misrepresentations of company tenders
- corruption of the electronic ordering or invoicing systems
- duplication of payment
- denying an order was placed
- denying an order was received
- denying receipt of goods
- denying that payment was received
- falsely declaring that a payment was made

For e-commerce implementation to be successful, information about the organisation needs to be made available to other participants in the trading community. However, people are becoming concerned at the amount of information required and the security of the data the other party collects. If people or organisations are not confident that data is properly protected, they may be unwilling to provide it. Public confidence can be adversely impacted if information is accessed without proper authorization.

6.3 Information at Risk

What type of information of any entity is at risk? An IT auditor is expected to identify such information from their origin or centre of creation. Any information emanating from lesser assured or partially assured system can not be called assured information as regards to its accuracy and integrity (Pathak and Baldwin, 2003). IT auditor makes efforts to ascertain the quality of information to identify whether such information is at a risk of being corrupt or potentially corrupt. Some of the potential information at risk may include the following:

- services and prices which are not normally provided to the general public
- cost structures, particularly those relating to tenders
- an individual's information – name, address, contact detail, previous purchases or services provided
- restricted information – information that should be shared only between specific parties, such as medical records, prison records and personnel files

Risks may be caused by either internal or external malicious activity – virus attacks, hacking, the interception of data by unauthorised person, unauthorised viewing or corruption of data, and data that is archived or disposed of improperly. Poor access protection of information can be another cause of risk, especially when dealing with the separation of private and public data.

Repudiation is another area of risk in electronic transactions. Although the system shows that the transaction took place, one of the parties denies that it occurred. Given that paper trails are limited in the electronic world, how does one party prove irrefutably that the transaction has taken place? A lack of authentication can lead to another area of risk in electronic transactions. Proper authentication is a critical component of an e-commerce transaction, since once a party has been accepted into the system; a legally binding transaction process has begun. Because paper-based controls are limited during an electronic transaction, an unauthorised party may be accepted and go undetected indefinitely.

These issues all deal with the question of data integrity. Many believe that risks involve activities that can be performed remotely through web resources. But although those are sources of risk, the reality is that almost all corruption of data takes place within the system. One of the major concerns associated with data corruption is the possibility that the data may become invalid. Some examples of malicious activity that can invalidate data include:

- amending catalogues without authorization
- destruction of audit trail
- tampering with the ordering process
- interrupting the transaction recording
- disrupting online tendering
- business interruptions

Business interruptions are a major risk; if companies cannot promptly and adequately resume business activities after a crisis, legal liabilities may arise when services or goods are not delivered or when payments are not made on time. The role of an IT auditor is important in a scenario that contains this amount of risk, and in assessing the impact of these risks on the overall activities of e-commerce. Inadequate funding may force some organisations to tolerate a higher than acceptable risk when implementing e-commerce. The need for an e-commerce site is becoming more apparent day after day, but so is the potential risk. An audit review program for e-commerce web sites will be a critical tool for IT auditors (Pathak, 2000).

E-commerce creates new dimensions for transactions, but these new dimensions require a set of security tools and an infrastructure that necessitate business processes being re-engineered. As e-commerce assurance continues to capture headlines in our daily lives, it is imperative that e-businesses have an Information Assurance Framework – a solid plan of action with the required tools, trained personnel, and tested procedures – that is capable of protecting valuable information regarding the privacy and financial aspects of the prospective customers.

The audit review process will provide the closed-loop cycle of continuous improvement that is imperative in today's e-commerce world. I have identified the framework that needs to be implemented by the IT auditors and they need to make the beginning of the arduous process of making it a reality. Auditors must understand that the solution is not a quick-fix and will build over time with the awareness of all employees and the support of management. The box shown below gives a brief but all encompassing structure of e-commerce audit. This structure shows all the pertinent aspects of such specialized audits to be kept in mind while performing an e-business audit.

E-business Audit Structure

1. **Information Discovery**
    - Organisation and Management Team
    - Commercial Objectives
    - Target Market Definition
    - Products and Services
    - Market Status
    - Competition
    - Financial Performance
    - Marketing and IT Strategies

2. **Business Analysis**
    - Value Chain
    - Supply Chain
    - **Marketing**
      - Promotional Activity
      - Online and Offline Integration
      - Key Metrics and Performance
      - Competitor Activity
      - Web Site Evaluation
      - Resources
    - **IT Infrastructure**
      - Hardware and Software
      - Networks
      - Connectivity
      - Intranet/Extranet
      - Security
      - Resources

1. **SWOT Summary**
2. **Benchmarking**
3. **Recommended Strategy Development Priorities**

A specimen of audit report issued by an auditor after performing detailed audit of various processes and procedures is depicted below.

Structure of the Report

1. Confidentiality Statement

2. Scope of the Audit
   - Project description
   - Test structure
   - Risk classification procedure

3. Executive Summary
   - Overall security assessment
   - Overall identified vulnerabilities sorted by risk factors
   - Summarized analysis of security risks which required immediate action
   - List and short description of all identified vulnerabilities

4. Tests and Results   For each performed test:
   - Test description
   - Tested services / applications? Test results
   - Risk classification
   - Recommendations
   - Log files

For services / applications with a risk factor higher than "0", the following information is provided in detail (if applicable):
   - Vendor, software version, protocol version, host, server, port or path
   - Configuration, authentication
   - Known vulnerabilities
   - Other / unpublished vulnerabilities
   - External system compromise
   - Description / code listing for the working exploit (for unpublished vulnerabilities and/or vulnerabilities discovered by you as an auditor)
   - Risk classification
   - Recommendation

5. Final Recommendations

6.4 Controls and Audit Evidences

In cyber commerce environment, controls relating to transaction integrity are often designed to fulfil certain basic objectives of an auditor. Some of these are shown below:

- validate input
- prevent duplication or omission of transactions
- ensure the terms of trade have been agreed before an order is processed, including delivery and credit terms, which may require, for example, that payment is obtained when an order is placed
- distinguish between customer browsing and orders placed
- ensure a party to a transaction cannot later deny having agreed
- to specified terms (non-repudiation), and ensure transactions are with approved parties when appropriate
- prevent incomplete processing by ensuring all steps are completed and recorded (for example, for a business to consumer transaction: order accepted, payment received, goods/services delivered and accounting system updated) or if all steps are not completed and recorded, by rejecting the order
- ensure the proper distribution of transaction details across multiple systems in a network (for example, when data is collected centrally and is communicated to various resource managers to execute the transaction) and
- ensure records are properly retained, backed-up and secured

In the cyber commerce environment, it is important that transactions generated from an entity's web site are processed properly by the entity's internal systems, such as the accounting system, customer relationship management systems and inventory management systems (often known as "back office" systems). Many web sites are not automatically integrated with internal systems. The way e-commerce transactions are captured and transferred to the entity's accounting system may impact the important matters as:

- the completeness and accuracy of transaction processing and information storage
- the timing of the recognition of sales revenues, purchases and other transactions and
- identification and recording of disputed transactions

When it is relevant to the financial statement assertions, the auditor considers the controls governing the integration of e-commerce transactions with internal systems, and the controls over systems changes and data conversion to automate process alignment.

There may not be any paper records for e-commerce transactions, and electronic records may be more easily destroyed or altered than paper records without leaving evidence of such destruction or alteration. The auditor considers whether the entity's security of information policies, and security controls as implemented, are adequate to prevent unauthorized changes to the accounting system or records, or to systems that provide data to the accounting system.

The auditor may test automated controls, such as record integrity checks, electronic date stamps, digital signatures, and version controls when considering the integrity of electronic evidence. Depending on the auditor's assessment of these controls, the auditor may also consider the need to perform additional procedures such as confirming transaction details or account balances with third parties.

7 IT Auditing and Security of Information Systems

There is no doubt about the essential role that information plays in current society. Furthermore, it looks certain that this role will be more important in the next century. Resultantly, it is not an exaggeration to nominate this society as the Information Society, just as other eras that were called Agricultural or Industrial. Therefore, informatics, or more general, information and communications technologies (ICT) have a predominant place in our technological societies.

On the other hand, it is obvious that protection controls are already required to make information and its technologies reliable and trusted. Otherwise, it is obvious that this need of security will be higher in the near future. Migration from accepted systems and procedures (commercial, administrative, technical, etc.) to new ones (electronic commerce, digital cash, tele-working, electronic mail, etc.) will not be accepted by the people without an improvement of security. However, computers and networks – without which it is impossible to conceive modern enterprises – represent a risk for information and its management.

This chapter is basically devised from professionals' point-of-view, hence least amount of scholarly references are provided. It starts with the preliminary discussions on information security, identification of computer assets, potential security threats and controls. The discussion further deepens into the aspects of security evaluations and certification criteria, network security, open system architecture, security services and mechanisms, etc. available. The last part of this chapter is interesting as it briefly describes various case laws from the US courts related directly with the main theme of this chapter so that auditors can remain aware about the legalities involved. The entire chapter, though focuses on information security aspects but all from the prism of an IT auditor and not from a security expert.

This way, threats and attacks of fictions are possible today for organisations and people using a PC connected with a telephone line. The actual threats to the security of information system emanates from your own employees, hackers, virus creators, competitors, etc., all of those can produce substantial losses for the information systems. Curiously, the same technologies that increase the productivity can also invoke losses because of laxity in the security. This adequately justifies an increasing attention to the information systems security and motivates management to increase its awareness for the security of the systems and its audit.

The security audit has become an important method to assure the working of the security controls and, hence, to assure the reliability and trust on the information and the technology related in maintaining these information systems. There are many risks associated with network use, so this field is one of the most interesting from a security point of view.

7.1 Information Security

In general, we can say that security means goods protection (also called assets or resources). However, although this definition fits into the security concept, it is not very useful; because nothing is said about the way to obtain a certain level of security. Therefore, a better definition could be: result of the balance between risk and controls for reducing it. Then when the risk is elevated, there should be higher protection controls. This is known as the *proportionality principle*. So, the more important task for a security auditor will be to check if implemented controls palliate estimated risk and also if the controls are the best possible in balancing the compensatory risk and the investment. Using this definition, an asset risk is a combination among threats that affect to that good, its vulnerabilities and its value.

This way, only if one among those three parameters was zero, the risk would be also zero. However, it is not possible to decrease the value of an asset, and it is very difficult to reduce threats so security is mainly based on reducing the vulnerabilities by the adopting reasonable cost-effective security controls. On the other hand, it is very important to show that security cannot be achieved in-total. As is known, even if the security investments are substantial, there is always some risk, called, *residual risk* that is not feasible to eliminate. But even if risk could be unlimitedly minimized, certain *risk threshold* security controls involve certain costs that are higher than the asset value that is being protected.

The risk under the threshold is usually assumed to be acceptable risk and is compensated by means of the contingency plan. Therefore, another main task for the auditor will be to find out the residual risk for the company and its system, assume it and decide carefully the security controls for compensating rest of risk.

The definition above is applicable to any other field, industrial security, nuclear security, personal security and, of course, information security. The next step in focusing on information security is to establish the information security goals, which are confidentiality, integrity and availability. Information security is comprised of Confidentiality, Integrity and Availability. *Confidentiality* means the information is only disclosed to authorized users, in pre-determined mode and time. *Integrity* aspect of information signifies that the information is modified which includes creation and deletion, by authorized people only.

Lastly, *availability* means that information can be used when and how it is required by authorized users. Over the years, the emphasis over these properties has been changing. In the beginning (of 50's and 60's) availability was the most important feature; but in these days of various privacy laws, confidentiality and integrity have taken higher magnitude.

There is no universal priority for those properties. Each of them will be more or less important depending on information, enterprise or organisation nature. For example, confidentiality can be essential for a pharmaceutical research and development laboratory of a company preventing from industrial espionage, but integrity could be basic for an equity fund data system; finally, availability maybe highly critical in an industrial shop floor production system.

For an audited system it is essential (and the first step to follow) to specify what is the priority among those properties, because security controls are different depending on which is more important (for example, if availability is the most important, information ciphering can be eluded. For example, in USA, integrity is slightly more important based on reliable surveys. Private enterprises often place availability and finally confidentiality in the order of priority. For governmental institutions after integrity, it is confidentiality and, at last, availability.

7.1.1 Computer Assets

The ICT security involves the protection of the information managed by these technologies. At first, we could say that these goods are hardware, software and data. It is rational that the second step for auditing is to identify the computer goods to protect. Among them, data is the most exposed to the risk and its value decreases quickly in time for specific uses. Data is exposed to more risk because it is accessed by more people than the others (users, analysts, programmers), and affected by the same threats as them. Hardware lifetime is around four or five years; whereas, software (personnel management, stocks control, production management...) can stay operative for ten or twelve years. According to several reports, among all losses suffered by companies due to lack of security only 5% are directly related to: hardware, software, computer consumables, etc.; so these are easily replaceable. The 95% remaining are indirect losses (linked to theft, modifications or destruction of information) that are priced with difficulty because they are intangible, e.g. loss of competitive advantage, credibility loss, penal responsibilities, etc.

Threats to Security

Classified by its *origin*, threats can be accidental, natural and intentional. Accidental threats can be divided into human errors, equipment failure, electricity supply, electromagnetic radiation, etc. Natural threats can occur for different reasons; for example, fire, floods, heat, earthquakes, hurricanes, etc. Threats that can affect the information and the information systems can be divided by different approaches, e.g. on the basis of origin, operation mode and importance. Finally, among intentional threats – made with the aim of damaging the information systems or its information – are fraud, material or immaterial sabotages and theft. Frauds are data or programs altered for obtaining some profit.

They typically are caused by inadequate programming controls, an example being the method known as salami that consists of truncating last decimals of economic operations and transferring this remainder to the account of the deceiving person, for instance the programmer account.

In addition, frauds are also tramps (illicit and not documented backdoors in programs) that allow disloyal programmers to access data and programs at any time. Another fraudulent technique commonly used is to transfer information from one program to another by unconventional channels. This method is called information leaks.

Sabotages can be material or immaterial, depending on the type of goods that are destroyed. Immaterial sabotages are more problematic, usually causing program or data deletion or alteration. These can be made by acting directly over the information system or also indirectly by using malicious programs that act by themselves. A well-known example is a virus.

Finally, thefts can also be material or immaterial; the latter ones are data or programs subtraction or duplication. Sometimes when data is allocated in the main memory of a computer, other users are able to access it. These data, sometimes known as residues, are produced because some operating systems do not delete this memory area when a user logs-off. The kinds of people who provoke these threats are mainly hackers, virus creators, crackers and disloyal employees, who pose the highest risk factor.

Therefore, it is not an exaggeration that between 75% and 80% of the computer crime is made by personnel of the company (insiders!). Only between 20% and 25% are caused by other attackers although those last ones are highly divulged by the media. This group is closely connected to the computer networks, will be explained in depth. By its percentage *importance* according to the losses that result (classified from high to low) are errors (on hardware, software, design, specification, codification, input, operations, etc.), dishonest employees, natural accidents and actions by others.

The first ones reach 40% of the total, followed by the others with 30%, 25% and 5%. Recently, the second and fourth ones are on the increase and third one is quickly decreasing.

7.2 Security Controls

A security control also called countermeasures, services or measures is a function supplied by a system or product that improves the security. Different security controls have to be adopted to counteract the threats. So it can be concluded that the purpose of a security control is to reduce the risk or its equivalent viz. threats, vulnerabilities and impact, associated to an asset, which is located in certain place at a certain time.

On the other hand, it is very important to distinguish between controls and their implementation in a system or product. This implementation is made by one or more security mechanisms. Furthermore, the same security control can be implemented by a different mechanism, acting in isolation or in collaboration with others e.g. computer networks.

These controls can be classified depending on the operation mode or its nature. According to the first one, there are the following types.

Preventive control attempts to decrease the probability of certain threats. An example is the use of access control software that permits the use of certain resources or data just for authorized people. A preventive control is also the utilization of ciphering systems that prevent against unauthorized reading (and perhaps modifications). Also in this type are firewalls that hinder the access to determined network addresses or certain information traffic.

Detection control that act to notify about an attack occurrence to mitigate it. In this group are hash functions which discover data modifications (accidental or deliberate). Audit logs also can send warning messages to an operator to alert about unauthorized accesses. Other examples are input data control procedures that check data input and reject those that do not belong to a certain range.

Correction controls act after the detection controls and correct accidental or deliberate attacks. For example, there are cyclic redundancy codes (CRC) and failure tolerance systems or devices. There is also a user authentication system that after a number of log-in attempts disables the user or even the terminal where she/he is trying to get in.

Recovery controls act to recover the previous state of the information system. This group belongs in the contingency plans. The first type is probably more advisable than the others, but it is also the more expensive one. One of the more interesting mentioned controls is called perimeter defence which consists of the construction of successive protection barriers: preventive, detention, correction and recovery that surround all the domains to protect. It is important to say that attacks against confidentiality can be only protected by preventative controls. According to their nature, security controls can be classified as:

Legal controls are those laws made for protecting the information and the systems that deal with it. Although some laws have protected computer goods in the same way as others, there is now emerging a set of specific laws that are specially oriented to guard information security. This type of legislation about intellectual property rights, data base distribution, personal data protection, electronic signature, etc. is currently applied in many countries.

Administrative controls are in charge of the security management and are based on the selection of policies and procedures that implement, fortify or complement the rest of the controls. Examples are the responsibility assignment, information classification policy, personnel policy, incident register procedures, auditing, etc. Those controls include risk analysis and contingency plans. It is important to note that without suitable security management, the rest of the cited controls are useless or even counterproductive.

Physical controls are commonly used for describing protection controls foreign to the information process equipment, which try to protect them from physical threats. Adopted controls usually are electric and electronic devices that prevent against fire or floods. The price of physical controls is not excessive (except uninterruptible power supply systems, UPS systems) and their support has no special problems. These types of countermeasures contribute to counteract floods, fire, power failures, electromagnetic jamming, assaults and thefts, not authorized physical accesses, etc.

Technical controls try to protect software (base or application) and data. These security measures can be implemented over hardware devices or over software products. The development of these controls has required very intense research, mainly during last decade and a half. As a result of this research very interesting theoretical models have appeared as: access control models (Graham and Denning matrix access, Harrison, Ruzzo and Ullmann matrix access, "Take-Grant"...), data flow control models (multilevel or reticular, Bell-La Padula, Biba, Clark-Wilson, Chinese wall...), private and public cryptosystems development (DES, RSA, Merkle-Hellmann knapsacks, based on elliptic curves, ...), development of electronic signature systems for data transmissions, etc. All of them have changed the way of understanding information security.

7.3 Security Evaluation and Certification Criteria

Due to their importance, recent works on security evaluation and certification must be mentioned in an individual section. Evidently, a standard and an objective test for evaluating security could be useful, since it will significantly reduce the security auditor's work. In this way, once the security of a system or a product has been evaluated and certified by a trusted organisation, the supervision of an auditor will not be needed because those systems will be guaranteed by this certificate

This need of a security principle was first understood by the National Computer Security Center (NCSC), dependent on the National Security Agency, that published in 1985 the *Trusted Computer Security Evaluation Criteria* (TCSEC), known colloquially as the *Orange Book* that covered different security hardware criteria, firmware and software, as well as security evaluations methodologies for operating systems working in a specified hardware.

Criteria are hierarchically divided into four divisions: D, C, B and A, where A level is reserved for systems with severe security controls. Divisions B and C are also divided into classes (three for B and two for C). Classes are further classified in a hierarchical way, using a digit besides the letter (this digit is also put after the character in level A). So, there are seven levels that sorted from less to more security: D; C1; C2; B1; B2; B3; A1.

Starting from the orange book, NCSC has promoted the "Rainbow Series", that is a group of documents with the aim of evaluating other components of the information systems, as passwords, networks, databases, etc. In September 1990, Germany, France, Great Britain and the Netherlands, under the European Union support, presented a draft document for the establishment of a standard for the evaluation of the information security which was called *Information Technology Security Evaluation Criteria* (ITSEC) version 1.0. Later, in June 1991, version 1.2, which was experimentally applied during the previous two years, appeared. ITSEC determines ten security function4 sets (functionalities). The first five are: F-C1; F-C2; F-B1; F-B2; F-B3, and they are hierarchically sorted and are equivalent to the five levels defined by the NCSC Orange Book, from C1 to A1. Furthermore, ITSEC specifies other evaluation levels to study how near is the evaluated target to the proposed security objective. Those are the *Confidence in the effectiveness* and the *Confidence in the correctness*. They are defined in seven evaluation levels from E0 to E6, hierarchically sorted from less to more confidence. So, E0 level describes no confidence of the evaluator on the target (system or product); E1 represents minimum confidence level and E6 the maximum.

Lastly, it is important to mention that organisations involved in previous works from EU, USA and Canada have made an effort to combine their criteria for establishing a single one, known as *Common Criteria for Information Technology Security Evaluation* (from now on, *Common Criteria*), where they have been working since 1993. The first version of Common Criteria was born in January, 1996 and was approved like the ISO-draft in April of the same year. After numerous tests and reviews, in May 1998 version 2.0 was published, which although is usually known as Common Criteria 2.0, has been formally called by ISO as *Evaluation Criteria for Information Technology Security* with the reference ISO/IEC15408.

7.3.1 Networks Security

Once we have outlined the foundations of IT security, general aspects of the communications and networks security can be settled. Currently, computer networks are exposed to numerous threats. Organisations cannot do without networks; they must assume that risk and use them to take a position in the market and to get a higher scale of interconnection to their machines. All this justifies that, during the last several years, the production of network security programs has been multiplied. The prestigious annual report EITO'98 (European Information Technology Observatory) established the highest growth areas as: access control, authentication, encryption and firewalls, that means how security professionals worry about those aspects. Risks linked to the computer networks are mainly motivated by:

- *Diversity of products*: hardware (firewalls, bridges, routers, gateways, etc.) and software (Windows NT, Unix, Netware, etc.) made by different manufacturers, each of them with a particular security approach and coexisting all of them in the same network
- *Numerous network access points*, many of them from public networks
- *Continual network reconfigurations*. Sometimes even the network administrator is not informed
- *Users and computer staff* with lack of knowledge and experience
- *High value of the information* that travels across computer networks

Therefore, it is not strange that according to a survey made by *Information Week* and Ernst and Young in 1996, 78% of the responding companies admit to have suffered losses caused by lack of security and 32% said to have had internal hacker attacks. Despite that, only 27% of those companies have more than three people working for the security department. We will next study particular network vulnerabilities, then we will focus on their threats and finally on their security controls.

Vulnerabilities

Vulnerability is the susceptibility of a system or of a component for suffering damages caused by a specific attack. Equivalently, it can be defined as a weakness of the protection system of a resource that can be exploited by an attack. In this sense, vulnerability comes first with the acceptance of the open systems interconnection model, which means systems specifications that are public. In fact, everyone can know any design detail or implementation aspect of a system, what is valuable information to detect security holes and to develop attack methods. A second factor is the networks magnitude. A few years ago only some institutions and individuals had access to networks.

Today there are millions of users that have access to them from any remote place around the world. At last, friendly use of current systems and IT technologies allows people with no specific preparation and without knowledge of the associated risks and unawareness of the information value, to manage, process, store or send significant data for them and their companies.

Summarizing, the same reasons that explain the extended acceptance of the network-based systems are causing their vulnerabilities. So, the solution is complex because we should reduce the vulnerabilities with no decreasing of the facilities given by networks. If we return to less flexible systems (as old batch systems), to system designs only known by a few (proprietary systems) or to not many connected systems(local process systems), we will turn back society to the fifties. In other words, the risk reduction should come with no detriment of its friendly use, design details transparency and even promoting the remote access facilities.

Threats

A threat is a potential violation of a system security; whereas an attack is the materialization of a threat. Deliberate threats, which affect present systems and information technologies, are multiform with an elevated technological level and usually unpredictable. In the case of networks security is essential the division between active and passive threats. *Passive threats* affect information confidentiality, and their distinctive feature is that they do not change either the state of the information or the system.

A known example is the interception of an information channel to catch the data (cipher or not) that travels through it. Particularly, a serious threat is the password sniffing. But even if communication is encrypted and an intruder cannot guess the content of the message, an attacker can read message headers, where they can find out the identity and nodes situation. Starting from this information and checking the messages (network address, frequency, length, etc.) she/he could conjecture the nature of them.

This is also a passive threat that is called traffic analysis. Usually, commented passive threats are very difficult to detect and to correct, which sometimes means that are unrecoverable. *Active threats* are those that change the state of the information (or the system) so they are easier to detect and correct than the first ones. Furthermore, under certain conditions (if a data backup copy exists) it is possible to recover the previous status of the information system. Active threats emerge when a device is connected to the transmission channel to modify, delete or generate messages. Active threats usually can be distinguished by interruption, modification and generation.

Interruption is a threat that affects the information availability and consists of interrupting a transmission. Usually this threat is called denial of service. Examples are the suppression of messages with a certain destination by a malicious intermediate node or the saturation of a resource by request flooding. For instance, sending the same message over a short period of time, to a certain communication port, this could get collapsed.

One threat of this type for the TCP protocol is the SYN flooding. *Modification* consists of the fraudulent modification of messages for example, and not authorized changes of data or programs. It is a threat that affects the information integrity. In networks, a known example is the user supplantation which occurs by changing IP message headers (what is called IP spoofing).

Finally, *generation* is the creation of false messages that pretend to be real. An example is message replication that consists of capturing a message and its transmission as many times as needed. IP hijacking could be also considered in this group; this threat consists of the interruption of an authenticated connection and the supplantation of one legitimate host by the attacker. So, this is a threat against messages authentication, or against its integrity.

7.3.2 OSI Architecture

The OSI (Open System Interconnection) reference model created by ISO (International Standardization Organisation) is a set of norms oriented to the interconnection of different computer systems, which due to this feature will be called open systems. An open system is that one, which can be interconnected with others according to certain norms dictated by an independent standardization institution, particularly ISO.

Therefore, the open systems interconnection model is in charge of the information exchange among these systems and will provide a convenient link for cooperative work among them. This interconnection is made by a set of rules denominated by protocols. From now on, we will consider as open those systems that cover the ISO standard. It is necessary to say that there is no commercial product that follows strictly those standards, mainly because they are costly and complex. However, all of them accept OSI model foundations.

The interconnection system is formed by a group of objects situated in different levels of the structure (sometimes called stack) that are denominated layers. A *service* is a set of functions, significant for the interconnection that a layer supplies to the upper one. That is to say, a layer of determined level of a system uses services supplied by the layer of the level that is immediately below.

A service defines functions but nothing is said about how to implement them because this labour is reserved for protocols. More specifically, a *protocol* is a set of rules that permits to establish and control data which is logically exchanged between two layers of the same architecture level. Therefore, the same level layers of a system exchange information according to certain protocol. Logic data flow passes through all levels, downward for the sender and the other way around for the receiver.

The OSI reference model defines seven layers: physical, link, network, transport, session, presentation and application. In this way, tasks for initiating, maintaining and finalizing a communication between two entities are shared among these layers. Although the first OSI standards did not pay much attention to security, in 1988 the OSI Security Architecture (ISO/IEC7498-2, 1988) appeared and since then security standardization works have been uninterrupted and very intense.

However, the first thing to fix is that this norm only covers the security aspects of the interconnection but does not cover either machines or system terminals security. Four basic concepts of OSI security architecture are: security threats, security services, security mechanism and their implementation levels. We covered first ones and the last three are left to study, which due to their importance for network auditing will be treated preferentially.

Security Services

OSI standards define a security service as a function supplied by a communication system in order to guarantee its security and the data transmissions. Security services described in the standard are: confidentiality, integrity, authentication, access control and non repudiation.

Those services can be invoked from different levels of the OSI architecture and also by other entities (users, programs, etc.) not defined into this standard. *Confidentiality* (called *data confidentiality* by the standard) protects data against passive attacks and can be identified by four types: selective field, connectionless, connection, traffic flow.

Selective fields' confidentiality protects against disclosing, but only for some specific fields of a message because, sometimes, not all fields have information that needs to be hidden. However, it is frequently faster and cheaper to hide the whole message than selecting those ones that need to be hidden.

Connection confidentiality protects all fields, or data items, of an entire message. On the contrary, *Connectionless confidentiality* protects against the disclosing of message datagram. In both cases, as we shall study, the appropriate mechanism to use is data encryption.

Finally, *Confidentiality traffic flow* protects against frequency analysis of the messages, which have a determined origin and destination. The adequate mechanism is traffic padding. *Integrity* service guarantees that messages (all fields or only some of them) are received without unauthorized alterations; that is to say, they are received as they were emitted.

Included into this service are absence of duplications (or more generally replications), insertions, modifications, or destructions. The adequate mechanisms are hash functions and CRC codes. This service has two main modes of working: connection and connectionless. *Connection integrity* tries to protect all fields of a message and guarantees that neither complete message nor any field have been duplicated, modified, replaced or destroyed. Therefore, this working mode counteracts active attacks: interruption, modification and generation.

Connectionless integrity protects individually to message fields (datagram) and, hence, only guarantees modification detection for those fields and sometimes its replacement. Both modes connection and connectionless integrity can be applied to selective fields, what are called *selective field connection integrity* and *selective field connectionless integrity*.

Authentication service ensures who are the participants in a communication. There are two types: *peer entity authentication* or *data origin authentication*. The last one guarantees that messages come from the source that emitted it. In the first case it is necessary to be sure about two aspects. First, when the communication starts peer entities are who they say they are, and second, during the connection no third party supplants the identity of one of them or pretends to repeat a previous connection. That is the case, for example, of the attack IP hijacking. Mechanism in charge is authentication.

Access control is oriented to control open resources, which are accessed through an OSI interconnection system. Those resources can be OSI or not, physical devices, programs or data. It acts after authentication, once this one has satisfactorily finished and permits or denies access to certain resources according to the authenticated identity of the entity which demands access.

This identity, in OSI terminology, authenticated identity, can be a user or other resource, for instance, a program in execution that demands access to certain resources. As we said, access control is a service supplied after authentication and that means it is designed according to the entity profile, permitting different types of access to a determined resource.

For example, given certain information (stored into a database) and the entity identifier can be authorized only by reading, writing, or deleting this information. This service is provided by the access control mechanism and is usually implemented by the access control table or matrix. *Non-repudiation* service avoids that a sender or a receiver of a message could deny its emission or reception respectively.

So, there are two different modalities: *non-repudiation with proof of origin and non-repudiation with proof of delivery.* For the first modality, when a message is sent, a receiver can be sure that it effectively was sent and that the sender is whom she/he says. For the second modality, a sender can prove message emission and the proper reception by the receiver. This is a basic service for any electronic commerce type, or more appropriately, for any electronic transaction. The main mechanism involved is electronic signature. An improvement to the non-repudiation service can be obtained by an electronic signature notary, also called Certification Authority.

7.3.3 Security Mechanisms

The standard defines *security mechanism* as a logical or physical device in charge of supplying a security service. However, a security service could require more than one security mechanism. This norm differentiates between specific and complementary security mechanisms. The first ones are implemented into a certain layer of the OSI model and supply a determined service or, more frequently, complement other mechanisms for joining or supplying a security service.

The second ones are not designed to offer any of the commented services, and due to the slight relation with auditing, we will not explore them. Specific mechanisms (from now on, just mechanisms) considered in the OSI standard are: encryption, electronic signature, access control, data integrity, authentication exchange, traffic padding, routes control and notarization.

Encryption

Encryption's immediate purpose is to supply confidentiality service for data or data flow. Furthermore, it is also an essential mechanism for achieving other services. This mechanism includes procedures and techniques for key management, who are able to generate and distribute them across the network in a secure way.

- **Control Objectives**
  - Stored or transmitted information, classified as sensitive (according to the corporate policy for information classifying), must be protected against unauthorized disclosing using encryption procedures

- **Audit Guidelines**
  - To check the information classification policies and review if information over certain sensitivity levels travels or is stored encrypted
  - To verify that encryption algorithms have public specifications and have been completely studied by the cryptological community, not finding any weakness. Encryption devices are made by a recognized reputable company. Length of keys (session, key ciphering keys, master keys, etc.) is adequate for the information sensitivity managed. It has established a key recovery system, in case keys were lost or not accessible. Session keys have an expiration date (crypto-period) according to transmitted data sensitivity. Key generation procedures have no weakness (keys are random or at least unpredictable). Encryption devices are as fast as the transmission channel, so there will not be originated bottlenecks. If encryption is only performed for data that leave or arrive at a local area, then the encryption device must be isolated and accessible only to the authorized people. Key distribution procedures cannot compromise them. There are instant key change procedures if it is suspected that unauthorized people have access to them. If asymmetric encryption is used for confidentiality and all employ-

ees' keys are generated in a centralized device, then private keys are not destroyed (for recovering them if it is strictly necessary)

Digital Signature

This mechanism consists of two processes: message signing and signature verification. In the first process, the signature is obtained from the message (or a specific transformation of it) and private information (called *private key*), only known by the signer. Thus, with the change in the message, the signature will also change. The second process applies public information (known by everyone) to the signature. The public information (*public key*) is related to the private information, but it is computationally impossible to obtain one from the other. Finally, the result of this process is compared with the message (or the mentioned transformation of it).

- **Control objectives**
  - To check, at any time (present or future), authorship and integrity of the information by those that require it
- **Audit Guidelines**
  - To review signing procedures to be sure that the required information is signed, and only that
  - To verify that Private and public key generation is secure (with special attention to random numbers generator algorithms) and that private keys are properly stored into secure storage devices (for example a smart card).
  - If all employee keys are generated in a centralized device, private keys must be destroyed
  - If the same algorithm (for example, RSA) is used for non-repudiation (digital signature) and for confidentiality (encrypt), then two different key pairs must be used for each purpose
  - Original and signed documents are stored for later signature validations.
  - When a public key expires (its lifetime must not exceed one or two years), it must not be destroyed, because it must be kept for later signing verifications
  - If an internal Certification Authority exists, then its certification key must be longer than 2048 bits (if RSA is used)

Access Control

This mechanism restrains access to determined resources. This decision is made after the identity has been authenticated and according to the type of access (read, write, etc.) that is required. Furthermore, in case of denied accesses, the mechanism could send a warning message or register it into audit logs. An access control system can make decisions based on: a matrix (called access control matrix or table) where all entities and their access privileges to the resources are registered, labels (that contain information about the entities and their privileges for this resource) associated to each resource, credentials presented by entities, access routes; etc. Out of all of them, access control matrix is the most commonly used method.

- **Control Objectives**
    - To concede access to the resources according to strict control access policies

- **Audit Guidelines**
    - To verify if a network operating system is certified by an independent evaluation and certification standard (for instance: TCSEC, TCPEC, IT-SEC/ITSEM, Common Criteria) and the classification obtained
    - To examine that access is based on a need-to know rule. People in charge of conceding access privileges are clearly identified. Access control mechanism is protected against intrusions. Database management system provides appropriate field-level sensitivity. All un-allowed accesses are prohibited (better than all not permitted is accepted). When employee changes job, then all his/her old access privileges are eliminated. There are different resource privileges: read, read/ write, delete execution, copy, etc. Network server is isolated and its physical access is restricted

7.3.4 Integrity

Data integrity means that the person or process in charge(source in a data transmission) adds some information, which is a function of those data. It can be used as a cyclic redundancy code (CRC) or, preferably because of its strength, a keyed hash function or a hash function is encrypted. On the other hand, when information is going to be acceded (or in reception in a data transmission), it first has to retrieve the added information and decrypt it if necessary. Second, starting from received data, this information must be recalculated (using same procedure as in the origin).

Finally, both results are compared, accepting them if are equal, or rejecting them (asking for its retransmission) in other case. Sometimes, a partial protection of the data items can be obtained using a time-stamp. In transmissions, there are two integrity modalities included into OSI standard: data item integrity and whole data flow integrity (message). For connectionless integrity, in addition to comments earlier, some sorting of the fields (datagram) as a numeration of them or a cipher block chaining encryption mode is required.

- **Control Objectives**
    - To detect unauthorized modifications of data and programs that require it, according to the information classification corporate policy

- **Audit Guidelines**
  - To check that servers have installed anti-virus programs that are periodically updated
  - At each connection, terminals check the server and download, automatically, anti-virus updated version (if it exists)
  - Employees know their responsibility for program installations that have not been acquired by the company (intellectual property rights)
  - Network programs have implemented CRC codes or hash functions, which are applied to all transferred messages

Authentication

The precise name used by the standard is authentication exchange, because two-entity communication must require, logically, mutual authentication. This mechanism is, without a doubt, the most important because it acts before the others and, once it is passed, the user is logged on and into the system. Techniques to use can be:

- certain information, like a password, only known by the entities
- determined cryptographic techniques
- possession of a credential

Traditionally, when a user wants to connect to a network, usually to a host, they are required to provide an identification code, which is commonly represented by ID, and some agreed information, supposedly not possible to falsify. This information is something only known by the user (and, of course, the system) as: a password, a physical device in the possession of the user (a conventional magnetic card), a biometric feature (fingerprint, iris, voice, etc.) or a distinguishing Behaviour (signature, typing cadence, etc.).

Those procedures have been used as secure for the local computers authentication (not connected to public transmission networks) in protected environments. However, for remote computer access, the mentioned procedures are entirely inadequate and their use represents a temptation for computer delinquents. Consequently, ISO/IEC 9594-8 (and ITU-T X.509) standard considers an authentication, denominated simple, much more secure that is based on computationally irreversible functions.

Strong authentication (also known as robust authentication), described in the mentioned standard, is based on asymmetric cryptographic techniques. Furthermore, this authentication requires that every user (more generally entity) has an doubtless identification, known as distinguishing identifier, of which acceptation and storage is responsibility of the Certification Authority.

There are three strong authentication types, which have a different number of information exchanges between implied entities. In this way, authentication is considered in one way (unidirectional), two ways (bi-directional) and three ways.

- **Control Objectives**
  - To restrict remote user access by the use of secure passwords

- **Audit Guidelines**
  - To verify the existence of strict policies for users' identification and authentication and for password selection and management. It is also necessary to verify that those policies are known by all employees
  - To review remote authentication procedures accomplished by dial-up telecommunication line, verify that they are based on call-back or in one-time passwords systems
  - Check that conventional passwords can not be used cyclically, stored by irreversible algorithms, immediately cancelled when employee leaves the company, consists of more that six characters (better eight), and includes upper and lower case letters and special characters. Those that come with new machines or devices are changed
  - Initial password is only used one time
  - Have a maximum (usually between one and three months) and minimum (one week) duration
  - The system logs out the user after a certain number (between three to five) of erroneous access attempts. The user account is not enabled until a certain time or until person in charge activates it
  - Network (or authentication) server is isolated and its access is restricted

7.3.5 Security Mechanisms Location

OSI stack is formed by seven layers, but usually only four of them are implemented by the security mechanisms. Implementation of each layer depends on the security requirements, which can be also classified into four groups. In this way, an encryption device at the physical or link layer is the solution when it is needed to connect secure networks by unsafe links. But even if the origin and destination networks are safe, if the route between their nodes goes through an insecure network (for example a public network), then it is essential to add security mechanisms at the transport layer.

However, if the user of a computer who wants to be connected is not sure about the security of his/her own networks, then it is required that security be extended to end to end. This type of security can be implemented at the network or transport layer. Both options are under consideration in the corresponding normalization committees. Finally, some users that only want to protect certain applications or only a few fields of those applications need to implement security at the application level (also called, end to end). Although in both cases security is placed at the presentation layer; for instance in: electronic mail applications like PGP or S/MIME, or in electronic commerce protocols like SET. In conclusion, and now focusing on the network topological organisation, there are two procedures to implement security into the domains to protect.

One of these is commonly known as defense in deep which consist of an independent security consideration for each network resource. In this way, the person in charge decides the security mechanisms to protect that specific resource. This decision can be based on the resource importance and the value of the data processed, stored, transmitted, etc. A disadvantage of this procedure is due to the mechanism multiplicity according to the manufacturer or model, technical staff to use, etc., which are probably different for each resource. That is the reason for the emergence of a procedure where security responsibility falls on a single machine or resource.

The security mechanisms are implemented into this resource, which is placed in a node and protects all network traffic input and output. After this, the network appears divided into an insecure external network (often called red network) and an internal network which is isolated from the other and is secure (often called blue network). Both are connected by a single node which is placed in the security device that controls all data traffic in both directions (only allowing what is explicitly authorized).

This procedure, which figuratively assures the network perimeter like medieval city walls, is known as *perimeter defence*, which is usually used for network protection. An earlier-mentioned device, which implements security measures in the perimeter defence, is the denominated firewall. there are basically three types of them: packet level, circuit level and application level. It has been mentioned that there are two networks that result after a firewall implantation: blue and red, but it is common to distinguish a third one, orange, where organisation servers are located (as the web) that have to be accessible for external users.

This network is protected by the firewall, but unlike the blue one, the protection is not full because in the other case those external users could not get access to the services. Consequently, from the blue point of view, the orange is insecure and, hence, access is not permitted from the orange to the blue one. Obviously, both types of defence increasingly used are perimeter and in deep.

In conclusion, we should say that even if implemented security measures are impeccable, they will not be effective without an appropriate management. Unfortunately, although ISO is treating the standardization of this important subject already, a few years are left for those efforts to take the form of a standard, and a few more for being conveniently followed by users and administrators.

7.4 Future Trends

The information and communications technologies belong to this kind of field that is quite variable, and it is very risky to predict the future. It appears obvious that during the next years complete and friendly automated tools for auditing systems will emerge. During the last several years different programs that scan certain networks looking for security failures have already appeared.

Examples are the Security Administrator Tool for Analyzing Networks (SA-TAN), used many times with opposite intentions, the Computer Oracle and Password System (COPS) and more recently the Internet Security System products (ISS). On the other hand, the broad acceptance of the certification standards and the unification of all of them into Common Criteria (Evaluation Criteria for Information Technology Security, ISO/IEC 15408) previously cited, will make unnecessary the security auditing of every isolated component of networks, because the main part of them will have its respective certificate. It will be only necessary to check if its security level is adequate for counteracting the expected threats. Also in the risk analysis and management field, closely related to the auditing, we will see the growth of automated methodologies that, unlike the current ones, will include sophisticated tools based on fuzzy logic, Bayesian probabilities, specific algorithmic techniques, etc.

All of them will allow a better and more complete study of the vulnerabilities and the proposal of new controls or the improvement of the current ones. This progress will signify considerable help for auditing. However, all we said does not mean that the auditing task of the future will be trivial.

On the contrary, it will produce a transformation of the auditing focus because information systems will be complex and formed by multiple interconnected machines (each of them certified with a certain security level) whose global security must be audited. Even if many automated controls are developed, there is always an enormous complex task left that is difficult to automate.

This is the auditing of the management controls, because without them all the other technical controls treated in this chapter become useless. One should remember that security is a multidisciplinary field and to obtain even the minimum level of assurance, the solid technical measures are to be chosen, appropriately managed and correctly regulated.

7.5 Exemplary Case Laws Related to Security Needs and Breaches in USA

(Sourced and adapted from various internet-based sources. Author can not assure about the truthfulness or validity of this information. However, to the best of author's knowledge, these are all possibly correct descriptions of the cases and interested readers are advised to refer the detailed case reports from the law libraries.)

7.5.1 Case Laws Related to Data Preservation

Antioch Co. v. Scrapbook Borders, Inc., 210 F.R.D. 645 (D. Minn. 2002)

Antioch brought an action for copyright infringement concerning decorative stickers. Antioch moved for an order for preservation of records to compel discovery, to expedite discovery, and to appoint a neutral computer forensics expert all based upon the belief that defendants have or would destroy relevant documents and materials. Defendants did not oppose the order for preservation of documents claiming they had no intention of destroying any relevant materials. Antioch provided a computer expert who testified through affidavit that data deleted from computers is retained on the hard drive but is constantly being overwritten by new data through normal use of the computer. The court reviewed the processes described in Playboy Enter. v. Welles and Simon Property Group v. mySimon and designed a process by which a computer forensics expert would create a mirror image and work with the parties to provide the relevant information.

Bartley v. Isuzu Motors Ltd., 151 F.R.D. 659 (D. Colo. 1993)

In this products liability case, the injured plaintiff hired an expert to conduct computer simulations of the Isuzu vehicle. Isuzu wanted access to all of the simulations. Plaintiff objected stating that after each simulation the data is changed. The court ordered the plaintiffs to retain all data showing all simulations as well as the premises upon which all simulations were made.

Danis v. USN Communications, Inc., 2000 U.S. Dist. LEXIS 16900, 2000 WL 1694325 (N.D. Ill.)

Plaintiff class filed a series of motions for discovery sanctions against defendant over a two-year period. The parties battled over discovery abuses. The court held that the CEO of defendant took no steps to safeguard documents but rather attempted to delegate the responsibility to a new in-house attorney with no litigation experience. The court held that he turned a blind eye to the destruction of documents but did not award sanctions, rather fined the CEO of defendant $10,000 to be paid to the court.

Strasser v. Yalamanchi, 783 So. 2d 1087 (Fla. Dist. Ct. App. 2001)

This is the second Strasser case. The court found that the fears raised by Yalamanchi that Strasser would destroy evidence, see Strasser 1, were well-founded and that Strasser had indeed destroyed evidence. The trial court gave an instruction based on negligent destruction of evidence and provides a detailed analysis of that claim.

7.5.2 Case Laws Pertaining to the Scope of Discovery

Adobe Systems, Inc. v. South Sun Products, 187 F.R.D. 636 (S.D. Cal 1999)

Several manufacturers of software filed suit against a wholesale jeweler contending that the jeweler was using copies of the software for which it had not purchased licenses. The manufacturers sought an ex parte order to prevent defendant from destroying evidence of its piracy of software. The court held that the jewelry wholesaler was not a sophisticated computer company and, therefore, that even if it attempted to delete these entire complex applications, telltale traces of the previous installations would remain.

Anti-Monopoly, Inc. v. Hasbro, Inc., 1995 U.S. Dist. LEXIS, 1995 WL 649934 (S.D.N.Y.)

Anti-Monopoly moved for an order compelling production of data in electronic format. The court held that "data in computerized form is discoverable even if paper 'hard copies' of the information have been produced." It continued to state that the responding party was responsible to design whatever programs were necessary to acquire the information electronically but that it would consider allocation of costs. The court does not provide any guidance at this point as to the allocation of costs.

Bartley v. Isuzu Motors Ltd., 151 F.R.D. 659 (D. Colo. 1993)

(See Data Preservation)

Bloss v. Ford Motor Co., 510 N.Y.S. 2d 304 (App. Div. 1987)

Plaintiff's counsel traveled to a warehouse maintained by defendant, Ford Motor Co., in this rollover case. On arrival, he was presented with 76 boxes of documents relating to the design and development of the vehicle and told he had only two days to review them. He learned that Ford had made an index of the documents but Ford would not provide that index claiming privileged attorney work product for material prepared for litigation. The court held that the preparation of the indexes did not require any special legal skill nor were they a communication between attorney and client; therefore, plaintiff had the right to see the indexes. This paper case is applicable to electronic information, especially with respect to electronic litigation support.

Braxton v. Farmer's Insurance Group, 209 F.R.D. 651 (N.D. Ala. 2002)

The plaintiff in this class action sought e-mails and other information from a nonparty. The defendant, Farmer's Insurance, objected. The court held that the information was potentially relevant and, therefore, that the subpoena would not be quashed.

Byers v. Illinois State Police, 2002 U.S. Dist. LEXIS 9861, 2002 WL 1264004 (N.D. Ill.)

Byers sued the Illinois State Police for discrimination. As part of discovery she sought an order compelling the police to produce archive e-mails authored by one of the individual defendants that related to her or her co-plaintiff. Defendants argued that it would be unduly burdensome to search backup tapes for archived e-mail. The court noted that e-mail has replaced informal chat around water coolers and in break rooms. It also noted, however, that e-mail is difficult to search. Defendants estimated that the total cost of responding would be between $20,000 and $30,000. Due to the cost, the court looked at the utility of the proposed project. Plaintiffs argued there was a high probability they would find relevant data because they had been told of the existence of one inflammatory e-mail. All of the individuals allegedly involved denied it and, through other sources, plaintiffs had not proved that this e-mail existed. Therefore, the plaintiffs would be required to pay the cost of recovery of e-mails if they decided those e-mails were important enough.

In re CI Host, Inc., 92 S.W. 3d 514 (Tex. 2002)

Plaintiffs sought production of computer backup tapes from CI Host. The parties agreed that the tapes contained some information protected from disclosure under the Electronic Communications Privacy Act. The Supreme Court of Texas denied the request for writ of mandamus and remanded the case to the trial court to modify its protective order forbidding disclosure of any trade secrets so that it included a protection of the privacy interests of third parties.

Columbia Communications Corp. v. Echostar Satellite Corp., 2001 U.S. App. LEXIS 1033 (4th Cir.)

Echostar asked the court to hold that Columbia had committed discovery misconduct and, therefore, Echostar should receive a new trial. The issue at trial was whether Columbia was ready, willing, and able to perform its part of a contract with Echostar. During discovery, Echostar had requested relevant databases essentially to show whether or not Columbia was ready, willing, and able. Columbia produced one database but shortly before trial "found" additional databases. Even though the trial court had found that the databases fell within Echostar's discovery requests, it found that there was no evidence Columbia had intentionally failed to comply and that the additional documents would only have been cumulative. It, therefore, refused to order a new trial. Fourth Circuit affirmed this as well as a variety of other matters raised on appeal.

Deloach v. Philip Morris Companies, Inc., 206 F.R.D. 568 (M.D.N.C. 2002)

Plaintiffs moved to strike portions of defendants' rebuttal expert report because it relied on computerized transaction data deliberately withheld from plaintiffs during discovery. Defendants claimed that they had not provided the information because plaintiffs' request was overbroad. The court looked through this argument and found that the information defendant provided to its own expert was not made available to plaintiff until after plaintiffs' expert could no longer use it, and that defendants' expert used the withheld information to rebut plaintiffs' expert report. The court held that the withholding of the data resulted in unfairness to the plaintiffs. As a sanction, the court ordered that the plaintiffs could respond to defendants' rebuttal expert report as to certain paragraphs and that defendants would not be allowed the opportunity to reply to plaintiffs' response.

Duff v. Marathon Petroleum Co., 1993 WL 388380 (N.D. Ill.)

In a two-paragraph memorandum order, the court simply holds that electronic information is discoverable.

Fennell v. First Step Designs, Ltd., 83 F. 3d 526 (1st Cir. 1996)

Following a motion for summary judgment, Fennell sought additional discovery under Federal Rule Civil Procedure 56(f) claiming that it had information that a certain memo was created after the fact to justify First Step's behaviour. The trial court did not grant additional time for discovery and Fennell appealed. Fennell provided "five suspicious facts" that did not convince either the district court or the court of appeals to allow further discovery. Additionally, the court of appeals noted that it would reverse the district court's discovery ruling for an abuse of discretion. This case should be used cautiously because it is a court of appeals case (abuse of discretion standard) and also because Rule 56(f) has different requirements than Rule 37.

Koen Book Distributors v. Powell, 212 F.R.D. 283 (E.D. Pa. 2002)

A client notified its attorneys that it had a potential malpractice action against the attorneys. While the attorneys attempted to find alternate representation for the client, that firm continued to represent the client. Subsequently, the client sought documents including e-mails that, among other things, concerned if and how to continue to represent the client and how to respond to the client's communications in light of a possible malpractice action. The attorneys claimed that attorney-client privilege and work product doctrine prevented the client from acquiring these documents. The court disagreed and ordered the production in unredacted form of all of the documents identified in the privilege log.

In re Lees, 727 N.Y.S. 2d 254 (Sup. Ct. N.Y. 2001)

A criminal defendant charged with rape and sodomy made an application to the trial court for an order directing the alleged victim and a third party to produce their computers so that he could search for e-mails between the two concerning false reports of rape for the purposes of impeachment at trial. The court outlined the procedures in New York State for such an order and granted the defendant a period of time in which to make a proper application.

McPeek v. Ashcroft, 202 F.R.D. 31 (D.D.C. 2001)

Plaintiff claimed that as a result of a complaint he filed in the work place, he received retaliation and was humiliated. Defendants searched for electronic and paper documents. Plaintiff asked that the backup system be searched. The court analyzed the difficulties of searching backup tapes, the question of cost, and ordered that defendants search a sampling of the backup tapes. After the defendant reports to the court with the results as well as the costs, the court will have another hearing at which the plaintiff can argue why the search should continue and who should bear the cost.

Northrop v. Inventive Communications, L.L.C., 199 F.R.D. 334 (D. Neb. 2000)

Plaintiff claimed that defendant had used plaintiff's software without a proper license. Defendant claimed it was a different software program. Plaintiff sought to compel discovery of the source code. Defendant filed for a protective order. The court ordered the defendant to provide the source code but only under the condition that plaintiff agree not to compete during the pendency of the lawsuit and for one year afterward, keep the source code confidential and post a performance bond.

Ohio v. Cook, 777 N.E. 2d 882 (Ohio App. 2002)

Defendant was convicted of child pornography and raised questions concerning probable cause for a search and authentication of a mirror image of the hard drive from his computer. The court found that the search warrant was issued as a result of a tip from the defendant's brother-in-law and was sufficiently justified. The mirror image of his hard drive had been examined by EnCase software and a report generated for trial. The defendant objected because he claimed that the state did not establish the reliability of the mirror image. The appeals court held that while some conflicts existed in the testimony, they relate to the weight of the evidence, not admissibility, and that the evidence was properly authenticated.

Procter and Gamble Co. v. Haugen, 179 F.R.D. 622 (D. Utah 1998)

The court held that Proctor and Gamble was allowed to specify search terms for the defendant to use in searching its databases to find if its supervisors were involved in fostering claims that Proctor and Gamble was involved in Satanism. The court set a procedure for defining the queries, having them run, and providing the information to the requesting party.

Simon Property Group L.P. v. mySimon, Inc., 194 F.R.D. 639 (S.D. Ind. 2000)

The court sets forth a process for discovery by which an expert from Computer Forensics, Inc. ™ was chosen to inspect computers. The expert was designated as an officer of the court and asked to search the data on the computers and provide a report to the court. The court, in turn, provided the report to the responding party to identify responsive and non-privileged documents and to create a privilege log and produce that material to the requesting party. The expert was asked to destroy any materials held in evidence at the conclusion of the case.

Southern Diagnostic Associates v. Luz Bencosme, 830 So. 2d 801 (Fla. Ct. App. 2002)

In an effort to get around the duty to preserve records and the duty to provide those in discovery, an insurer determined not to keep records but to delegate that responsibility to a non-party. The court did not find this to be an acceptable method of document retention and ordered the trial court to tailor an order to remedy the wrong.

Stallings-Daniel v. The Northern Trust Co., 2002 U.S. Dist. LEXIS 4024, 2002 WL 385566 (N.D. Ill.)

Plaintiff in an employment discrimination case wanted to do extensive electronic discovery. The court held that plaintiff's requests for electronic discovery were largely speculative because she had very scant evidence that she would find anything and, consequently, the court denied her motion initially and subsequently denied her motion for reconsideration.

Strasser v. Yalamanchi, 669 So. 2d 1142 (Fla. Dist. Ct. App. 1996)

Frequently responding parties cite to this Strasser case for the proposition that alleged misconduct of a responding party does not necessarily invite intrusive discovery abuse. One should be careful in citing to this case because, based upon Strasser II (see Data Preservation), the responding was indeed involved in destruction of evidence while claiming not to be.

Times Publishing Co. v. City of Clearwater, 830 So. 2d 844 (Fla. App. 2002)

The newspaper brought an action against the City of Clearwater to require them to release all e-mails sent from or received by two city employees using government-owned computers. The City of Clearwater had provided what it considered to be public e-mail but the Times wanted all the e-mail. The city had a computer resources use policy that stated that no employees would have an expectation of privacy in their e-mail. The question for the court became whether all e-mail stored on public computers is public record. The court decided that it was a matter for the legislature to determine.

Tulip Computers International B.V. v. Dell Computer Corp., 2002 U.S. Dist. LEXIS 7792 (D. Del.)

In this patent infringement case, Tulip sought e-mail evidence from Dell Computer and provided a procedure whereby e-mails would be given to a computer forensics firm to search, based upon Tulip's search terms. The e-mails would be given to Dell who would produce the e-mail subject to review for privilege and confidentiality.

U.S. v. Tucker, 150 F. Supp. 2d 1263 (D. Utah 2001)

The court analyzes the elements of knowing possession of child pornography over the Internet and determined that viewing the images on a computer constitutes control over the images. The court used as some evidence the fact that defendant had taken the time to delete image links from his computer cache file showing that he had knowledge that the links were there and what they were and that he, therefore, had control over them. The evidence also showed that he had willingly acquired the images and that they were not there on his computer due to ignorance, mistake or accident in that he had paid a user fee and acquired a password to access the websites.

In re Verizon Internet Services, Inc. v. Verizon Internet Services, 240 F. Supp. 2d 24 (D.C. 2003)

Verizon sought to quash a subpoena for the identity of users of Verizon's services who allegedly downloaded music from the Internet. Verizon argued that the information was transmitted over their system and did not reside on it therefore it was outside the power of the subpoena. The court analyzed the Digital Millennium Copyright Act and its legislative history in detail, considered its constitutionality, and concluded that Verizon must comply with the subpoena.

Westrienen v. Americontinental Collection Corporation, 189 F.R.D. 440 (D. Or. 1999)

Plaintiffs wanted access to all of defendants' computers. The court held that they were not entitled to unbridled access but must identify what it is they are seeking.

7.5.3 Case Laws Related to the Records Management

In re Cheyenne Software, Inc., Securities Litigation, 1997 WL 714891 (E.D.N.Y.)

The court found that defendants had failed in their discovery obligations and ordered defendants to bear the cost of downloading and printing up to 10,000 pages of e-mails responsive to appropriate key word searches. The defendants were allowed to withhold documents identified by the searches based only on privilege. Specifically, the court stated defendants could not object on relevance. In addition, the court held that defendant had erased electronic data but held that plaintiffs had not established prejudice. Irrespective, the court ordered defendants to pay $5,000 to the court and $10,000 to the plaintiffs.

Columbia Communications Corp. v. Echostar Satellite Corp., 2001 U.S. App. LEXIS 1033 (4th Cir.)

(See Scope of Discovery)

Duff v. Marathon Petroleum Co., 1993 WL 388380 (N.D. Ill.)

(See Scope of Discovery)

Koen Book Distributors v. Powell, 212 F.R.D. 283 (E.D. Pa. 2002)

(See Scope of Discovery)

Kozlowski v. Sears, Roebuck and Co., 73 F.R.D. 73 (D. Mass. 1976) (as amended Dec. 8, 1976)

This paper case has been used by many in both electronic and paper discovery to stand for the proposition that if a company creates a certain record-keeping procedure, that company must bear the cost of searching the records for responsive documents. In Kozlowski, Sears, Roebuck and Co. organized complaints by name of claimant rather than by type of product. The court held that Sears created the record-keeping system and, therefore, Sears would need to look through all of the records to find those records that were relevant to this products liability case.

Lewy v. Remington Arms Co., 836 F. 2d 1104 (8th Cir. 1988)

The court in this products liability case intimates that there are rules concerning records management and document retention, however, does not provide much guidance to corporations in what must be retained. It is clear, however, their blanket record destruction policy will likely be unacceptable. The policy must take into account different types of records. Once litigation is anticipated or begins, the parties have the responsibility to maintain electronic records that might be discoverable or to apply to the court if it finds the necessary procedure too burdensome.

New York State Nat'l Org. for Women v. Cuomo,1998 U.S. Dist. LEXIS 10520, 1998 WL 395320 (S.D.N.Y.)

The court instructed attorneys that they may not take the obligation to preserve records cavalierly but that they have a duty to advise their clients of pending litigation and of the requirements to preserve potentially relevant evidence, including electronic evidence. Clients cannot be expected to know all litigation that may be pending and, therefore, it devolves to the attorney to inform the client of the obligation once it arises.

Public Citizen v. Carlin, 2 F. Supp. 2d 1 (D.C. 1997)

This early case provides an excellent analysis of the differences between paper records and electronic versions of the records. It can be used to educate courts and other parties as to why it is important to have the electronic versions of documents as well as the paper versions. In conjunction with Premier Homes (see Reliability), Public Citizen can be particularly useful.

Southern Diagnostic Associates v. Luz Bencosme, 2002 Fla. App. LEXIS 15684

(See Scope of Discovery)

Times Publishing Co. v. City of Clearwater, 830 So. 2d 844 (Fla. App. 2002)

(See Scope of Discovery)

White v. Office of the Public Defender for the State of Maryland, 170 F.R.D. 138 (D. Md. 1997)

An attorney formerly employed by the Maryland Public Defender sued for racial discrimination. The court found three bases for imposing sanctions on the plaintiff for destruction of a diary that she called a manuscript autobiography. It considered Rule 3.4(a) of the Rules of Professional Conduct, Rule 37 of the Rules of Civil Procedure and the court's inherent authority. The court went through a two-step process. First, it considered five elements: the act of destruction; the discoverability of the destroyed evidence; the intent to destroy; the timing (that is, if the destruction occurred after litigation began or was contemplated); and the prejudice to the other party. The court held that based upon all of these factors, sanctions were appropriate against the plaintiff, the destroying party.

7.5.4 Case Laws Pertaining to the Use of Experts

Antioch Co. v. Scrapbook Borders, Inc., 210 F.R.D. 645 (D. Minn. 2002)

(See Data Preservation)

Gates Rubber Co. v. Bando Chemical Indus.,167 F.R.D. 90 (D. Colo. 1996)

Gates acquired an order allowing it to access Bando's Denver computer to seek deleted files. The "expert" Gates hired purchased a copy of an un-erased program, loaded it onto Bando's computer and attempted to locate deleted files. In the process of unloading the new program onto the computer, the expert overrode at random 7 to 8 percent of the data on the Bando computer. The court analyzes its ability to impose sanctions for destruction of evidence based upon Rules of Procedure

37 and also the inherent powers of the court. The lengthy case provides an excellent understanding of use of experts, destruction of evidence, and sanctions.

Playboy Enter. v. Welles, 60 F. Supp. 2d 1050 (S.D. Cal. 1999)

The court first noted that by requesting "documents" under the Rules of Civil Procedure the requestor automatically requests electronic evidence. Based upon testimony that e-mails had been created that might be relevant, the court determined that the burden upon Welles was outweighed by the need for the requested information and, therefore, that the requesting party would be allowed to find an expert to image the hard drive. The court would provide a protective order for the expert to sign and the information would only be provided to the producing party. The producing party would then review the material and produce anything responsive and non-privileged for the requesting party.

Simon Property Group L.P. v. mySimon, Inc., 194 F.R.D. 639 (S.D. Ind. 2000)

(See Scope of Discovery)

7.5.5 Case Laws Related to the Costs and Allocation

In re Air Crash Disaster at Detroit Metropolitan Airport,130 F.R.D. 634 (E.D. Mich. 1989)

Northwest Airlines sought computer data from flight simulation runs from McDonnell Douglas Corporation. McDonnell Douglas provided the material as hardcopy. Northwest again asked for the computer tape because its expert would need to load manually about 95 pages of single-spaced printout in order to perform his tasks. McDonnell Douglas claimed it did not any longer have the material in the format requested by Northwest. The court ordered McDonnell Douglas to prepare a computer tape in the format requested by Northwest but directed that Northwest would bear the cost since the tape did not currently exist.

In re Brand Name Prescription Drugs Antitrust Litigation, 1995 U.S. Dist. LEXIS 8281, 1995 WL 360526 (N.D. Ill.)

Class plaintiffs sought e-mail from drug manufacturer. The drug manufacturer did not dispute having discoverable e-mail but claimed that class plaintiffs should bear the cost of retrieving it. The court looked at limited factors and concluded that since the drug manufacturer chose an electronic storage method, the necessity for a retrieval program or method is an ordinary and foreseeable risk, therefore, the responding party would be required to bear the cost of retrieving the e-mails. In the event class members wanted paper copies of any e-mails, they would be required to pay the costs.

In re Bristol-Myers Squibb, 205 F.R.D. 437 (D.N.J. 2002)

The court emphasizes the importance of the Federal Rules Civil Procedure 26 meeting and the Rule 16 conference to anticipate and to prevent problems related to electronic discovery. The court learned that class plaintiffs agreed to pay for paper copies of documents that, unbeknownst, the plaintiffs had stored electronically and could have been produced inexpensively in electronic format. The responding party entered many documents into a litigation software program and then printed hard copies for plaintiffs in an attempt to get plaintiffs to pay the bill.

Byers v. Illinois State Police, 2002 U.S. Dist. LEXIS 9861, 2002 WL 1264004 (N.D. Ill.)

(See Scope of Discovery)

Fennell v. First Step Designs, Ltd., 83 F. 3d 526 (1st Cir. 1996)

(See Scope of Discovery)

Oppenheimer Fund, Inc. v. Sanders, 437 U.S. 340 (1978)

The United States Supreme Court took certiorari in this case to resolve a dispute among the circuits as to whether the discovery rules apply to authorize a district court to order a defendant to help identify the members of a plaintiff class so that individual notice can be sent or if the rule of class actions, Fed. R. Civ. Proc. 23(d), applies. The United States Supreme Court held that, even though the request resembles discovery, the class action rule applies. The question then became, who should bear the cost of compiling a list? The U.S. Supreme Court held that in this case the class members (respondents) should bear the cost of hiring the outside party to locate the information.

Rowe Entertainment, Inc. v. Wm. Morris Agency, Inc., 205 F.R.D. 421 (S.D.N.Y. 2002)

The Southern District of New York defined eight factors to consider when allocating costs of electronic discovery. Those factors are: specificity of the discovery requests; likelihood of discovering critical information; availability of such information from other sources; purposes for which the responding party maintains the requested data; relative benefit of the information to the requesting party; total cost associated with production; relative ability of each party to control cost; and, resources available to each party.

Sattar v. Motorola, Inc., 138 F.3d 1164 (7th Cir. 1998)

The court required Motorola to loan proprietary software to the requesting party or to allow that party access to Motorola's computer system to view the data. In an effort to encourage the parties to work out any problems, the court ordered them to share the costs of printing 210,000 pages unless they could create a better solution.

Strasser v. Yalamanchi, 669 So. 2d 1142 (Fla. Dist. Ct. App.1996)

(See Scope of Discovery)

Williams v. E.I. du Pont de Nemours and Co., 119 F.R.D. 648 (W.D. Ky. 1987)

This early case stands for the proposition that materials produced by litigation support are not covered by the attorney work product or attorney-client privilege and must be provided to the requesting party because they do not evidence any legal analysis but rather are more a ministerial and administrative function.

Williams v. Saint-Gobain Corp., 2002 U.S. Dist. LEXIS 12798 (W.D.N.Y.)

Defendant produced certain e-mails on the eve of trial and plaintiff moved for sanctions. Plaintiff cited federal regulations requiring defendant to maintain documents including e-mails concerning reorganisation and claimed that this showed that defendant had the documents and in bad faith refused to produce them. The court refused to find a bad faith element but ordered that discovery would continue and that the parties would both provide responsive information to the other.

Zubulake v. UBS Warburg LLC, 02 Civ. 1243 S.D.N.Y. (May 13, 2003)

The court provides a detailed analysis of the different types of data available for discovery and determines that the proper question is the accessibility of data rather than the media it may be stored on or the reason for its creation. The court rejects two of the Rowe Entertainment factors and creates seven factors to determine whether cost shifting should occur. First, it determines that the default answer is that there should be no cost shifting. Second, if the question is data in an accessible place, there should be no cost shifting. If the data is difficult to access, the new seven factors should be applied although not weighed equally. However, prior to the analysis, the court wants the responding party to restore and produce responsive documents from a small sample to assist in the fact intensive analysis.

7.5.6 Case Laws Related to the Spoliation and Sanctions

Applied Telematics, Inc. v. Sprint Communications Co., 1996 U.S. Dist. LEXIS 14053 (E.D. Pa.)

Applied Telematics asked the court to enter a default judgment as a sanction against Sprint because it contends its expert was not able to analyze all of the data due to defendants destroying routing plans. Sprint claimed that when it received Applied's discovery requests, it notified Applied that the system was not used for record-keeping but was used to route calls and that, due to its normal document retention policy, each weekly backup destroyed the data from the previous week. The court held that after receiving the complaint and request for document production, Sprint had a duty to preserve information. This duty did not arise instantly but arose at a reasonable time after Sprint understood the complaint and document request. The court analyzed the degree of fault of the defendant, degree of prejudice suffered by the plaintiff and reviewed a variety of sanctions available. The court ordered an adverse inference and attorneys' fees against Sprint.

Computer Associates International, Inc. v. American Fundware, Inc., 133 F.R.D. 166 (D. Colo. 1990)

Computer Associates moved for a default judgment as a sanction based upon American Fundware's destruction of evidence. The court held that American Fundware must have been aware that certain source code would be the subject of a discovery request long before it stopped destroying older versions. The court further found that American Fundware was subject to a duty to preserve the source code. It failed to preserve the source code intentionally destroying portions of it. Based upon findings that American Fundware acted willfully or in bad faith, that Computer Associates was seriously prejudiced by the actions, and that alternative sanctions would not adequately punish American Fundware and deter future discovery violations, it imposed the most severe sanction available, that is, striking the defendant's answer with respect to liability, entering default on the issue of liability against all defendants, ordering the parties to attempt to settle the remaining issues, and, if settlement did not occur, notifying the court so the court could proceed.

Crown Life Ins. Co. v. Craig, 995 F.2d 1376 (7th Cir. 1993)

The Seventh Circuit Court of Appeals reviewed a district court order sanctioning Crown Life for discovery abuse by entering a default judgment. The court of appeals used an abuse of discretion standard and found that the sanction was proportionate to the discovery failure based upon Crown Life's wilful failure to comply with discovery orders.

Danis v. USN Communications, Inc., 2000 U.S. Dist. LEXIS 16900, 2000 WL 1694325 (N.D. Ill.)

(See Data Preservation)

GTFM, Inc. v. Wal-Mart Stores, Inc., 2000 U.S. Dist. LEXIS 16244, 2000 WL 335558 (S.D.N.Y.)

GTFM sought transactional documents from Wal-Mart in this trademark infringement case. Wal-Mart's counsel responded that it did not have the centralized computer capabilities to track the purchase and sale of goods for a particular period of time. Plaintiffs then attempted to discover the information through other sources. Approximately one year later, GTFM deposed a Wal-Mart vice president who revealed that Wal-Mart's computers did in fact have the capability to track the purchase and sale of goods. The court held that counsel for Wal-Mart had a duty to find the person within the organisation who had knowledge of the computer capabilities and held that Wal-Mart had misrepresented its computer capacity. The court ordered defendant to pay all of plaintiffs' attorneys' fees and costs unnecessarily expended due to the failure to disclose accurate information.

Lexis-Nexis v. Beer, 41 F. Supp. 2d 950 (D. Minn. 1999)

In this employment case, the corporate employer sought sanctions against its employee for providing information to his new employer. Through computer forensics, the corporate plaintiff was able to determine that the employee had a variety of files on his laptop computer that he claimed he never had.

Linnen v. A.H. Robins Co., 1999 WL 462015 (Mass. Super. Ct. 1999)

Linnen is one of the first pharmaceutical products liability cases. In Linnen, the plaintiffs went to the court ex parte and acquired a document preservation order. After it was served on the defendants, the defendants waited for some period of time prior to stopping the recycling of their backup tapes. During discovery, defendants balked at the request to restore many of the backup tapes to search for responsive information. The court ordered the defendants to restore the backup tapes and search. Further, it ordered that a "spoliation inference" would be given, that is, that the jury be instructed that an adverse inference may be drawn from the fact the documents were destroyed by the defendants.

Procter and Gamble Co. v. Haugen, 179 F.R.D. 622 (D. Utah 1998)

(See Scope of Discovery)

Residential Funding Corp. v. DeGeorge Financial Corp., 306 F. 3d 99 (2nd Cir. 2002)

The trial court held that the delay in providing electronic records by Residential Funding was not done in bad faith or with gross negligence and, therefore, that an adverse inference instruction would not be given. The Second Circuit vacated and remanded because it found that the wrong standard had been used. The Second Circuit instructed the trial courts that an adverse inference instruction could be imposed when discovery was delayed by ordinary negligence and that a finding of gross negligence or bad faith was not necessary.

Simon Property Group L.P. v. mySimon, Inc., 194 F.R.D. 644 (S.D. Ind. 2000)

The court held that inadvertent disclosure of privileged documents does not waive the privilege.

Strasser v. Yalamanchi, 783 So.2d 1087 (Fla. Dist. Ct. App. 2001)

(See Data Preservation)

Trigon Insurance Co. v. U.S., 204 F.R.D. 277 (E.D. Va. 2001)

Plaintiff Trigon Insurance discovered that certain documents had been destroyed by the government. The court held that the federal government has an obligation to maintain records that begins when a party has noticed that the evidence is relevant to litigation and that the destruction of those documents can lead to sanctions.

Wm. T. Thompson Co. v. General Nutrition Corp., 593 F. Supp. 1443 (C.D. Cal. 1985)

The court analyzes discovery sanctions under both Rule 37(b) and under the inherent power to sanction litigants for abusive litigation practices and affirms a special master's decision.

White v. Office of the Public Defender for the State of Maryland, 170 F.R.D. 138 (D. Md. 1997)

(See Records Management)

7.5.7 Case Laws Pertaining to Inadvertent Disclosure

In re Bridgestone/Firestone, Inc., Tires Products Liability Litigation, Master File No. IP 00-9373-C-B/S, MDL No. 1373 (S.D. Ind. 2001)

In this order the judge considers the second inadvertent disclosure of the same document in which Ford claims a privilege. In the case management order there was a claw back provision. The court held that producing the document once was inadvertence, producing it again while at the same time vigorously asserting in court the importance of its confidentiality was inexcusable and constituted a waiver of any privilege.

In re Dow Corning Corp., 261 F.3d 280, (2nd Cir. 2001)

The court considered corporate minutes redacted to remove attorney-client privileged material. This case of paper discovery may have significant impact on the ability to redact electronic information.

Simon Property Group L.P. v. mySimon, Inc., 194 F.R.D. 644 (S.D. Ind. 2000)

(See Scope of Discovery)

U.S. v. Keystone Sanitation Co., Inc., 885 F. Supp. 672 (M.D. Pa. 1994)

The court held that the inadvertent disclosure of e-mail messages from one attorney to another when those messages were relevant to show an attempt to transfer assets to avoid environmental liability waived the attorney-client privilege. The court identifies five considerations to be balanced in determining whether waiver occurred.

7.5.8 Case Laws Related to the Method of Litigation

Adobe Systems, Inc. v. South Sun Products, 187 F.R.D. 636 (S.D. Cal 1999)

(See Scope of Discovery)

America Online, Inc. v. Anonymous Publicly Traded Co., 542 S.E. 2d 377 (Va. 2001)

A publicly traded company filed litigation anonymously against what it believed were former employees who it alleged were making defamatory material representations about the company. It issued a subpoena duces tecum against America Online, Inc. for the identity of people making comments on an Internet chat room. AOL moved to quash; the trial court refused to quash the subpoena; AOL appealed. Virginia Supreme Court reversed and remanded because it found that Virginia law would not allow an anonymous litigant under these circumstances.

Antioch Co. v. Scrapbook Borders, Inc., 210 F.R.D. 645 (D. Minn. 2002)

(See Data Preservation)

In re Bristol-Myers Squibb, 205 F.R.D. 437 (D.N.J. 2002)

(See Costs and Allocation)

Dodge, Warren and Peters Ins. Servs., Inc. v. Riley, 130 Cal. Rptr. 2d 385 (Cal. App 2003)

Plaintiffs acquired an injunction requiring defendants to maintain electronic evidence pending discovery. Defendants claimed that the injunction should not have been issued because the rules of civil procedure cover the same field and require the preservation of documents; therefore, a protective order or injunction is not necessary or authorized. The court held that post-destruction remedies are not adequate at law and that the injunction was improper.

In re Lees, 727 N.Y.S. 2d 254 (Sup. Ct. 2001)

The criminal defendant asked for computer information from the alleged victim and a witness that he claimed would show that the alleged victim had manufactured the story of the alleged crime. The court analyzes orders for production of evidence and explains to the pro se defendant what process he will need to follow to acquire the information.

Procter and Gamble Co. v. Haugen, 179 F.R.D. 622 (D. Utah 1998)

(See Scope of Discovery)

Rowe Entertainment, Inc. v. Wm. Morris Agency, Inc., 205 F.R.D. 421 (S.D.N.Y. 2002)

(See Costs and Allocation)

Sattar v. Motorola, Inc., 138 F.3d 1164 (7th Cir. 1998)

(See Costs and Allocation)

Tulip Computers International B.V. v. Dell Computer Corp., 2002 U.S. Dist. LEXIS 7792 (D. Del.)

(See Scope of Discovery)

Williams v. E.I. du Pont de Nemours and Co., 119 F.R.D. 648 (W.D. Ky. 1987)

(See Costs and Allocation)

Williams v. Saint-Gobain Corp., 2002 U.S. Dist. LEXIS 12798 (W.D.N.Y.)

(See Costs and Allocation)

7.5.9 Case Laws Related to Criminal Issues of Security

New Jersey v. Evers, 815 A. 2d 432 (N.J. 2003).

Criminal defendant challenged the validity of a search warrant because the affidavit in support of the search warrant violated his reasonable expectation of privacy as well as California and Virginia law and that the warrant did not meet the probable cause standard of New Jersey law. The New Jersey court provided a detailed analysis of the exclusionary rule as well as the federal constitutional standard and concluded that the search warrant was valid and the conviction could stand.

Ohio v. Cook, 777 N.E. 2d 882 (Ohio App. 2002).

(See Scope of Discovery)

South Dakota v. Guthrie, 654 N.W. 2d 201 (S.D. 2002).

The defendant claimed to have an electronic suicide note from his wife whom he was accused of murdering. Defendant waited until after the prosecution had rested its case in chief to produce the suicide note. The prosecution recalled one of their experts to refute the evidence and ask that the defendant be required to pay the cost. The court found that the amount of cost was excessive based upon the ability of the defendant and his attorney to pay the cost but ordered that the defendant's attorney pay a portion of the cost.

Thompson v. Thompson, 2002 U.S. Dist. LEXIS 9940 (D.N.H.).

This federal litigation arose in the context of a divorce proceeding. The plaintiff husband brought a claim in federal court arising under the Electronic Communications Privacy Act and the Wiretap Act against the defendant for copying his stored e-mail. The court held that copying stored e-mail did not constitute interception of electronic communications and, therefore, the case was dismissed.

Trigon Insurance Co. v. U.S., 204 F.R.D. 277 (E.D. Va. 2001).

(See Spoliation and Sanctions)

7.5.10 Case Laws Related to the Reliability

Premier Homes and Land Corp. v. Cheswell, Inc., 240 F. Supp. 2d 97 (D. Mass. 2002).

After defendants' consultants began mirror imaging electronic evidence, plaintiff's counsel disclosed that one of its employees had manufactured evidence which likely would have become apparent through the metadata. The court provides an analysis of how electronic documents can be fabricated and how that can be determined.

St. Clair v. Johnny's Oyster and Shrimp, Inc., 76 F. Supp. 2d 773 (S.D. Tex. 1999).

In an entertaining opinion written by Judge Samuel B. Kent (whose opinions are always entertaining) the court notes the difficulties in authenticating information from the Internet.

7.5.11 E-Sign Statute and Case Laws

In re RealNetworks, Inc., Privacy Litigation, 2000 U.S. Dist. LEXIS 6584, 2000 WL 631341 (N.D. Ill.).

Class members objected to arbitrating their dispute because they claimed that the arbitration agreement contained in the electronic license agreement was not written. The court held that the Federal Arbitration Act and the Washington Arbitration Act requirement of a writing could be satisfied by an electronic communication. The court holds that it is a writing because it could be printed and stored.

Rio Properties, Inc. v. Rio International Interlink, 284 F.3d 1007 (9th Cir. 2002).

Plaintiff attempted to serve process on defendant, a Costa Rican company, by attempting to serve process on its international courier and its attorney, both of whom refused to accept service. Plaintiff, a Nevada corporation, then went to the court and asked that it be allowed to serve process through e-mail. The trial court agreed and the Ninth Circuit affirmed, based upon the extraordinary circumstances.

Sea-Land Service, Inc. v. Lozen International, LLC, 285 F. 3d 808 (9th Cir. 2002).

The court uses a variety of evidentiary material including e-mails, faxes, and oral testimony to confirm that defendant had read and understood the terms of a contract. The case also considers the admissibility of an e-mail and questions of foundation.

Specht v. Netscape Communications Corp., 306 F. 3d 17 (2nd Cir. 2002).

This case concerns an arbitration clause that appeared on a computer screen imbedded in a user agreement. The Second Circuit held that the arbitration clause did not bind the parties for a variety of reasons. Primarily it found the user was not on inquiry notice because license terms submerged in another screen did not put consumers on constructive notice of the terms, and the language was not conspicuously displayed anywhere else.

U.S. v. Miller, 70 F. 3d 1353 (D.C. Cir. 1995).

The court held that the use of an automatic teller machine card and entry of a personal four-digit code could amount to bank fraud. The defendant claimed that it was more akin to check kiting. However, the court held that the entry of the electronic information amounted to a false misrepresentation.

7.5.12 Case Laws on Privacy

Braxton v. Farmer's Insurance Group, 209 F.R.D. 651 (N.D. Ala. 2002).

(See Scope of Discovery)

Chance v. Avenue A., Inc., 165 F. Supp. 2d 1153 (W.D. Wash. 2001).

Plaintiffs filed a class action against Avenue A. for placing "cookies" on their computers after class members visited certain Internet sites. Class members claimed that this violated their privacy right by allowing Avenue A. to monitor their electronic communications without their knowledge, authorization, or consent. The court provides a thorough analysis of "cookies" and action tags but determined that, based upon the current state of the law, Avenue A did not violate the Computer Fraud and Abuse Act, 18 U.S.C. § 1030; the Stored Communications Act, 18 U.S.C. § 2701; the Wiretap Act, 18 U.S.C. § 2510, but did not reach the Washington state law claims because it chose not to exercise supplemental jurisdiction.

In re CI Host, Inc., 92 S.W. 3d 514 (Tex. 2002).

(See Scope of Discovery)

In re DoubleClick Inc. Privacy Litigation, 154 F. Supp. 2d 497, (S.D.N.Y. 2001).

Plaintiff class members brought this case against DoubleClick, the largest provider of Internet advertising products, based on DoubleClicks' targeting Internet users for banner advertisements. Based upon personal information it gathered without the knowledge of the Internet users, class members brought this action under Electronic Communications Privacy Act, 18 U.S.C. § 2701; the Federal Wiretap Act, 18 U.S.C. § 2510; and the Computer Fraud and Abuse Act, 18 U.S.C. § 1030. The court held that class members did not have a cause of action under any of these federal acts. Furthermore, it declined to exercise supplemental jurisdiction over the state claims.

New Jersey v. Evers, 815 A. 2d 432 (N.J. 2003).

(See Criminal)

Pharmatrak, Inc. Privacy Litigation, 220 F. Supp. 2d 4 (D. Mass. 2002).

This case is another in the series of cases with Chance v. Avenue A. and In re DoubleClick Inc. Privacy Litigation.

U.S. v. Bach, 310 F. 3d 1063 (8th Cir. 2002).

The expectation of privacy created by Congress in 18 U.S.C. § 3105 is greater than the expectation of privacy created by the Fourth Amendment to the United States Constitution and, therefore, a violation of the statute is not necessarily a violation of the Constitution for purposes of suppression of evidence in a criminal case.

7.6 Kind of Audits Called Security Audits

7.6.1 Internet/Perimeter Audit

This is a view from the Internet towards your company. It examines all exposed devices (examples include firewalls, routers, servers, desktop devices, etc). The Internet audit sees your company's assets that are available to the world, whether or not you intended them to be viewed by others. This snapshot will identify vulnerabilities to threats and provide you with the necessary information to guard against them.

7.6.2 Website Audit

While it is a problem if your web page is defaced, it is even more disastrous to have someone enter your database servers through your web site. If you are conducting information exchanges, or Point Of Sale (POS) e-commerce on your site, any vulnerability can be extremely serious. Once inside, the attacker will have access to customer credit cards, employee information, business processes, trade secrets and more. A properly conducted web site audit will mitigate your exposure and contribute to your business assurance.

7.6.3 Penetration Audit (Ethical Hacking)

We establish a controlled environment with the client so they can see what we are doing and how we are doing it. The Penetration Audit is designed to identify vulnerabilities and exploit these vulnerabilities to determine what parts of a client's information we can access. All of this information is logged and recorded in a findings report. From the findings report we can then make recommendations as to how to mitigate these vulnerabilities and proactively prepare against future attacks.

7.6.4 Wireless Audit

We will examine your wireless configuration to determine whether the proper encryption tools are being utilized and provide your staff with the knowledge they need to have a safe wireless presence.

7.6.5 Network Audit

Statistical evidence shows that the majority of malicious acts come from the inside. That's inside your network. This Audit takes an internal view of your network and determines the vulnerabilities found there. Our report of findings and recommendations of your internal security will assist your staff in mitigating vulnerabilities and enhancing its strengths.

7.6.6 Security Policies and Procedures Audit

Policies and procedures are the heart and soul of your company's security. The key to successful policies and procedures are how they are communicated and practiced. You can have the best policies and procedures documented, but if they are not communicated or practiced, they are worthless. That is the same as not having any at all, therefore making you vulnerable to extensive litigation. Our review will give you a clear understanding of possible shortcomings, missed opportunities, and an overall sense of how well your policies and procedures are being practiced. This will increase your security practices while sharply lowering your exposure to litigation.

7.6.7 Facilities Audit (Physical)

Legally an organisation is required to have a safe and secure facility in which to conduct business. A Facilities Audit will enable you to validate the security you have and determine what areas need improvement. We will walk your perimeter, walk up and down your halls, and look in ceilings and under floors. Looking at camera angles, interviewing staff, checking access controls and badge issuance policies are only a small piece of overall physical security. Could an outsider gain access to your facility through the loading dock? Do you use water for fire suppression in the data centre? DSA will enable you to mitigate your security risks and provide a safe and secure working environment.

7.6.8 Business Continuity Plan (BCP) and Disaster Recovery (DR)

Since the terrorism attacks of 9/11/01, it has become abundantly clear that every company must have a working Business Continuity and Disaster Recovery Plan. If you do not have one, or have not updated what you have, you leave yourself wide open to litigation from victims, federal and state governments and even a class-action lawsuit from your own shareholders. Your information, services, and the ability to transact business must be available, on-line, to everyone all the time. No longer do you have the luxury of taking several hours, let alone days, to recover after a catastrophic event. Also you have a fiduciary responsibility to protect the safety of every one at your facilities. In addition to the safety of your people, you must always protect your data from any potential loss. We will provide you with a review of your current BCP and DR plans. We will then give you our recommendations for any corrections needed to improve these plans.

7.6.9 Regulatory Compliance Audits

Companies are subject to federal regulations and therefore must comply with these regulations or be subject to law suits and/or criminal prosecution. Here is a short list of common regulations.

HIPAA: Health Insurance Portability and Accountability Act – This highly complex and extensive requirement pertains to any company that retains any kind of medical record on anyone. It requires specific measures be imposed to maintain the security of these records. Security auditors assist clients in their efforts to comply with this act.

GLBA: Gramm Leach Bliley Act – This pertains to any bank, broker/dealer, or insurance company that retains financial records. This too requires that specific measures be imposed to maintain the security of these records. Auditors (Security) often work with companies in their efforts to become compliant.

Sarbanes Oxley Act: This law applies to publicly traded companies with respect to accountabilities, financial audits, and consulting. It requires that specific measures be taken regarding the separation of financial duties from the duties of executives and board of directors'. Many private and nonprofit companies have chosen to comply, since some of the same people participate in other organisations. Security auditors with other operational auditors are expected to be helpful in assisting clients in their efforts to comply with this law.

NERC: North American Energy Reliability Council, Urgent Action Standard 1200 - This standard applies to the Utility industry's generation and/or distribution of electrical power. Organisations in their efforts to comply with this extensive and robust standard have opted for IT auditors' assistance.

The Patriot Act: This law gives the federal government at times much needed extensive power to prevent terrorism in America and around the world. As with any such broad reaching legislation, sometimes well meaning individuals and organisations can accidentally be disrupted as the U.S. government continues its war against terrorism. Once again, IT auditors with the security specility auditors have a niche where they can assist enterprises in their efforts to be in compliance with the Patriot Act and maintain secure operations.

This is just a small sample of the many government regulations which apply to enterprise operations.

7.7 How Can Security Audit Help the Enterprises?

7.7.1 Protecting the Physical Safety of Your Employees, Vendors, and Visitors

If there is a disaster with no warning (fire, tornado, earthquake, gas leak, explosion, bomb threat, etc.), do your employees, vendors, and visitors know what to do? Do you know how to account for everyone in case someone is missing? Do they know where to go? Whom to call? What if someone is disabled, how do you get them out? It is these questions and many more that you must ask yourself when drafting or improving on your Disaster Recovery Plan. This plan must be well thought out and communicated to everyone. Someone's life could be ruined and you will get sued if something goes wrong.

Protecting how your information is generated, communicated, stored, backed-up, restored, and accessed: The most valuable asset a company has is information. This includes client information, transaction information, credit card information, social security numbers, dates of birth, company financials, proprietary technical information, pricing and price breaks, purchasing history, credit scores, medical records, direct access to client and/or vendor databases and more.

Typically information is generated by a transaction or inquiry by a customer. When a computer terminal or website executes a transaction, is this information vulnerable to unauthorized access? When a transaction is executed, this information is communicated to other parts of the company or maybe even to other companies via phone lines or wireless connections. Phone lines or wireless communications that are not properly encrypted can provide access to product supply, shipping, banking, and accounting. Where is the information stored? Physically, where is the server and who has access to that area? Is that area vulnerable? Who and how many people have access to the data? Can someone who has inappropriate administration rights access this information unnecessarily? How is this information backed-up?

How often is the information backed-up? Are the same back-up tapes being used over and over again? Are the back-up tapes stored off-site? Who has access to the back-up tapes? If there is a disruption of the data, how does the company restore the data? Has the company done a complete restore? When was the last complete restore? Have things changed since the last restore? Is there a cold site (back-up data center)? Is the cold site operational? For example, companies often tell they have a cold site, but when it is examined for its operations, it is found the sites are not configured, powered, or set up properly. Can someone gain access to classified information? This information includes HR files, employee compensation, access codes to vendors or clients, proprietary product technical information, company financials, tax records, pricing, purchasing history, client information and much more.

Proving due diligence with any organisation is extremely important: Security auditor gives the ability to the enterprises to prove that they have had an independent audit that can validate company's security. This process will prove that enterprise measured the risks posed to the organisation, and made an informed decision, and chose the appropriate course of action. Protecting company public image is a constant public relations campaign.

Security audit enables enterprises to protect employees, vendors, visitors, and information. Security auditor enables organisation to show that the company is stable and secure thus encouraging other organisations to do business with the enterprise. Mitigating risks of lawsuits, negligence, and noncompliance with regulations requires constant attention to detail in the operation of an organisation. With the results of an audit, security auditor gives recommendations and alternatives as to how to mitigate various risks. By practicing due diligence, this endeavour will substantially lower if not eliminate a company's susceptibility to negligence.

These security auditors have the capacity to assist the organisation in its efforts to comply with regulatory issues. Proactively planning versus reactively spending is essential in protecting company assets in the case of a catastrophic event. Having the foresight to protect an organisation from the risk of loss in a catastrophe will make organisation able to survive such an event with minimal financial or public image loss. It will also make the enterprise more competitive. Security auditor can help examine, improve, and put in place an effective disaster recovery plan. Without security, nothing else matters.

Turning security into revenue is a strategy that is popular with many enterprises. Often independent security auditors provide a list of recommendations and alternatives. Once these recommendations are implemented through the appropriate amendments and rectifications to its vulnerabilities controls, security auditors perform a follow up for a Validation Audit. If the results of this Validation Audit are in line with data security best practices, these independent security auditors often award the enterprise with a certificate of "Best Practices Validation". Audited organisations can make use of this Best Practices Validation for marketing purposes to prove to their clients/customers, vendors, and investors that the particular enterprise is committed to data security. It has been noticed that such kind of marketing can yield substantial interest and subsequent revenue for these security audited organisations.

8 Information Technology Governance and COBIT®

Sue Bushell writes in CIO web magazine (05/07/2003) that historically, boards have seldom been involved in IT issues, intervening mainly when IT problems threatened the viability of the business. Boards rushed to intervene in some of the online retail companies, including Amazon, when fulfilment problems threatened the credibility of the company and buyers were still skittish about online buying. Boards have also intervened in some companies in which IT was seen as integral to the business model. Otherwise, it has been rare for an IT issue to attract the attention of a board of directors. As leading global businesses increasingly recognise the imperative for strong IT governance, some boards are stepping up to adopt a much stronger oversight role, and leading institutions are proposing those organisations as role models for the rest of the business world. This Chapter is an effort to bring the pertinent facts and fictions (if there are any!) together with an intent to inform the IT auditor, the role to be played in the corporate or enterprise IT governance.

She further commented in the brief on the applicability and impact of control objectives for business and related technologies (COBIT) in these words, "... Strong framework tools are essential for ensuring IT resources are aligned with an enterprise's business objectives, and that services and information meet quality, fiduciary and security needs," the institute says. CobiT is designed to ensure alignment of IT resources with an enterprise's business objectives so that information and services meet quality, fiduciary and security needs, and to provide a mechanism to balance IT risks and returns. CobiT defines 34 significant processes linked with 318 tasks and activities, and defines an internal control framework for all of them. The institute says CobiT is a useful and powerful framework for communicating effectiveness and value to the business. It also warns its usefulness can occasionally be undermined by resistance from IT executives, who may see CobiT as a threat when it is introduced in an enterprise, as it often is, via the audit route.

Management specialists dealing with the IT governance, look at the increasing importance of IT governance and how CobiT can simplify companies' transition to an organized structure that seamlessly integrates the business objectives with IT. Many believe that IT will be the major driver for economic wealth in the 21st century. Information and the technology that supports it represent companies' most valuable assets. What is even more important is that today's competitive and rapidly changing business environment requires increased quality, functionality and ease of use from organisations' IT systems. It is clear that most enterprises rely on IT for their competitive advantage and cannot afford to devote anything less to it than, for example, financial supervision or general corporate governance. There-fore, the time has come for company board members to create committees that proactively take charge of IT governance.

Alan Greenspan, chairman of the US Federal Reserve Board, put it: "A firm is inherently fragile if its value-added emanates more from conceptual as distinct from physical assets. Trust and reputation can vanish overnight. A factory can-not."

8.1 Why Do we Need IT Governance?

At its core, IT governance has two responsibilities: it must drive and enable busi-ness value, and mitigate risks. However, it is important to remember that IT gov-ernance is not a "unique" discipline – it is essentially a component of corporate governance. By applying the principles of corporate governance, IT governance can, for example, focus on the alignment of IT and business strategies, thoroughly review potential IT investments and measure performance.

The key responsibility, however, in realising IT governance lies with com-pany's board members. This doesn't necessarily mean that they must become tech-nology buffs overnight. What it boils down to, is that these members must equip themselves with a high-level understanding of their changing roles regarding IT and should consider attracting more IT-related business skills to the boardroom. According to recent predictions by leading analysts groups such as Giga, Gartner and Compass; there has already been a recent shift towards the following IT gov-ernance responsibilities:

- **Strategic Alignment** - focused on aligning IT with business and collaborative solutions
- **Value Delivery** - concentrating on optimizing expenses and proving the real value of IT
- **IT Asset Management** - focusing on knowledge and infrastructure and
- **Risk anagement** - safeguarding IT assets and implementing a disaster recovery strategy

John Lainhart IV, a leading member of the ISACA task group on IT governance suggests in one of his writings (available at IT Governance Institute website) that within the last decade, IT has changed how nearly every business executive does his or her job. Currently, IT governance includes such elements as:

- **Capital Resources** (information systems, technology and communication)
- **Strategies and Regulations** (business, legal and other issues)
- **Human Resources** (all concerned stakeholders, including directors, senior management, process owners, IT suppliers, users and auditors)

IT should be governed by practices that help ensure an enterprise's IT resources are used responsibly, its risks are managed appropriately and its information and related technology support business objectives. Businesses today rely on information technology (IT) as an integral part of their overall enterprise strategy.

As the logical next step, a new field of thought called IT governance has been under development for several years. No business, it seems, is immune to some form of IT attack, fraud or bad planning, whether from malicious external hackers, inexperienced managers or from dissatisfied employees. For example, the U.S. State Department recently confirmed that one of its confidential Web sites was hacked, causing the shutdown of several internal Internet servers. In other news stories, many leading-edge companies reported disastrous delays and cost over-runs from uncontrolled IT projects with unspecified budgets and poorly defined objectives. Business managers must step in and provide high-level thought and guidance for IT projects. IT governance is the process by which an enterprise's IT is directed and controlled. Effective IT governance helps ensure that IT supports business goals, maximizes business investment in IT and appropriately manages IT-related risks.

IT governance also helps ensure achievement of critical success factors by efficiently and effectively deploying secure, reliable information and applied technology. George Spafford writes in his article 'the benefits of standard IT governance frameworks' (at itmanagement.earthweb.com/netsys/article.php/2195051): "In the wake of 9/11 and corporate debacles such as Enron, organisations are taking a serious look at their information technology (IT) groups and questioning the governance models necessary to minimize risks and maximize returns. At a very broad level, organisations can approach governance on an ad hoc basis and create their own frameworks, or they can adopt standards that have been developed and perfected through the combined experience of hundreds of organisations and people. By adopting a standard IT governance framework, enterprises realize a number of benefits."

8.2 Introduction to COBIT®

In theory, IT governance might seem like just another important agenda point, but in practice there lies a great deal of challenges ahead for many companies. And this brings us to Control Objectives for Information and related Technology (CO-BIT). First published by the Information Systems Audit and Control foundation (ISACA) in 1996, COBIT – now in its third edition – is supported by the likes of IT Governance Institute, Meta Group and Gartner. COBIT aims to bridge the gap between business risks, control needs and technical issues - presenting IT activities in a manageable and logical structure. One of the greatest strengths of COBIT is its ability to provide clear management guidelines. According to COBIT, managers need to understand the status of their IT systems and decide what security and control they should provide.

What this essentially means is that there is a need of continuous improvement in IT security and control – deciding how much, however, is the challenge. By implementing COBIT Management Guidelines, companies can for example benchmark and measure their process against peers and enterprise strategy, achieving a competitive level of IT security and control. COBIT also focuses on performance management by utilising the principles of the Balanced Business Scorecard. Through tools such as Key Goal Indicators and Key Performance Indicators, organisations can measure the outcome of their processes and assess how well it's performing. COBIT answers the perpetual question: "What is the right level of IT control in order for it to support enterprise objectives."

Historically, senior managers have not had a solid grasp on IT issues and have not been as deeply involved in IT issues as they were in financial, strategic and other business decisions. IT governance provides the tools to enable them to be more effective in the IT arena of the business. Simply put, good governance – enterprise and IT – is good business. Enterprise governance, the system by which companies are directed and controlled, drives and sets IT governance. At the same time, IT should provide critical input to, and form an important component of, strategic planning for enterprise governance. In many cases, IT influences the strategic opportunities and benefits identified by the enterprise. Whether for sales, operations, human resources, and legal or manufacturing, enterprise activities require data and IT services to meet business objectives.

IT must be aligned with and enable enterprises to take full advantage of reliable, accurate and usable information. By so doing, businesses maximize benefits, capitalize on opportunities and gain a competitive advantage. COBIT is a comprehensive framework of control objectives based on 36 international source documents, ensuring a global view and a best practice point of view. Available as a complimentary download from *www.isaca.org*, COBIT is the result of years of research and cooperation among global IT and business experts and provides an authoritative, international set of generally accepted IT practices for business managers and auditors. This edition contains a new publication with detailed management guidelines to provide guidance on business risks, control needs and technical issues. The management guidelines help monitor business processes by using critical success factors (CSFs), key goal indicators (KGIs), key performance indicators (KPIs) and maturity models (MMs). By addressing COBIT's control objectives, business managers can ensure that an adequate control system is provided for their IT environment. They can then focus on high-risk areas and determine cost-effective ways to mitigate those risks.

8.2.1 COBIT and the Reality

Theory is one thing, but putting it into practice is another. Currently, COBIT is utilized by a number of well-known national international organisations. Phillips International uses COBIT as part of a company-wide quality improvement Programme and has, for example, developed a scoring process that uses the framework's maturity models to reflect is own organisational and process needs. Brussels-based global messaging services and interface software developer, SWIFT, introduced COBIT as part of the development process for a new systems planning group – all to implement sound mission objectives. Lastly, research authority, Meta Group recently commented that 30% to 40% of Global 2000 companies deploying new technologies and entering new markets with e-products in 2003 will adopt a COBIT -like risk assessment and balanced risk/reward reporting process. Opportunities continue to arise to support better stewardship for businesses. Enterprise stakeholders want assurance that executives running the enterprise on a day-to-day basis are taking all possible steps to protect the business and make the best use of its assets.

Organisations demonstrating that assurance – and an IT governance program is one way of doing so – can reap the rewards of stakeholder support. E-commerce, for example, is a growing business opportunity for many organisations. When exploring e-commerce options, though, enterprises must implement and clearly exhibit effective control of IT and information for trading partners and customers. Without the trust of partners and customers, companies do not have a chance of succeeding in the e-commerce arena. IT governance enables businesses to inspire that trust, through clearly demonstrated control over the IT function. Business threats are just as numerous as business opportunities. Perhaps the most rampant are increased security threats and vulnerabilities, through information warfare and cyber threats. Rarely a day goes by that evidence of hacking or illicit data manipulation isn't trumpeted in the press.

What are the potential business drivers which are to exist to opt for COBIT, are aptly summarized in one of the documents called "COBIT MAPPING" issued by the IT Governance Institute, US. These are shown below:

- there is a need for IT governance
- services delivered by IT are to be aligned with business goals
- IT processes are to be standardized/automated
- a framework for overall IT processes is needed
- processes are to be unified
- there is a need of a framework for a quality management system
- a structured audit approach is to be defined
- mergers and acquisitions are occurring
- IT cost-control initiatives are desired
- part or all of the IT function is to be outsourced
- compliance with external (e.g., regulators, organisations or third-party) requirements is of concern

In case, the enterprise wants to avoid opting for COBIT, the potential risks faced are enumerated as follows:

- misaligned IT services, divergence
- weak support of business goals due to misalignment
- wasted opportunities due to misalignment

- persistence of the perception of IT as a black-box
- shortfall between management's measurements and management's expectations
- know-how tied to key individuals, not to the organisation
- excessive IT cost and overheads
- erroneous investment decisions and projections

For the in-depth coverage of COBIT, readers are advised to go to the website of ISACA (*www.isaca.org*) or the sister website at IT Governance Institute, USA.

9 Database Management Systems and Auditing

Database technology is changing rapidly as evolving technology creates new requirements. In this age of open systems, database management systems (DBMSs) must be portable across many diverse hardware platforms. The database is at the heart of client/server architecture, acting as the data server for client data requests. Client/server technology is also revitalizing the distributed database concept, requiring improved capabilities for data synchrony and replication between databases. Specialized DBMSs are emerging to support the data warehousing concept. The recent introduction of the massively parallel processing hardware architecture mandates changes in the DBMSs to exploit these powerful processors effectively. Finally, the electronic data to be managed has changed dramatically. In addition to the "old" character-based data, DBMSs must now support mechanical drawings, blueprints, charts, graphs, maps, electronic documents and publications, photographs, images, and even multimedia sound and video. The requirements of this new electronic age have led to the latest innovation in database technology: the object data management system. This chapter presents the basic concepts of databases and describes various approaches to database management, including popular products. An IT auditor is expected to have basic understanding of database concept and the available relational database management systems being used by the clients. The weaknesses and strengths of these database management systems help an IT auditor in identifying the risks involved and the overall audit risks.

9.1 Concepts of Database Technology for Auditors

A database is a collection of structured data elements with a particular organisation; this physical structure is the way data is stored by the database management system. A database is also a collection of logically similar records; those records contain data elements, which are collected and stored in the database. In a database, the elements required for an application are defined as needed, giving more flexibility than the standard file structure. Access to the database can be made according to the database structure and is controlled by the DBMS. The database system is composed of three components: (1) the data, (2) the schema and subschema that describe the arrangement of the data, and (3) the programs that perform operations on the data. A structural component of the schema (a view of the entire database) is the subschema; each subschema describes the database as seen and accessed by one particular user or application. Usually, there are indices, used by the system somewhat like an index in a book, maintained by the DBMS to locate requested information more quickly. Each request for data made by an application program must be analysed by the DBMS. The request is stated in terms of the logical name of the data (used in the application). It is converted by the DBMS into a set of physical file addresses, so that the physical data can be retrieved and transmitted by the DBMS to the application program.

9.1.1 Data Independence

Prior to the development of databases, data files were designed for, and viewed as belonging to, one or more closely related application programs. The data was stored in the logical and physical relationship required by the application. When new applications were developed, it was more practical to create new data files containing the specific data and format requirements. This made it possible to avoid program amendments in existing applications, since generally any change in data structure required a program amendment. Data could be obtained only from existing files in inflexible formats, unless extraction and reformatting programs were written. This data-dependent style of processing resulted in program maintenance problems, piecemeal development efforts, and duplication of data.

The database concept separates the data requirements from the application requirements. Both requirements are evolving processes that are not necessarily compatible. A database provides for the integration and sharing of common data among different programs. In a database approach, the data elements (fields and segments) are stored with little or no redundancy, and the physical (or real) file structures may bear little resemblance to the logical records and files being processed by application programs. From a data processing point of view, a database is a means of gaining flexibility by creating and maintaining data independently from the application programs that access that data.

9.1.2 Database Management Systems and its Functions

The data that an organisation generates, manipulates, and stores for the continuing operation of the organisation is one of its most important assets. A shared collection of information that satisfies the organisation's needs best is often a database. Various DBMSs have been developed to build and manipulate databases. The DBMS translates data requirements of application programs and executes data management functions (store, update, delete, retrieve) on behalf of those programs. As and when an application program using a DBMS; requests data, the DBMS looks up the description of the data. This description is defined when the database is implemented. If there is an index, the DBMS uses it to find the data. The DBMS also determines whether the program has permission to access or update the data, information that is defined when the database is constructed. If the application program is used to update a record, the application program instructs the DBMS to return the modified data to storage.

The Database Administrator

The database administrator (DBA) is the manager of the database. One responsibility of the DBA is security and information classification—not everyone should have access to all of the information. This duty may be shared with a data security administrator in a large database environment. (In fact, the access to information is a primary audit concern.). The DBA is responsible for the design, definition, and maintenance of the database. Other functions include setting policies and procedures for backup and recovery, determining appropriate access permissions for applications programs and users, and resolving any conflicts among users of the data.

Data Organisation

A database system can be described as being information-oriented, then user-oriented or data-oriented. Information-oriented data is meaningful to the organisation as a whole; user-oriented data relates to how a user of the information wishes to manipulate or retrieve the information; and data-oriented data means storing the data only once and being able to access and retrieve it easily. The data in a database is stored in fields that represent units of information (e.g., the number "4891100" is seven digits, which, taken as a whole, could be the telephone number 4891100 or an invoice amount of $48,911.00). Interpretation of the data depends on the user and the computer application program processing the data. Perhaps the easiest way to describe the database concepts as implemented is to describe how a hospital may create, manipulate, retrieve, and store data. The patient information shown can be used to identify patients for billing, treatment, insurance reporting, and such, each of which is an application system in the database. One application program in the billing system is the invoicing of patients for treatment received. In this case, the invoice is triggered by treatment, which may have been triggered by an appointment register. Each of these activities represents a different database application.

The receptionist making appointments in a doctor's office does not need access to the patient's entire file, only to the information necessary to make the appointment. When the receptionist enters the appointment in the appointment register, it may be done via a terminal that allows only appointment transactions to be entered. This transaction simultaneously causes the scheduling of a doctor and an examination room for the day and time of the appointment. Figure C5-6 illustrates the physical organisation of data within a human resources system, as stored on disk versus the logical organisation of the data as defined within the database.

Database Structure

There are three common database structures: hierarchical, network, and relational. This section will address each structure in general, while describing a popular DBMS for each.

Hierarchical

In a hierarchical database, data is organised in a tree structure. IBM's IMS (Information Management System) uses hierarchical architecture and concepts. The uppermost data element in the hierarchy is called the root. The root is linked to data elements or nodes on a lower level, each called a child. The higher level node to which the child is linked is called a parent.

A hierarchical structure has only one root. Each parent can have numerous children, but a child can have only one parent. Subordinate segments are retrieved through the parent segment. Reverse pointers are not allowed. Pointers can be set only for nodes on a lower level; they cannot be set to a node on a higher level. Navigation to individual database records takes place through predetermined access paths.

Network

The network structure is more flexible, yet more complex, than the hierarchical structure. Data records are related through logical entities called sets. Within a network, any data element can be connected to any item. Unlike in IMS, a data element called a member (the equivalent of a child in IMS) can have more than one owner (parent). Because networks allow reverse pointers, an item can be both an owner and a member of the same set of data. Members are grouped together to form records, and records are linked together to form a set. A set can have only one owner record but several member records. A popular network database is Computer Associates' IDMS (Integrated Database Management System). IDMS uses the Data Definition Language (DDL) and the Data Dictionary Definition Language (DDDL) to define the schema and the subschema of the database. Since a schema is a conceptual description of the entire database, it includes the name and definition of all files, areas, records, elements, and data set relationships. The subschema is a subset of the schema. It can restrict a program's view of the database to the data the program needs and the Data Manipulation Language (DML) commands used to access the database. DML converts application program commands to access data into calls to the IDMS interface module that handles communication with the physical database. The source code for the schema and subschema are stored in the Integrated Data Dictionary (IDD). The compiled version of the subschema can be stored in the IDMS load library or the load area within the IDD.

Relational

Both hierarchical and network database structures define data by their relationship to applications. Relational database technology separates data from the application and uses a simplified data model. Based on set theory and relational calculus; relational database models information in the structure of a table) with columns and rows. Columns, called domains or attributes, correspond to fields. Rows, called tuples, correspond to records. Relational databases have grown in popularity over the last several years because they are easier to set up and maintain than other DBMSs. Relationships are defined at the data value level so that physical pointers do not have to be set up. As a result, application programs are more independent of the data structure. Adding or deleting a field from the database does not require the program to be recompiled. In addition, relational databases are more flexible in supporting user requests for data because files are loaded into the DBMS. Application programmers define how their applications view the data. The user need not be concerned with the access path or the pointers used to retrieve the data.

IBM DB2, Oracle 9i, Microsoft SQL Server, and Sybase database technology, and most PC-level database software (e.g., Paradox, dBASE, and Access), use relational architecture and concepts. In addition to the underlying database, most of these products include a data manipulation language for developing a database application; a forms builder for defining the user interface to that application; and a query tool, such as Structured Query Language (SQL), that facilitates the retrieval of information from the database by the end user. See Appendix C5-1 for more information on SQL.

Data Manipulation Language

The data manipulation language (DML) interfaces between the application program and the DBMS to perform a function (e.g., open a file, insert a record). IMS uses DL/1 commands to manipulate data. IDMS and other networks usually use the CODASYL DML standards.

Data Dictionary

The data dictionary (DD) describes various attributes of the data elements. In some DBMSs, it also contains information about the physical location of the data. It may include the data name, the segment on which it occurs, and the programs using the field. A DD can be used to ensure that data is defined uniformly. It also supplies the application programmer and the user with information as to what data is available and in which database it is located. DDs are classified as passive or active. Active DDs are updated automatically whenever there is a change in the DBMS. A passive DD is not integrated with the DBMS, and must be maintained separately. IMS has a passive DD, IDMS has an active integrated DD, DB2 has the DB2 Catalog that performs some active DD functions.

Data Integrity

The integrity of data is the degree to which it can be relied on as being valid. This includes the accuracy, timeliness, authorization, completeness, non-duplication, sequence, and other qualities of the data. While the application systems should incorporate many of these data integrity qualities, DBMSs also provide certain techniques and controls for maintaining the integrity of the data. The following techniques can be found in most relational database products.

1. Referential Integrity

Referential integrity controls help ensure the integrity of relationships between entities in different tables or, when a table references information in another table, that information exists and the attributes of that information remain proper. For example, a table of invoices references a table of customers to establish which customers owes which invoices. If the customers associated with those invoices are allowed to be deleted from the customer table or modified, the relationship to invoices would be lost. Most relational database management systems (RDBMSs) incorporate referential integrity controls.

2. Locking

Locking ensures that no user can access data in a table that another user is updating until that update is complete. This ensures that two or more users do not overwrite each other. Automated locking is a basic control built into most DBMSs. Depending on database and application design, locking controls can lead to deadlocking or deadly embrace situations.

3. Edit/Validation Routines

Edit and validation routines can be associated with tables to edit or validate data before it is updated to the table. These routines are established when the table is created.

9.1.3 Relational Database Management Systems (RDMS)

Relational database management systems (RDMS) are finding a place in the delivery of a wide variety of services through computer networks, intranets, and the Internet. These systems are a consistent, powerful method of storing, reading, and manipulating information. RDMS, provided by vendors such as Oracle, IBM, Informix, Microsoft, and others, are the backbone components of client/server applications. They simplify system design and application programming by providing a common data retrieval and manipulation interface. The relational model uses a common language called structured query language (SQL) to access and manipulate data. Most database vendors comply with an accepted SQL standard that makes their databases compatible with a variety of applications and utility programs. Auditors should understand the importance of database systems and how they are used within an organisation. Audit procedures must be tailored to suite the objectives of a particular database application.

Applications

Relational databases are commonly used as data repositories or warehouses. Users can download information from a legacy system and store it in a repository or warehouse until they want to run reports on demand. This saves a lot of time and bypasses the former need to have mainframe programmers write report programs, and eliminates the steps that were necessary to execute programs. Another advantage is that database systems take the processing load off of mainframe and other systems. A database used in combination with reporting tools, often referred to as executive information systems (EIS), further improves accessibility of information by replicating databases in remote locations across a network. A major drawback of this and a concern of auditors, however, is that replication multiplies the potential of increasing the probability of the occurrence of a data integrity error and increases the complexity of administering database security. Errors may also be difficult to detect. Because important business decisions rely upon the integrity and the timeliness of EIS, auditors should be concerned about the effectiveness of controls which ensure that data elements are synchronized for timeliness, and that the relationship between the EIS data and the legacy system data is consistent. Auditors can use manual or automated controls to test for this consistency. Increasingly, relational databases are being used to support integrated enterprise resource planning (ERP) application packages (e.g., SAP R/3, Baan, Oracle Financials). ERP effectiveness relies on the integrity of a relational database as a common platform for storing, retrieving, and manipulating an organisation's production, planning, sales, and financial data. To further complicate an auditor's task, many organisations are beginning to offer corporate information to clients by making databases available over the Internet through Web servers which Internet users can access. Users click on a link which executes a common gateway interface (CGI) server program that calls up a database on an organisation's internal network. Internet users can read or write to the database depending upon the business purpose and their system privileges. The availability of corporate databases over the Internet requires an auditor to understand not only basic database risks and controls but also those that crop up as a result of the interface between the database.

Data Files

The data files include the master tables, control tables, transaction tables, and other user application tables. Tables files are organised into table spaces which are distributed among data files. The key to successful setup and tuning of a database application is minimizing the contention between user processes and system processes used for reading and writing to a disk. The risk is that a poorly planned disk configuration which does not take user processes into account will create performance bottlenecks that affect database availability. As part of a database audit, especially a pre-implementation review, an auditor should determine if a study was conducted that details which table spaces an application writes to most often, and whether these table spaces are distributed among separate disks to minimize input and output contention. Procedures should also be in place to monitor database performance in reading and writing to a disk, against predetermined performance benchmarks. Critical databases should be mirrored on separate disks for faster recovery from system, file, or component failure. Mirroring is an exact duplication of each database written to a separate set of disks. This is also known as the redundant array of inexpensive disks (RAID) 1 strategy. The RAID 5 strategy entails storing a database across several disks. This is also called striping. RAID 5 uses a parity check algorithm to recreate missing blocks of data during a data recovery situation.

Redo Logs and Archived Redo Logs

When the first redo logs is filled up, the log process begins writing to a second file, and so on. When the last redo log file is filled up, the system begins overwriting the first redo log. The recovery risk from this overwriting situation is mitigated by running an Oracle database in archive log. The redo logs should be written to a disk which is separate from the archived redo logs, so if one disk fails either the redo logs or the archived redo logs will be available to enable an effective recovery. A database containing critical business data should always mirror the redo logs for a quick and secure recovery. It may also be advisable to mirror the archived redo logs as well. The control files should be mirrored on two or three separate disks to ensure their availability during a recovery scenario. It is probably not possible to recover a database online if there is no control file available.

Network Configuration

The architecture of database systems that contain critical programs and data should be designed so that they are nearly 100 percent available to networked end-users and remote users.

In a configuration where a database server is networked to application servers and a replication server; there will likely be heavy network traffic between the database server and the other servers. This traffic should be restricted from other network traffic. The network design needed for such traffic is to be a high availability design that uses multiple network interfaces for each server, along with the Fiber Distributed Data Interchange (FDDI) transmission medium which serves as the backbone of the servers network.

Backup Procedures and Database Recovery

With real-time, online systems the impact of a database failure can be tremendous. In addition to planning and implementing a robust and stable RDMS with its corresponding hardware architecture, there must be adequate procedures in place to ensure that a database can be recovered in full or at least from a known point in time. Database systems, their host operating systems, and many third-party tools provide a variety of methods for backing up and recovering databases. The Oracle database supports the concept of logical backups and file system backups.

1. Logical Backups

Logical backups read the entire database or portions of a database and dump (i.e., export) the data into a binary file. This binary file also includes a stored sequence of commands that is used to rebuild a database during an import operation. The data can be imported back into the same database or a different database. Oracle's full mode export operation procedure dumps the entire database, while the user mode dumps all of a user's objects, and the table mode dumps a table or set of tables into a binary file. Logical backups must be made while a database is up and running. Depending on how a database is used and the nature of its supporting application, logical backups may be made of selected critical objects at more frequent intervals than full-mode backups. A backup in a full-mode procedure may include all objects or only objects that have changed since the last backup. Logical backups only restore a database up to the point in time of the last backup.

Logical backups are made a table at a time, while the database is up and running. Unfortunately, many tables are interrelated and there is a risk that a database transaction may be reflected in some tables but not in others if a user transaction is executed during a logical backup procedure. When this happens, the database becomes inconsistent. To prevent this situation, backups should be scheduled during off-hours when users and batch processing applications are not accessing the database. Application and network controls can be used to help enforce this by curtailing access during certain hours of the day, for instance. Backups can also be executed during a restricted session mode so that users, other than a database administrator, cannot access the database during export.

2. File System Backups

File system backups rely on the host operating system commands to create backups of a database system on a block-by-block basis. File system backup tools recognize only operating-system-level objects such as file names that represent Oracle table_spaces, redo logs, and control and configuration files. File system backups can be performed while a database is up and running (i.e., hot backups) or when it is shut down (i.e., cold backups). Cold backups are usually made on tape devices for off-line data storage. It is advisable to make frequent backups of heavily used table_spaces to facilitate a quick recovery. The Oracle archive process is an example of a hot backup. This process copies redo logs to online disks instead of tape devices, to facilitate a rapid recovery in case the redo logs become unavailable.

3. Backup Strategies

A schedule should be developed and implemented to ensure both incremental and full file system backups. These backups should be made on reliable physical devices and storage media. It would be optimal to be able to perform a full file system backup of a database on a daily basis; however, due to the size of some databases this may not be feasible. Usually, a full file system backup is done offline or online during the weekend. This weekly backup, in conjunction with the redo logs, restores a failed database up to the point in time of the last backup. Shutting down a database can be a significant event since it clears out memory buffers and, in some cases, severely affects performance. Overall, the following recommendations help to ensure successful file system backups and recoveries:

- include all Oracle data files; online redo logs, the control files, and the Oracle configuration files for a full file system backup
- perform frequent, online backups for large, critical databases
- perform a backup after database reorganisation or other structural change
- perform full system backups on at least a weekly basis
- perform full system, offline backups on at least a monthly basis
- store generations of backups daily at an off-site, secure location so that a database can be restored up until the last backup, even if the data centre is destroyed or made unavailable
- back up frequently changing table spaces often
- perform logical backups only under controlled conditions to protect the integrity of a database
- perform cumulative backups as well as incremental logical backups because the latter are only appropriate for databases with large tables which are updated infrequently
- store database configuration and setup files, such as init<System/Instance ID>.ora and config.ora, off-line in logical and hardcopy form

The real key to a successful backup strategy is balancing (1) the impact of shutting down a database for a full file system backup (2) the frequency of incremental backups, and (3) the need for quick, online recovery. An auditor should review the backup schedule and the backup methods used (e.g., online, offline, logical backups, and file system backups). It may be necessary to perform a business impact assessment of a database application and end-users to gauge the impact of data loss and the cost of each hour of database downtime on the business. A backup strategy and backup procedures should be consistent with the affect that downtime will have on the business.

Disk Recovery Scenarios

Testing database recovery can be difficult under full production conditions. Also, the risk of affecting production may be too significant to test database recovery in a production environment. Database recovery must be tested prior to rolling out a new database application. Figure C5-13 presents the eight combinations of disk failure events or scenarios under which database recovery procedures must be developed and tested. These are:

- loss of system
- loss of data files
- loss of online redo log
- loss of control files
- loss of online redo logs and data files
- loss of control files and data files
- loss of control files and online redo log
- loss of control files, online redo logs, and data files

The auditor should ensure that there are appropriate plans that address each scenario and test for recoverability.

9.1.4 Database Security

Database security and access controls deal with controlling user processes. A user process may represent an actual person working from a console or networked PC, who logs into the system either through an application program or through database tools such as Oracle SQLPlus or SQLDBA. A user process may also be a server program which runs under a powerful database user ID with multiple users accessing and using the program, although the database process may run as a single-user process. Database security may be partially or completely dependent on the security of networked platforms such as client PCs, application servers, or a database's host operating system. Many applications are developed with database IDs and passwords embedded in the program code. This allows a program to call up and manipulate a database by using the functionality of the program. Depending on the security over access to program code, this built-in functionality can be a severe security weakness. An effective audit of database security requires an auditor to spend a significant amount of time documenting the technical architecture, reviewing the flow and processing steps of client/server programs, and identifying the control points in the database client/server architecture. The key control objectives are that the system properly authenticates all users before they can access a database and further restricts users access to their authorized objects.

1. Login and Authentication Controls

A user is most clearly identified by a database login ID. The ID may represent either a person or a program. Oracle users may log in and provide authentication with a user ID and password. This login process may be done after a user logs in to a database host operating system or through a networked interface which may allow a PC user to log in to an Oracle database from an Oracle client program. The create user command sets up a new Oracle user ID account, and the identified by operand assigns a password to that new account. The account data are stored in the Oracle table called dba_users. Passwords are stored in secure, encrypted form. The table, dba_users, contains all Oracle user records including two system-supplied user accounts – sys and system. Each of these accounts has well-known default passwords. The sys_user account has the default password, change_on_install. The sys account owns all the system tables, the system views, and the data dictionary. It is critical that the default password for sys be changed during the installation process. The system account owns all of the tables used by the Oracle tools and also has a default password – manager. This password should be changed during the installation process as well. These default passwords are probably the most obvious potential holes in Oracle security. An auditor can test whether these passwords were changed by using them IDs to attempt to connect to a database. Users may log into a database through programs such as SQLPlus or through other means such as networked connections. When a user who is logged into a database host operating system types the command sqlplus, the system will prompt the user for an Oracle ID and password. The password cannot be viewed while it is being entered. Alternatively, a user may log into a database by entering the connect string command, sqlplus ID/password. In this case the password appears in clear text as the user enters it.

This method should be discouraged whenever possible. In-house developed or third-party programs which connect to a database as part of their startup process may present another password security problem. In Unix systems, if a program requires a user to type in the start command along with the connect string, Oracle ID/password, the password will be stored in memory. If a user executes the ps (process) command in Unix, the clear text password will be listed along with the start command. These types of programs should be modified so that the system prompts the user for the Oracle password rather than giving him or her the option of using a connect string. The database administrator manages and controls Oracle passwords. Controlling password format, frequency of password mandatory change, and reuse of passwords is the responsibility of the database administrator. There should be documented procedures that clearly indicate responsibility for creating and deleting user IDs and controls over passwords.

2. Operating System Authentication

Oracle and many other database programs also provide a mechanism that grants authenticated operating system users automatic access to a database. An Oracle ID in the dba_users table that is prefixed with the characters OPS$ sets up an account that authenticates the user and permits him or her to connect to an Oracle database without supplying an Oracle ID and password. The OPS$ user simply types the command, sqlplus/, and the system automatically connects that user to the database. The Oracle ID name that follows the OPS$ prefix, however, must be identical to the Unix operating system account name.

Other operating system accounts may still connect to an OPS$ account if an Oracle password has been defined in connection with it in the dba_users table. In this case, a password is required for other operating system users without an OPS$ account, but it will not affect those with such an Oracle account. Use of the OPS$ accounts should be carefully controlled because they expose a database to all of the potential security holes that exist at the operating system level. In most cases it is advisable to forgo use of OPS$ accounts unless absolutely necessary. OPS$ accounts for remote users can be disabled by using the startup parameter, OPS$OFF. This helps to protect the database from weaknesses in the Unix remote system, trust mechanism. During an audit review of the dba_users table, the auditor should note any OPS$ accounts and cross-reference them to the Unix audit work plan, especially the login and password controls. In a Unix environment, the Oracle directories and files are owned by a database administration account such as oradm or oracle. The group owner is the dba group. Any user who can log in under the administration account or is a member of the dba group may access the database by executing the command, called connect internal, by using the SQLDBA or Oracle server manager shells. This allows users to connect to a database under the sys user account, without providing password authentication (see Section C5.08 [1][a]). The auditor should closely scrutinize controls over the use of the Oracle administrator account. Membership in the dba group, in the etc/group directory should be limited to the Oracle administrator account.

In many cases, a detailed audit of privileges will not be necessary, because user access to a database may be completely controlled by an application program, and the user will not have any direct access to the database. Many applications will run under a privileged Oracle account that owns all of the application data and programs within a database. In this case, the primary objective of a review of database privileges is to ensure that the privileged Oracle account cannot mistakenly access system tables. Only open systems which allow users dynamic query access to a database may require detailed auditing of system privileges.

Roles make the assignment and management of privileges easier by grouping privileges together and then assigning these groups of privileges to individual users. A database administrator can create roles or use predefined default roles. Oracle has approximately 80 predefined roles. Many of these roles are based on the key words "alter," "create," and "drop," as applied to various objects in a database. A comprehensive listing of database roles can be found in the system documentation.

A database administrator can create custom roles to support specific applications that require a few classes of user to have access to an application's database objects. The set role command grants temporary access to objects when a user logs into a database, and the set role none command removes the privilege when a user exits the application. Roles can also be protected by requiring an additional password. This helps to ensure that a user cannot access database objects except through an application program.

Mainframe Database, Functions and Security

IBM's Information Management System (IMS) uses Program Specification Blocks (PSB), Program Control Blocks (PCB), and the Database Dictionary (DBD) to define the database structure. The DBD describes the physical structure of the database. It contains the name and the length of the segment, and the relationship among the segments. The PCB defines which segments of the DBD the program can view, the relationship between the segments, and the processing codes they can use (e.g., retrieve, delete, insert). The processing options associated with an application program are described in the PROCOPT parameter on the PCB. The PSB is composed of one or more PCBs that define how the application program can view the data. Typically, a DBA establishes naming convention standards so that the PSBs are readily identifiable to the application program and to the database. (See Figure C5-14 for an example of a layout of a DBD, PCB, and PSB.)

IMS has the capability to describe logical databases (i.e., that use the data for a specific application) that can be composed of already-defined physical databases. Logical databases do not have a separate existence. Instead, segments that compose the local databases are defined, as required, from the underlying physical database that connects two or more physical databases in a DBD. They are passed to the application program on request after the DBMS has determined that the defined program can access the data elements requested. Conversely, logical database segments are accepted from the application program and inserted, replaced, or deleted as appropriate. To optimize processing, an indexed database can allow alternate keys to access data elements. In the earlier example of the hospital environment, the patient's name relates to the patient's files and can be used as a key to accessing that data. The receptionist making appointments can enter the patient's name, and the insurance clerk can enter the patient's Social Security number; both gain access to the same set of patient information. The index also allows access using a key other than the one used to store the data.

On-line capabilities for IMS are provided through the Data Communication (DC) feature, which allows users on-line execution of the IMS system with user access via terminals. Two or more IMS systems can transmit transactions to each other through the capabilities of the Multiple Systems Coupling (MSC) feature. The transaction processing facilities of IMS/VS (virtual storage) permit the messages entered via terminals to be processed by application programs. Application programs may communicate via transactions that are messages. There are two general categories of transactions:

- DC transactions processed by the DC feature
- Fast Path (FP) transactions processed by the FP feature

The primary difference between these two features, from an audit viewpoint, is that FP transactions can originate only from terminals, whereas non-FP transactions can originate from a terminal or from an application program. When an application program is scheduled for execution, IMS/VS must first have available the DBD and the PSB control blocks previously created by the DBDGEN and PSBGEN procedures. These control blocks are merged and expanded into an IMS/VS internal format called application control blocks (ACB). The ACBs must be created before the on-line system is started in a process called ACBGEN. The DC feature provides two types of transaction processing: (1) message processing programs (MPP), and (2) batch message processing (BMP). A batch program may use an ACB or a PSB; DC must have an ACB. IMS restricts access to data through a combination of terminal, password, transaction command, and user identification (ID) security. Terminals are classified as physical, logical, and master, as follows:

Physical terminals are the hardware devices as defined in the OS/VS SYSGEN (the operating system generation or startup program) via data definition statements in the IMS startup. Physical terminals are defined in OS/VS SYSGEN so that IMS knows they exist. Without such definition they cannot interact with the system. They are protected by restricting access. Logical terminals are the names related or assigned to physical terminals so that IMS/VS can construct and transmit messages. One physical terminal can have one or more logical terminals associated with it. Logical terminals exist so that if a particular physical terminal breaks down, another one can be substituted to receive data that might be queued for processing. Logical terminal security is established by defining which transactions and commands can be entered via the logical terminal. The master terminal is a logical terminal that acts as the operational hub of IMS/VS. This terminal has complete control over IMS/VS communication facilities, message scheduling, and database operations. Note that because the master terminal is a logical terminal, it can be reassigned dynamically to another physical terminal. The operating system console can be used as an alternative master terminal. Often, the master terminal is named CTRL and the operating system console is named WTOR. However, they may be assigned any name (of one to eight alphanumeric characters) that relates to the physical devices defined during the OS/VS SYSGEN. Obviously, the master terminal requires the greatest security protection because it is capable of entering all commands.

Passwords provide another level of security that identifies a user, thereby enabling the user to access the data. Passwords can be used to limit or restrict access to physical terminals, logical terminals, transactions, commands, and databases. The problem with passwords is that they must be controlled (e.g., through frequent changes) and users must be educated to ensure that they remain secret.

The final mechanism for security within IMS/VS is the user ID verification, which defines which physical terminals require sign-on processing. Sign-on processing is accomplished through the use of the SIGN command which requires entering up to eight characters of user ID and user data. Thus, the SIGN ON/OFF command is designed to safeguard physical terminals.

The application programs that process transactions are called transaction processing programs. On-line transactions are processed by message processing programs. BMP (batch message processing) programs generate transactions to access on-line databases. A transaction entered at a terminal may result in more than one message being processed. An example is a transaction that permits information to be entered for updating a database. The transaction is edited on-line and, when all processing is complete, a message is generated for later batch message program processing. This means that once a batch of transactions is processed, the master file is actually updated.

IDMS/R

Computer Associates' Integrated Database Management System/Relational (IDMS/R) combines relational and network capabilities and provides for ad hoc end user requests and small applications (like a relational database) and, for high-volume applications, the power of a network structure. All functions are integrated into one DBMS in a central location that maintains all data and performs access, input/output (I/O), and space management functions. IDMS/R features allow end users to create applications of various sizes. All data is shared, eliminating duplication. Several forms of internal security are provided as well. The Automatic System Facility (ASF) generates the structure for the development of applications. This includes data definitions, screen formats, processing logic, and documentation, as necessary. IT staff can use ASF to reduce development time and create relational production applications for regularly scheduled processing and ad hoc queries. In addition, private applications can be developed with IDMS/R, helping end users to meet their independent information management demands. On-line capability allows users to bypass backlogs that often exist in a central IT department. IDMS/R can be used to create prototype network database applications. Its combination of relational and network capabilities allows migration from relational to network structure by redefining data records. IDMS restricts access to terminals, programs, tasks (transactions), users, and systems. It defines each in the IDD and assigns them security codes. The user requesting access must have a matching security code to obtain access through the resource; IDMS allows up to 255 security codes. IDMS also controls security through the USER statement, the authorization set on the OPTIONS statement, the PROGRAM REGISTRATION statement, and the subschemas defined to the users. Users are defined in the IDD either by a SYSGEN USER statement or a DDDL ADD USER statement. Encrypted passwords are assigned in the user entity definition. User standards also can contain clauses that restrict or allow access. It should be understood clearly at this stage that program security enforced through AUTHORIZATION specification is not absolute. It is possible to create an executable version of a program without using the DML preprocessor. In order to do it, one should be able to code directly only the statements coded automatically by the DML processor (e.g., IDMS control blocks and DML calling sequence). It is possible to access database areas directly without any kind of checking being performed at the IDMS Central Version level. In order to do so, a COBOL program can be used. If AUTHORIZATION IS ON, all the relevant calls to the database can be coded into the program. If program registration is enforced, you can use an existing program name already registered with the subschemas you want to access. Such a program will be able to access not only a database area, but also the data dictionary areas by specifying the relevant subschema names. These names are standard and usually are IDMSNWKX, IDMSNWKS, IDMSNWKA, and IDMSRSSA. For instance, a program that will always be registered with these subschemas is the DDDL compiler IDMSDDDL. Using such a name, the user-defined batch program could for instance modify a USER047 record (a user definition). The layout of these records can be found in IDMS/R Network Reference Manual. The only way to secure such a type of violation is by protecting areas of the dictionary. This can be done by having the sensitive database areas default to retrieval mode at startup time by way of the IDMSAREA statement at SYSGEN time. These areas are only to be "varied on-line in update mode" by the DBA during scheduled updates to the database areas. Although this does not eliminate the exposure, the window of vulnerability is narrowed. This solution is applicable only to the dictionary and cannot be used to secure data areas. Data areas can be secured using external security packages.

DB2

IBM's DATABASE 2 (DB2) is a relational structure with a data definition (DDL), manipulation (DML), and control (DCL) language, called SQL, that creates, retrieves, manipulates, and controls access to physical data organised within tables.

The user creates and defines tables with the SQL DDL. SQL is used to invoke all table operations as well (e.g., selection, deletion, update, summation of data within the table). The language can be embedded in an application program, or it can be interactive from an on-line terminal. The Query Management Facility (QMF) is DB2's on-line query system and interactive report writer. It allows users to perform calculations, modify, and manipulate accessible data. DB2 security is provided on a column/row level and on a table level. Protection and authorization are provided through two features: views and SQL DCL GRANT/REVOKE privileges assigned to tables in the DB2 Catalog. The strength of these controls is dependent on the DB2 system options and exits in place. DB2 interfaces with CICS, IMS/DC, RACF, and other security packages to determine if a user should be given access to DB2. Generally, if DB2 does not recognize the user ID, it assigns the default ID IBMUSER. In addition, in DB2, more than one user can have the same user ID. This limits accountability greatly. Views are not actual tables, but rather a subset of real tables. Their data is extracted when they are accessed. Views can limit user or program access to data. They are created using the SQL CREATE command. For each view or table created, a record containing its information is stored in SYSTABLES of the DB2 Catalog. SYSTABAUTH is updated with information pertaining to the creator of the views and tables. Other authorization tables can also be set up to assign who has access to the views and tables, the type of access they have (e.g., read, update), and which programs can use which tables or views. The security administrator can specify which commands a user is allowed to use. To ease maintenance, these commands are grouped into five privilege levels. The user is then assigned a level. Users' access can be controlled by either granting them a privilege or by selecting commands that they can use. All the DB2 tables and related data storage requirements, programs, and authorizations are defined within the DB2 catalog.

Oracle RDBMS Server Version 7 and 8

Before a user can access any database information, he or she must possess the proper "privilege." Oracle defines database privilege as the right to execute a particular type of SQL statement or the authority to access another user's database object. There are two privilege types: object and system. Each object privilege allows a user to perform a particular action on a specific table, view, procedure, function, or package. For example, assume that the user Scott owned a table called product, and executed the following command: GRANT SELECT ON product TO PUBLIC. In this case, all users (PUBLIC) could select records from Scott's product table. System privileges allow a user to perform a particular type of SQL command. For example, the system privilege SELECT ANY TABLE enables the user to query any database table, regardless of its schema or owner. There currently are more than eighty distinct system privileges, each allowing a user to perform a particular kind of database operation.

The DBA can simplify the administration process and group together a set of privileges together by creating a role. For applications with several users, roles greatly reduce the number of GRANT commands necessary for the DBA. Roles may be password-protected and dynamically enabled or disabled, which provides additional security administration flexibility. Oracle database has the ability to audit all its actions. Auditing is appropriate for investigating suspicious activity and monitoring database activity. Auditing operations may be focused on SQL statements, privileges, or database objects. The DBA must set the AUDIT_TRAIL parameter in the initialization file and execute the cataudit.sql script to install data dictionary tables and views. Regardless of whether database auditing occurs, the Oracle Server always will audit database instance startup, shutdown, and any connection to the database with administrator privileges. Auditing records may be written either to the SYS.AUD$ table or to the operating system's audit trail file.

9.1.5 Distributed Database Systems

With the advent of local area networks (LANs), client/server system concepts, and work group capabilities, more and more information that was historically housed in one centralized legacy system is being distributed to the end users. This need to distribute data across the organisation has increased interest in distributed database technology. Most of the major DBMS vendors have incorporated distributed database (DDB) functionality in their latest offerings. The move toward client/server systems is seen as the response to decades of interest in distributed data processing. In a centralized system, the data files, programs, and directories reside in the same processing system. In a distributed system, the programs, directories, and files associated with a particular request are spread among different processors, closer to the origin of the data.

It is this separation that creates the unique audit and other problems associated with distributed database systems. A DDB exists when an information network has two or more computers, each of which has permanent files attached. The set of permanent files forms the DDB. DDBs provide certain potential advantages not offered by centralized databases. The DDB allows files to be located at the point of need in a geographically dispersed organisation and thus offers the potential for reduced communication costs and reduced response time. The designer of a DDB system is faced with several challenging design factors that do not exist in a centralized database system. These factors must be considered carefully if performance is to be satisfactory to the system's users. The designer must decide how to split the files, how to split the directories, where to locate the programs, and how to design the communications network to support the message flow between nodes or parts of the system created by splitting the components of the database. Many of these issues must be addressed in client/server developments.

9.1.6 Object Data Management Systems

Object data management systems (ODMSs) or object databases are rooted in object-oriented (OO) technologies. The object concepts first were introduced in the class construct in Simula-67. Subsequently, many OO programming languages followed, such as Smalltalk, Objective C, C++, and Java. In recent years, C++ and Java have gained widespread popularity among application developer communities. OO's goal approach is to provide a solution. Hence, a programmer must partition a complex problem into manageable pieces by defining concepts or classes that resemble the application's logical makeup. This study's progression is known as data abstraction where the application developer defines the world as a set of objects, each with its own characteristics or data fields, and the corresponding procedures governing data field use. When properly applied, OO programs are easier to understand and maintain. The ODMS traditionally has focused on creating a tight, continuous integration of the OO programming language and the storage mechanism of objects. The domination of relational technology and the lack of industry standards for object databases have hindered marketplace acceptance of object database vendors.

9.1.7 Relation and Object: A Comparison

The relational database model is based on the concept of a table. Each instance of an interested entity is represented as a row in a table. The table has a set of columns, which correspond to the attributes of the entity being modeled. Each column has a data type, which is predefined by the database vendor and usually limited to character, number, time, or binary large object type. As a result of the table architecture, a relational database lacks the object technology's modeling constructs: encapsulation, inheritance, and polymorphism.

Encapsulation enables the application developer to specify a unique set of methods that can operate on a given object. In other words, objects may not be modified except through the developer's own methods. On the other hand, each column of a row in a relational table can be directly accessed. Since objects cannot be defined in a relational setting, inheritance and polymorphism, which deals with the reusability and flexibility of object-oriented codes, cannot be implemented. In response to the previous limitations, the ANSI SQL committee is working on a next generation SQL language standard, called SQL3. The goal of SQL3 is to allow user-defined data types in the definition of a database object, and support object-oriented features such as encapsulation, inheritance, and polymorphism. The market acceptance of this SQL revision is, however, yet to be seen. Two trends in software technology are fueling the drive toward object data management. First, the increasingly widespread use of workstations and networking requires a different approach to software development. Software now supports small workgroups, increasingly being used in situations requiring quick response to change.

A key to implementing a workgroup strategy is automating the flow of information throughout the organisation. To achieve this, workgroup software must capture the changing nature of the policies and procedures that govern the group's work, as well as those of the organisation as a whole. The second trend stems from the need to make massive amounts of information available to users with different needs. Increasingly, users need information from many sources. They also need to have the information presented in a usable format. Newer applications, such as computer-aided design (CAD), computer-assisted software engineering (CASE), expert systems, electronic mail, and network management, challenge the development and operational abilities available in traditional data management techniques, where data is separate from the application. The storage of raw data and the application procedures governing its use are considered to be separate functions. This approach is perhaps too limited for complex applications. For example, consider a document that is used by several applications.

The document is composed of various data components (text, graphics, format characteristics, and printer information). An application using the document would have to define how the data components fit together to form the whole. This process would have to be replicated by every application using the document, and the development and maintenance of redundant application code is an inefficient process. In addition, maintaining data separate from the application makes it hard to modify either the schema of the data or the application without modifying the other, making it difficult to respond to change rapidly.

An object-oriented approach to data management addresses those problems. In the above example, an object-oriented approach would define the object (the document) in terms of its characteristics (text, graphics, format specifications, and printer information) and the procedures governing their use (how those characteristics are used to make a complete document) once and only once. Then the object is to be stored as a resource that can be reused.

Security Considerations for Object Data Management

There has been very little work done in the area of unauthorized or inadvertent access in object data management systems. There are two components to securing data in an object data management system: Ensuring that users cannot access data for which they are not authorized; and ensuring that users cannot corrupt physical data structures through the programming language, query language, or end-user tools. This is a prerequisite to preventing unauthorized access. Among the architectures discussed, ODMSs based on extended database architecture have the potential to provide security by maintaining sensitive data on a physically secure network server that can be accessed only over the network using a query-language processor residing on that server. As long as the query-language processor is secure from user access to physical memory locations, and from having normal data access features compromised, the only objects a user can download and cache on a workstation are those that are authorized.

However, query-language security may be inefficient for many ODMS applications, particularly in situations where queried objects were already in the workstation cache, since the resulting extraneous computations could hinder performance. ODMSs using programming language architecture can provide some security by using code to check access authorization by checking requests against an authorization list. This kind of protection is similar to the protection based on a query-language processor in an extended relational database system in situations where the user is restricted to execute on a server or other machine to which physical access is limited. In both architectures, authorization to access data can be defined in a variety of ways. Users can be limited in accessing particular attributes, relationships, or methods based on access lists attached to each object or other constraint, such as the date. Authorization can be based on methods, composite objects, versions, and hierarchies of types, making security more complex than in a relational DBMS.

In addition to having a means to authorize access to object data, a system may need a way to authorize access to object methods. To maintain security, access to an object should not imply authorization to access associated objects. Database programming language architectures can provide an efficient method for security by basing the method on object types, such as pages, segments, or files. This method requires that objects be stored in physically separate areas, depending on authorization criteria. Authorization based on object characteristics is not provided. Instead, the server machine checks access to a physical unit according to user ID or group. To the user, this scheme will appear to be based on logical units such as object types, attributes, methods, or individual objects, when the protection is actually provided by physical means. Although this form of protection has its limitations, it may be adequate for many of the applications discussed above; and from a performance perspective, it is well suited for simple kinds of protection.

9.1.8 Data Warehouses

The current vision of the data warehouse has evolved from the information centre and end-user computing ideals of the early 1980s. The advancements in RDBMSs, distributed computing architectures like LANs and WANs, and the improving price/performance of mass storage devices have contributed greatly to the viability of the data warehouse. Impediments to progress of the data warehouse, like high cost of data storage and awkward or inefficient access tools, are being removed. Also, organisational, market, and economic pressures are forcing businesses to change dynamically, placing more pressure on the information technology department to respond quickly to changing environments.

The following paragraphs discuss some of the more salient aspects of data warehousing technology. It is important to note that this discussion relates to data warehousing technology in a very generic sense. Many organisations will implement warehouse technologies that may be very different from those described here. The objective is not to document fully all data warehousing approaches, but to describe a "typical" implementation and, from that perspective, identify significant control issues that it implies.

Data Warehousing Objectives

Simply stated, the overall objective of the data warehouse is to provide a framework for delivering corporate information to knowledge workers. This delivery must be accomplished such that the workers receive it in a usable format when they need it. The following are some of the issues that typically face information-dependent organisations. These issues can be resolved through implementation of a thoughtfully designed data warehouse. Current information systems typically are long on processing power, but short on usable data. In this context, usable refers to the accessibility of data to those who need it to do their jobs. An impressive array of hardware and software products is available off-the-shelf, but without access to timely and accurate data, these tools add little value to the organisation. Widespread implementation of personal productivity tools has led to extreme levels of data redundancy. A business may have literally hundreds of copies of data resident on multiple machines throughout the organisation. No individual has, or could be expected to have, full knowledge of all data resources. As personal computers proliferate, potentially, those responsible for data administration know less and less about their organisation's data.

Timeliness is a critical factor in the delivery of information to knowledge workers. Stale information cannot support such dynamic actions as those required to remain competitive in today's business environment. Consistency of data across applications is another critical issue. If multiple independent applications supply input to a decision support system, it is imperative that the data is consistent across these application boundaries. In many organisations, this is not the case. When applications are designed, implemented, supported, and used by many different organisations, there is ample opportunity for inconsistencies to work their way into the data. Implementing a data warehouse can address these and other data-related problems. The design, implementation, and control of the warehouse environment are critical elements of a successful solution to these issues.

9.2 Operational Systems Compared to Informational Systems

A key to understanding the data warehouse and its effects on the organisation is the distinction between operational systems and informational systems. As dependence on information technology increases, bringing vast increases in the volume of data maintained for organisational support, this distinction becomes more important. A brief discussion of some characteristics of typical operational and informational systems follows. Because all organisations are different, so are their supporting systems. Some of the more common features of both types of systems and a contrast of the two are discussed below to enhance the understanding of the data warehouse. Operational systems are those whose purpose is to maintain the books and records of the organisation. The day-to-day events that occur in the operation of an entity are recorded and tracked by operational systems.

The performance of these systems can be a critical issue, particularly if the business processes are closely tied to or automated by information technology. Data stored in operational systems is typically organised by application, for example, loans, CDs, demand deposit, and safe deposit box for a financial institution. Operational systems within a single organisation may be architecturally or technologically diverse because of different sources or diverging evolutionary tracks. Other characteristics of operational systems are their update volatility, which is one record at a time for interactive systems, and the period of time that their data reflects, typically thirty to ninety days. Conversely, informational systems are needed to support dynamic decisions.

The major implication of this requirement is that information is needed today, not after it is "stale." Effective decisions cannot be based on outdated information. Where operational databases typically are organised by application, informational databases must be organised by broader categories, like customer. Using the financial institution example again, an informational database may be oriented by customer, whose record would comprise all account relationships held with the institution. The interactive update volatility of the informational database is typically very low, with the information being refreshed on a periodic (usually daily) basis via a mass database load. The time period reflected in the typical informational system is much longer than that of the operational system. Normally from one to five years of data will be stored to allow users to analyse time series for statistically and economically significant periods.

A key point to consider when contrasting the two types of systems is the need to combine or consolidate information from multiple sources when running decision support systems, whether they consist of queries or batch reports. Because operational systems can be architecturally diverse, the task presented to the systems analyst or programmer to combine information from multiple sources into a single report or query can be staggering. Using the financial institution example again, consider that the loan processing system is an internally developed application residing on the mainframe. The demand deposit and CD systems are packages for which no internal maintenance is performed, and for which little internal knowledge of data structures exists. The safe deposit box processing system is a commercial PC-based package residing on a local area network. To structure an ad hoc query that imports data from each of these systems is virtually impossible, and a query that does not retrieve data from each of these applications does not reflect the customer's full account relationship with the institution.

Also, in a typical organisation each of these systems may be supported by different project teams. For a user to pull together such a broad-based query may require significant planning and political skills. More likely, the user will request reports from multiple applications and tie them together manually with the aid of a commercial productivity application. Ken Orr, a noted expert in data warehousing theory and technology, sums up this situation with the term "Data in Jail" to describe data that is known to be there, but users just can't get it out. When the systems analyst replies "maybe next month" to a user's request for an ad hoc that shows the customer's full account relationship, he or she is giving a reasonable answer. The hard part to swallow is that the analyst gives this answer because the task is truly formidable, not because he or she does not want to help. Information technologists can suffer undeservedly from diminishing reputations because of the roadblocks presented to them by incompatible technologies. Data warehousing can serve to remove some of these roadblocks.

10 EAI: Auditors Should Know Potential Risks to Enterprise

Information systems (IS) have become the organisational fabric for intra- and inter-organisational collaboration in business. As a result, there is mounting pressure from customers and suppliers for a direct move away from disparate systems operating in parallel towards a more common shared architecture. In part, this has been achieved through the emergence of new technology that is being packaged into a portfolio of technologies known as enterprise application integration (**EAI**). Its emergence however, is presenting investment decision-makers charged with the evaluation of IS with an interesting challenge. Enterprise application integration (EAI) is a kind of technological Velcro, enabling computer systems to accommodate such change. EAI allows diverse systems to connect with one another quickly to share data, communications, and processes, alleviating the information silos that plague many businesses. The benefits of assimilating new systems without prolonged programming efforts are apparent following merger and acquisition activity. EAI solutions provide a way to connect the systems of collaborators, partners, and others for as long as necessary, decoupling when the relationship ends. EAI is, in essence, the soluble glue for the modular corporation.

Enterprise application integration (EAI) is being considered by the most North American executives as theirs one of the top jobs pending to be performed. It seem that they are write in saying so as EAI is an exciting concept that promises to combine diverse technologies, systems, and data into a cohesive, efficient unit. Imagine the ability to integrate diverse technology, separate systems, multiple platforms, and specific job functions into a unified operation that processes business requirements from start to finish. That is very exciting to many business executives. Organisations often complain about the bewildering choices facing their selection of new technologies. Yet, the decision of whether to adopt new technology remains an important one, as many companies are increasingly being forced to develop new sub-systems that act as enterprise integration links, thus, bridging established systems (legacy) with new ones. The motivation for this would appear to be due to the ubiquitous nature of information systems (IS) and technological innovation, which as a result leaves many companies with the quandary of how best to evaluate the impact of their new systems and technologies on the organisational infrastructure.

However, knowing that EAI introduces new and complex challenges helps companies understand and respect the challenge before they invest deeply in EAI. The term enterprise application integration (EAI) refers to the plans, methods, and tools aimed at modernizing, consolidating, integrating and coordinating the computer applications within an enterprise. In the mid-1990s, a new approach to system integration known as Enterprise Application Integration – EAI – was introduced. The basic concept of EAI is mainly in its externality of enterprise integration with lower costs and less programming using existing applications. EAI is a business computing term for plans, methods, and tools aimed at modernizing, consolidating, and coordinating the overall computer functionality in an enterprise. Typically, an enterprise has existing legacy applications and databases, and wants to continue to use them while adding or migrating to a new set of applications that exploit the Internet, e-commerce, extranet, and other new technologies. EAI may involve developing a totally new outlook of an enterprise's business and its applications, determining how existing applications fit into the new view, and then devising ways to efficiently reuse what already exists while adding new applications and data.

Previously, integration of different systems required rewriting codes on source and target systems, which in turn, consumed much time and money. Unlike traditional integration, EAI uses special middleware that serves as a bridge between different applications for system integration. All applications can freely communicate with each other through a common interface layer rather than through point-to-point integration. Thus, EAI eliminates extensive programming.

The need to integrate across applications is being driven by customer demand for access to information and the desire of the business for a single point of contact with their customer base. The challenges are significant because of the variety of technologies in need of integration and because integration cuts across lines of business. This section distinguishes among four different, but highly related targets of EAI:

1. Data-level integration
2. Application-level integration
3. Process-level integration
4. Inter-organisational-level integration

I further discuss the technologies that assist with this integration in the categories as shown below:

1. Asynchronous event/message transport
2. Transformation engines
3. Integration brokers
4. Business process management frameworks

Enterprise application integration (EAI) – the plans, methods, and tools aimed at modernizing, consolidating, and coordinating the computer applications within an enterprise has of late acquired importance. Given that the need to integrate across applications is an age-old challenge, why is EAI suddenly in the spotlight? For the answer, you need only to look at yourself – and your behaviour and expectations – in your role as a customer of any company.

Your relationship with your bank, for example, is most likely via a browser where you expect to be provided access to the full range of banking services conveniently integrated on a single screen, e.g. "myvendorbanker.com", allowing you to query the status of your checking/savings/investment accounts, reconfigure your mortgage, buy/sell stocks/bonds/funds directly, transfer money to other accounts (not necessarily at your branch or even your bank), enact payments (automatically and/or electronically), take advantage of bill consolidation and presentation, and expect these transactions to be done instantaneously.

That the transactions cross multiple business lines, require coordination among many applications/databases resident on different technology platforms with different architectures, and must be done perfectly (consider how delighted you would be as a customer if your bank reported your account balances correctly only most of the time!) is of very little concern to you. As a customer, you have come to expect this level of service.

There is little doubt that the impetus behind EAI is the business need to respond to customer demand. EAI, however, is not an easy problem to solve. Perhaps that is why it has been an ongoing, continuous struggle. It is common in most organisations to have multiple applications (custom, legacy, and packaged), multiple platforms, multiple databases, multiple transaction processors, multiple data entry points, multiple versions of the same data, and incompatible business data.

This state evolved over time as waves of new technology swept over the landscape. Different groups, operating independently of one another, built application systems at different times. Early programs in areas such as inventory control, human resources, sales automation, and management were designed to run independently, with no interaction among the systems. They were custom-built in the technology of the day for a specific need and were often proprietary systems. As a result, organisations are stuck with incompatible architectures and with hard to maintain (but even harder to eliminate) legacy applications. It is not uncommon for organisations with EAI requirements to underestimate the time, effort, and inherent risk associated with successful implementation.

A lack of standard methodologies, complex legacy systems, and communication disconnects between business units are only a few of the reasons why anywhere from one-third to two-thirds of all EAI initiatives fail. With sobering fact in mind, this Chapter will address three areas. First, I will cover the primary reasons why EAI holds so much promise. Subsequently, I will discuss a series of EAI planning and technical risks that could derail an EAI implementation.

I will finish with an overview of areas where vendor provided software applications can assist to avoid this risk. The main lessons for an IT auditor to learn through the discourse in the chapter are to understand the intricacies involved and the potential changes taking place in the internal controls during and after the implementation of enterprise applications integration.

10.1 The Promise of EAI

It's being touted as a panacea for successful integrated business operations, and although expectations may sometimes outweigh results, today's EAI technologies can achieve integrated success. By now, everyone is familiar with the alphabet soup of business system types that EAI strives to integrate: Application-to-Application (A2A), Business-to-Business (B2B), Business-to-Consumers (B2C), Customer Relationship Management (CRM), Supply Chain Management (SCM), Enterprise Resource Planning (ERP), an so on and so forth.

EAI is the methodology, the technology, and the kind of glue that helps enterprises shape a variety of old and new systems, multiple protocol and data sources, and varying processes into a cohesive unit. EAI establishes a powerful and flexible infrastructure layer that manages data across the enterprise including legacy and custom applications. With EAI, entities can keep older applications that support their core business, integrate new applications with existing systems to enhance their value, and reduce their cost of upgrading technology in the future. Successful EAI helps organisations communicate more effectively, makes users more productive, builds customer satisfaction and loyalty, and improves partner relations. Therefore, it is precise to say that when planned and executed properly for the right type of requirements, EAI can certainly help an organisation deliver better business.

10.2 Improvement in Productivity

Everyone wants better productivity, every software product promises it, however, EAI can deliver it across a range of areas. Let's begin with the wealth of knowledge that is embedded in core legacy systems. Not only does EAI help to keep these systems alive, it exploits there processing capabilities to distribute business critical data to other departments, users, and systems. What's more productive-building on strength of legacy systems or replacing them? Now consider the full range of legacy, custom, and packaged applications in use by most of the business entities.

These systems all relate to the greater business strategy in some manner – but does any company want to deploy paper trails, extra data storage, complex proprietary integration embedded in an application, or even sneaker nets to share business information? When implemented properly, a separate plug-and-play EAI layer is definitely more productive in processing data through diverse applications, minimizing maintenance efforts, and scaling to support the growth of the enterprise. Think about the vertical islands of functionality that exists in organisations. Sales knows how to enter and process orders.

Accounting knows how to make and receive payments. Warehouse personnel can track inventory and ship goods. Each of their departments share some functional overlap, but just as sales people weren't hired to balance the company's books or accountants to ship orders, or warehouse managers to make sales calls, the systems that support these business processes weren't built to intuitively collaborate with each other either. Its also likely that these systems were built and deployed by different personnel at different times using different technologies, which further complicates the ability to collaborate business processing. EAI can greatly improve collaborative productivity by automating the business processes inside and outside the organisation without being blocked by functional islands.

10.2.1 Data Flow Streamlined

Overtime, data takes on a life of its own. At the highest level, data may appear relatively straight forward, but as it makes its way from an initial entry into every department and through multiple systems, data stores and reports, it will be squashed, separated, twisted, expanded, duplicated, and otherwise changed until companies end up with many different pockets of unique information. As the business changes and as data becomes increasingly granular, new systems will model, store, and access data differently. This is perhaps the biggest productivity benefit that EAI can offer-the ability to streamline data so that it flows easily between different applications.

10.3 EAI Reaches Beyond Your Borders

Business partners can be more demanding than customers. They have the right to expect you to communicate in real time, to meet the highest standards of effectiveness, and to nurture joint customer relationships. EAI is not just for internal processing-a wealth of EAI technologies is designed to improve communication and productivity across the extranet in support of business partners and suppliers. When you summarise the idea of IT-based productivity, it may just boil down to improving your ability to respond more quickly to business challenges whether they are the challenges of improving system performances, streamlining communication, satisfying customer demands, or meeting competitive threats. A well-planned EAI implementation can help you meet your business challenges through increased productivity. Several limitations with EAI implementations have been identified, however, beginning with the situation that EAI implementation involves an extensive long-term investment in design. Although the time required to implement EAI is less than that required for ERP's business process reengineering phase, it is nonetheless time-consuming work. Secondly, successful EAI implementation requires that there exist strong communication, coordination, and cooperation between information technology and business personnel. While the EAI approach initially slows down the speed of implementation due to the need to ensure agreement and integration among personnel, overall it can prove to be beneficial as compared to the "push-oriented" ERP implementation (which enforces standard business processes to business personnel first, then requires business personnel to later internalize those processes). Finally, EAI architecture requires business-mapping processes. Because EAI does not use standardized business process like ERP, a critical aspect is the need to combine separate systems' business processes.

10.3.1 Lowered Costs

With EAI software licences and deployment costs starting at several hundred thousand dollars and up, some may seriously question whether EAI really lowers the costs. But when an organisation performs the proper analysis and implements the right-sized EAI solution for their enterprise, the cost to implement EAI will save significant money particularly as the enterprise fully embraces EAI over time. Whether a company's intent is to improve internal operations or improve business-to-customer or business-to-business operations, EAI will lower the cost of business.

Modelling Cost Isolation

Consider how often a change to business processing requires corresponding application and/or data modelling changes. Also consider the impact of normal software upgrades to an environment in which application source has been customized to support point-to-point integration. It's less expensive to modify and enhance a separate middle layer of integration technology than it is to modify, test, and maintain redundant changes in multiple applications.

Business Process Structure

Nothing breeds interest in integrated systems like the success of integrated systems. With increased interest comes increased cost. Business systems will grow and multiply, requirements to integrate these business systems will increase, and as they do, the complexity of the integrated environment and cost to maintain it will exponentially increase. A structured EAI framework makes integration much more manageable, flexible, and affordable. Companies can plan and introduce new applications within the context of the overall business process and can design new data requirements in context of the overall integrated business process flow, rather than integrating business processes by customizing one application at a time.

Clean Data

As discussed earlier, data can take many paths and forms overtime. Redundant and/or inaccurate data is extremely costly to maintain and clean. EAI reduces the need for redundant data and minimizes repetitive data entry requirements, which in turn reduces errors and improves the accuracy of data that exists in systems. The cost of clean data can account for two-thirds of total cost and effort of implementing most data warehouse projects, and as far back as 2001, The Data Warehousing Institute estimated that inaccurate data was costing US business $600 Billion per year.

Functional Legacy Systems

Many companies have invested a lot of time and effort in core systems. Similar to the old adage that if something aren't broke don't fix it, EAI's adage should be that if something aren't broke...integrate it! EAI extends the life cycle of all business applications that participate in the integrated environment by allowing them to share data and processing without requiring major rework. While the value of continuing to use an existing system often is not readily apparent, the cost to replace or significantly revise an existing application is obvious.

The very fact that companies can run their business across an integrated environment also helps them lower costs by reducing their dependence on specific systems technologies, platforms, and hardware. By integrating multiple systems to share data and processing, EAI helps companies spread workload across machines and platforms, and allows companies to coordinate business processing across a mix of legacy an new system technologies. In this manner, companies can adopt their technology to support the way they do business rather than adapting their business processes to work around technical restrictions.

Both approaches consume a huge amount of time to build integrated systems but ERP seems to takes longer to implement. While ERP forces the adoption of standard business processes, EAI enables enterprise integration over business object levels. ERP thereby supports a centralized business strategy while EAI naturally accommodates decentralized business processes. Although EAI still requires time for mapping business processes, there is no tremendous time-consuming work for implementing standard business processes such as ERP software into organisations. Clearly, ERP implementation requires the reengineering of a business process prior to the adoption of ERP; however, EAI implementation enforces business-mapping processes to EAI architecture.

True enterprise integration means both technical and behavioural integration. It is not simply integrating different systems, applications, or business processes dispersed across an enterprise. It is integrating structural changes, different behaviours, and various information systems in an enterprise. Enterprise integration is costly and time-consuming; thus management should be cautious in the design of the project.

In terms of enterprise integration, there are two different approaches: internalization and externalization. These two extremes are moving together due to changes prompted by Internet technology. An enterprise can choose between internalization and externalization. It would not matter whether an organisation uses the push-oriented bottom-up ERP approach or the pull-oriented top-down EAI approach. Companies are more concerned about the true enterprise integration with standardization of communication and business through the network. Component-based development (CBD) can facilitate enterprise integration [12]. This would enable an enterprise to have agility and flexibility as well as standardization and compatibility through the Internet (allowing for efficient e-commerce, e-business, m-commerce, for example).

Many new technologies have emerged during the period from the early 1990s to the present. With new achievements in information technologies, companies are vulnerable if they do not respond to those technologies in a fast and proper way. Core competencies, however, are nearly always built from understanding the differences and similarities between the ways of doing business and desired new technologies [3]. Often technology appears to lead industries, but it is very important to examine the compatibility of new technology to be implemented and the capability of one's organisation. The same is true in enterprise integration. Organisations should not blindly rush into new technologies. Top management should first strive to understand their business and needs for enterprise integration, and then select a methodology of enterprise integration.

To achieve agility and flexibility in organisations, there should be a greater degree of communication, coordination, and cooperation in human factors as well as information technologies [5]. In this sense, global organisations have implemented the concept of integrating business processes. Enterprise integration is now both the internalization and externalization of organisations, fulfilling the needs of both internal business processes and external customers.

Bibliography and Further References

Adobor, Henry and Ronald S McMullen (2002), "Strategic Partnering in e-Commerce: Guidelines for Managing Alliances," *Business Horizons*, 45 (2), pp. 67-76.

Ageshin, Evgeniy (2001), "E-Procurement at Work: A Case Study," *Production and Inventory Management Journal*, 42(1), pp. 48-53.

AICPA (1973), American Institute of Certified Public Accountants Committee on Auditing Procedure, Internal Control- Elements of a Co-coordinated System and its Importance4 to Management and the Independent Public Accountants, Statement of Auditing Standards no. 1, New York, AICPA.

Aladwani, A. M. (2001), 'Change Management Strategies for Successful ERP implementation', *Business Process Management,* vol. 7, no. 3, pp. 266-275.

Allain, Halley (2002), "The Supply Chain: The Weal Link for Some Preferred Suppliers?" *Journal of Supply Chain Management*, 38(3), pp. 39-48.

Al-Mashari, M. & Zairi, M. (2000), 'The Effective Application of SAP R/3: a Proposed Model of Best Practice, *Logistic Information Management,* vol. 13, no. 3, pp. 156-166.

Amoroso, E.; Sharp, R. (1996). "Internet and Intranet. Firewall Strategies". *PCWeek*, ZD Press.

Anderberg, Ken; Carren Bersch; Sean Kelly and Ray Peckham (2001), "Banking on Storage Technology," *Communication News*, 38(11), pp. 6.

Anderson, S. C. (2000), 'The Globally Competitive Firm: Functional Integration, Value Chain logistics, Global Marketing, and Business College Strategic Support', *Customer Relationship,* vol. 10, no. 2.

Aneth M; Susan A Sherba & William V Lapthien (2002)," Towards Large Scale Information Integration," Proceedings of the 24th International Conference on Software Engineering, May 19-25, pp. 524-534. (*http://doi.acm.org/10.1145/581339.581403*)

Angeles, Rebecca (2000), "Revisiting the Role of Internet-EDI in the Current e-Commerce Scene," *Logistics Information Management*, 13:1, pp. 45-57.

Angeles, Rebecca; Cynthia L Corritore; Suvojit Choton Basu and Ravi Nath (2001), "Success Factors for Domestic and International Electronic Data Interchange (EDI) Implementation for US Firms," *International Journal of Information Management*, 21(5), pp. 329.

Ann, M., Rice, R., Malhotra, A., King, N. & Ba, S. (2000), 'Technology Adaptation: The Case of a Computer-Supported Inter-organizational Virtual Team', *MIS Quarterly,* vol. 24, no. 4, pp. 569-600.

Anonymous (1997) AICPA/CICA Unveils New Assurance Service, The CPA Journal, New York, 67 (11), pp. 9.

Anonymous (2000)," BTOB Web Price Index," B to B, 85:6, pp. 24.

Anonymous (2001)," Business Software Solutions-CRM Update," Accountancy (London), 128:1300, pp.1.

Anonymous (1999), "AICPA Retooling its CPE," *The Practical Accountant*, 32(4), pp. 10.

Anonymous (2000), "Do's and Don'ts of e-Commerce," *The Practical accountant*, 33(5), pp. 35-36.

Anonymous (2001), "E-Business Update," *The Journal of Business Strategy*, 22(3), pp. 3.

Argyris, C. & Schon, D. A. (1991), "Participatory Action Research and Action Science Compared: a Commentary, Sage, Newbury Park, C.A.

Arlinghaus, Barry P (2001)," Information Gathering, Technology and Enterprise Systems," Tax Executive, 53:5, pp. 354-364.

Armstrong, A. & Hagel, J., III (1996), 'The Real Value of On-line Communities', *Harvard Business Review*, vol. 74, no. 3, p. 134-141.

Atkins, Derek et al. (1996). "*Internet Security*. Professional Reference". New Riders.

Atkinson, P. & Hammerley, M. (1994), "Ethnography and Participant Observation", *Qualitative Health Research*, vol. 10, no. 3, pp. 324-339.

Auditors, I. o. I. (1998), "Share Service Centres An Unforeseen Result of EMU, predicts KPMG", *Management Services*, vol. 42, no. 1, p. 7.

Avarini, A., Tagliavini, M., Pigni, F. & Sciuto, D. (2000), "A Framework for Evaluating ERP Acquisition within SMEs", in *AIM International Conference*, Montpellier, France, pp. 1-11.

Avishalom Tor, Max H. Bazerman (2003) Focusing failures in competitive environments: explaining decision errors in the Monty Hall game, the Acquiring a Company problem, and multiparty ultimatums, Journal of Behavioral Decision Making. Vol. 16, Iss. 5; p. 353

Badaracco, Jr. (1991), Knowledge Links: How Firms Compete through Strategic Alliance, *Harvard Business School Press*.

Bagranoff, Nancy A, Jan Ellen Eighme & Harvey Kahl Jr (2002), "Who Moved My Ledger?" *The CPA Journal*, 72(10), pp. 22-27.

Bahrami, H. (1992), 'The Emerging Flexible Organization: Perspectives from Silicon Valley', *California Management Review*, vol. 34, no. 4, p. 33-52.

Bancroft, N. (1996), Implementing SAP /R3, Manning Publication, Greenwich.

Bancroft, N., Seip, H. & Spriegel, A. (1998), Implementing SAP R/3: How to introduce a large system into a large organization, ed. Manning, Greenwich, CT.

Bansal, Praveen (2002)," Smart Cards Spread Across Europe," The Banker, 152:913, pp. 122-123.

Barbara, M. (2001), 'Will users of ERP Stay Satisfied?' *Sloan Management Review*, vol. 42, no. 2, pp. 13-21.

Barnes, David; Mathew Hinton; Suzanne Mecgkowska (2002) Developing a Framework to Investigate the Impact of e-Commerce on the Management of Internal Business Processes, Knowledge & Process Management, 9 (3), pp. 133.

Barrier, Michael (2002), "The Crisis in Governance," *The Internal Auditor*, 59(4), pp. 50-54.

Barron, H. H. (1999), 'Technology, Diversity and Work Culture-Key Trends in the Next Millennium', *HRMagazine*, vol. 44, no. 11, pp. 58-59.

Beer, Stafford (1995), The Brain of the Firm, 2nd edition, NY, John Wiley

Belisle, Denis J (1999), "From Reform to Effective Delivery," *International Trade Forum (Geneva)*, Issue: 2, pp. 30-33.

Benbasat, I., Goldstein, D. K. & Mead, M. (1987), 'The Case Research Strategy in Studies of Information Systems', *MIS Quarterly*, vol. 11, no. 3, pp. 369-386.

Benjamin, R. I. & Levinson, E. (1993), "A Framework for Managing IT-Enabled Change", *Sloan Management Review*, pp. 23-33.

Berg, Allan (2001),"Can Information Assurance Efforts be United," Security Management, 45(3), pp. 160-162.

Berger, P. & Luckmann, T. (1967), The Social Construction of Reality, Anchor Books.

Bertheaud, Rick (2002), "2 Low Cost Options for Integrating IT," *Financial Executive*, 18(6), pp. 56-59.

Bette, A.S. & Jackie Gilbert (2001) Ethical Issues in e-Commerce, Journal of Business Ethics, 34 (2), pp. 75-86.

Biermann, E, Cloete E & Venter L.M. (2001) A Comparison of Intrusion Detection System, Computers & Security, 20 (8), pp. 676-683.

Bingi, P., Sharma, M. K. & Godla, J. K. (1999), "Critical Issues Affecting an ERP Implementation", *Information System Management,* vol. 16, no. 5, pp. 7-14.

Blackler, F. (1995), "Knowledge and the Theory of Organization: Organizations as Activity Systems and the Reframing of Management", *Journal of Management Information Systems,* vol. 30, no. 6, pp. 863-885.

Blake, M Brian; Hamilton Gail & Hoyt Jaffery (2002)," Using Component-based Development & Web Technologies to Support a Distributed Data Management System," Annals of Software Engineering, 13:1, pp. 13-34.

Boudreau, M.-C. & Robey, D. (2000), "Organizational Transition to Enterprise Resource Planning Systems: Theoretical Choices for Process Research", *Working paper,* vol. Georgia State University USA.

Broadbent, M., Weill, P. & St Clair, D. (1999), 'The Implications of Information Technology Infrastructure for Business Process Redesign', *MIS Quarterly,* vol. 23, no. 2, pp. 159-182.

Brock-Smith, J and Donald W. Barclay (1999), "Selling Partner Relationship: The Role of Inter-dependence and Relative Influence," *The Journal of Personal Selling and Sales Management*, 19(4), pp. 21-40.

Buchanan, D. & Bobby, D. (1992), *The Expertise of the Change Agent,* Prentice Hall, New York.

Burns, T. & Stalker, G. M. (1994), The Management of Innovation - The Organization of Innovation, Oxford University Press.

Bussler, Christoph, Dieter Fensol & Alexander Maedche (2002),"A Conceptual Architecture for Semantic Web-enabled Web Services" ACM SIGMOD (Special Issue: Special Section on Semantic Web & Data Management), 31(4), pp. 24-29, *www.doi.acm.org/10.1145/637.411.637415* .

Busta, Bruce (2002), "Encryption in Theory and Practice," *The CPA Journal,* 72(11), pp. 42-48.

Caldwell, B. & Stein, T.(1998), "Beyond ERP: New IT agenda", *Information Week,* November.

Carnall, C. A. (1997), Strategic Change, Butterworth-Heinemann, Oxford.

Carroll, Brian, (2002), " When the SEC knocks," *The Journal of Accountancy*, 194(2), pp. 35-38.

Cashell, James & George D AldhizerIII (1999), "Web Trust: A Seal of Approval", Internal Auditor, Altamonte Springs, June, 56 (3), pp. 50-54.

Cashell, James D. and George R. Aldhizer III, (1999), "WebTrust: A Seal of Approval," *The Internal Auditor*, 56(3), pp. 50-53.

Cassell, C. & Symon (1994), Qualitative Methods in Organisational Research – A practical Guide, Sage, London.

Cerny, K. (1996), "Making local knowledge global", *Harvard Business Review*, vol. 74, no. 3, p. 22-38.

Chadha, J.S.K., (2001), "The Storage Technology Equation Extends to Remote Users," *Communication News*, 38(8), pp. 16-20.

Chakraborty, Goutam; Vishal Lala and David Warren, (2002), "An Empirical Investigation of Antecedents of B2B Websites' Effectiveness," *Journal of Interactive Marketing*, 16(4), pp. 51-72.

Chan, P. S. & Land, C. (1999), "Implementing Reengineering using Information Technology", *Business Process Management*, vol. 5, no. 4, pp. 311-324.

Chapman, Christy (1998a), "Update," *Internal Auditor*, Feb.,11-12.

Chapman, Christy (1998b), "Just Do It: An Interview with Michael Hammer," *Internal Auditor*, June, 38-41.

Chapman, Christy, (2002), "Power Tools 2002: Audit Software Survey," *Internal Auditor*, 59(4), pp. 28-39.

Chatterjee, Debabroto; Rajdeep Grewal and V Sambamurthy (2002),"Shaping up for e-Commerce: Institutional Enablers of the Organizational Assimilation of Web Technologies," *MIS Quarterly*, 26(2), pp. 65-89.

Checkland, P. (1981), *System Thinking, System Practice*, J. Wiley, Chichester.

Cheswick, W.R.; Bellovin, S.M. (1994). *Firewall and Internet Security*. Addison-Wesley.

Chiasson, Theodor; Kirstie Hawkey; Michael McAllister; and Jacob Slonim, (2002), "An Architecture in Support of Universal Access to Electronic Commerce," *Information and Software Technology*, 44(5), pp. 279-289.

Christensen, C. M. (1997), *The Innovator's Dilemma* , Harvard Business School Press, Boston M.A.

Chung, S. H. & Charles, A. S. (2000), "ERP adoption: a technological evolution approach", *International Journal of Agile Management Systems*, vol. 2/1, pp. 24-31.

CICA (2001),"AICPA/CICA WebTrust 2.0: principles and criteria," Canadian Institute of Chartered Accountants;. Toronto, Canada.

Cody, W.F.; J.T. Kreulen; V. Krishna; & W.S. Spangler (2002)," The Integration of Business Intelligence & Knowledge Management," IBM Systems Research Journal, 41:4, pp. 697-713.

Coltman, Tim; Timothy M Devinney; Alopi S Latukefu and David F Midgley (2002), "Keeping E-Business in Perspective," *Communication of Association of Computing Machinery*, 45(8), pp. 69-73.

Conhaim, Wallys W (2002),"BI using Smart Techniques," *LINK UP*, 19(3), pp. 15.

Cooper, R. & Kaplan, R. (1998), "The Promise and Peril of Integrated Cost Systems", *Harvard Business Review*, vol. 76, no. 4, pp. 109-119.

Corbitt, Terry, (2002)," Getting e-Business off the Ground," *Management Services*, 46(11), pp. 20-21.

CPA Journal (1999)," WebTrust: a progress report," July, pp. 13–4.

Crafton, Thomas W., (2002), "Do You Really Know Your Customer?" *Strategic Finance*, 84(4), pp. 55-57.

Craig Jr JL (2000)," AICPA modifies WebTrust to respond to marketplace," TheTrusted-Professional[June], http://*www.nysscpa.org/trusteprof/archive/0600/6Tp8a.htm*.

Cronin, Mary, (1999), Doing Business on Internet, Van Nostrand Reinhold, 2nd Edition

Curtis, M. (1999), "A look at European Shared Service Centers", *The Internal Auditor*, vol. 56, no. 5, pp. 44-48.

Dale, Young, Carr Houston & Rainer Kelly Jr., (1999), "Strategic Implications of Electronic Linkages," *Information Systems Management*, 16(1), pp. 32-39.

Darke, P., Shanks, G. & Broadbent, M. (1998), "Successful Completing Case Study Research: Combining Rigour, Relevance and Pragmatism", *Information System Journal*, vol. 8, pp. 273-289.

Davenport, T. H. (1998), "Putting the Enterprise into the Enterprise System", *Harvard Business Review*, vol. 76, no. 4, pp. 109-119.

Davenport, T. H. (2000a), "The Future of Enterprise System-Enabled Organisations", *Information System Frontiers*, vol. 2, no. 2, pp. 163-180.

Davenport, T. H. (2000b), Mission Critical: Realising the Promise of Enterprise Systems, Harvard Business Press, Boston, M.A.

David, W. D. L. & Liam, F. (2000), "Diagnosing Cultural Barriers to Knowledge Management", *The Academy of Management Executive*, vol. 14, no. 4, pp. 113-127.

Davis, B. (2000), "Enterprise E-turn", *The Engineer (London, England) [H.W. Wilson - AST]*, vol. 289, no. 7503, pp. 23-4.

Davis, Randy, (2002), "The Wizard of OZ in CRMland: CRM's Need for Business Process Management," *Information Systems Management*, 19(4), pp. 43-48.

Davis, S. & Botkin, J. (1994), "The Coming of Knowledge-based Business", *Harvard Business Review*, vol. 72, no. 5, pp. 165-170.

DeGeus, A. (1988), "Planning as Learning", *Harvard Business Review*, vol. 66, no. 2, pp. 70-74.

Dehanayake, Ajantha; Henk Sol & Zoran Stojanovic, (2002), "Methodology Evaluation Framework for Component-based System Development," *Journal of Database Management*, 14(1), pp. 1-25.

Deloitte (1999), *Annual Research Report on ERP*, Deloitte Consulting, Deloitte.

DeLone, W. H. & McLean, E. R. (1992), "Information System Success: The Quest for the Dependent Variable", *Information System Research*, vol. 3, no. 1, pp. 60-75.

Depart. of Defense (U.S.A.) (1985). Trusted Computing Systems Evaluation Criteria, December. Govt. of USA.

Deshmukh, Ashutosh & Jeffrey Romine, (2002), "Accounting Software & e-Business," *The CPA Journal*, 72(11), pp. 52-54.

Devraj, Sarv; Ming Fan and Rajiv Kohli, (2002),"Antecedents of B2C Channel Satisfaction and Preferences," *Information Systems Research*, 13(3), pp. 316-333.

Dhillon, G., Coss, D. & Hackney, R. (2001), "Interpreting the Role of Disruptive Technologies in E-business", *Logistic Information Management*, vol. 14, no. 1/2, pp. 163-170.

Dias, DM, S.L. Palmer, H.H. Shaikh and T.K. Sriram, (2002), "E-Commerce Interoperability with IBM's Websphere Commerce Products," *IBM Systems Journal*, 41(2), pp. 272-286.

Dickens, L. & Watkins, K. (1999), "Action Research: Rethinking Lewin', *Management Learning*, vol. 30, no. 2, pp. 127-140.

Doherty, Neil & Fiona Ellis-Chadwick (2003) "The Relationship Between Retailers' Targeting & E-Commerce Strategies: An Empirical Analysis", Internet Research, Bradford, 13 (3), pp. 170.

Drucker, P. F. (1988), "The Coming of the New Organisation", *Harvard Business Review*, vol. 66, no. 1, pp. 45-53.

Dykstra, Gail (2002),"2002 SIIA Annual Conference," Information Today, 19:6, pp. 1 & 46.

Eisenhardt, K. M. (1991), "Better Stories and Better Constructs", *Academy of Management Review,* vol. 16, no. 3, pp. 620-627.

Elifoglu, Hilmi I, (2002), "Navigating the Information Super Highway: How Accountants can Help Clients Assess and Control the Risk of Internet-based e-Commerce," *Review of Business,* 23(1), pp. 67-71.

Epelle, A., (2002) FIS Assurance: A New Growing Profession," Business Day, *http://www.bday.org/article_862.shtml#* top1 browsed on December 31.

European Information Technology Observatory 98 (EITO'98). ISO 7498-2: 1987. Information Processing Systems. Open Systems Interconnection. Basic Reference Model. Part 2: Security Architecture. ITSEC *Information Technology Security Evaluation Criteria.* European Union, June 1991.

Evans, P. & Wurster, T., S. (1999), "Getting Real About Virtual Commerce", *Harvard Business Review,* vol. 77, no. 6, pp. 84-94.

Everdingen, Y. V., Hillegersberg, J. v. & Waarts, E. (2000), "ERP Adoption by European Midsize Companies: Searching for ERP Systems Offering a Perfect Fit", *Communication of the ACM,* vol. 43, no. 4, pp. 27-31.

Fan, Yushun; Wei Shi; Cheng Wu (1999), "Enterprise-wide Application Integration Platform for CIMS Implementation", Journal of Intelligent Manufacturing, 10 (6), pp. 587.

Farhoomand, A. F., Tuunainen, V. K. & Yee, L. (2000), "Barriers to Global Electronic Commerce: A Cross Country Study of Hong Kong and Finland", *Journal of Organizational Computing and Electronic Commerce,* vol. 10, no. 1, pp. 23-48.

Fawcett, Stanley & Gregory M Magnan, (2002), "The Rhetoric & Reality of Supply Chain Integration," *International Journal of Physical Distribution & Logistic Management,* 32(5), pp. 339-361.

Ferrando, T. 2000, 'ERP systems Help with Integration', *American City & County [H.W. Wilson - AST],* vol. 115, no. 11, p. 12.

Fielding, N. G. & Fielding, J. L. 1986, *Linking Data,* Sage, CA: Beverly Hills.

Figg, J, 'Continuous Auditing' Undergoes Study," *The Internal Auditor,* 56(5), (1999), pp. 14-16.

Ford, W; Baum, M. S. (1997). *Secure Electronic Commerce.* Prentice Hall.

Ford, Warwick (1994). *Computer Communications Security.* Prentice Hall.

Fordham, David R, Diane A Riordan and Michael P Riordan, "Business Intelligence: How Accountants Bring Value to the Marketing Function," *Strategic Finance,* 83(11), (2002), pp. 24-30.

Francalanci, C. 2001, 'Predicting the Implementation Effort of ERP Projects: Empirical Evidence on SAP/R3', *Journal of Information Technology,* vol. 16, pp. 33-48.

Freemantle, Paul; Sanjiva Weerawarana and Rania Khalaf,"Enterprise Services," *Communication of Association of Computing Machinery,* 45(10), (2002), pp. 77-82.

Frigo, Mark L,"Strategy and the Balance Scorecard," *Strategic Finance,* 84(5), (2002), pp. 6-9.

Fruitman, Paul, "In IT, Communication is Key," *Computing Canada,* 27(18), (2001), pp. 8.

Fuchs, P. H., Mifflin, K. E., Miller, D. & Whitney, J. O. 2000, 'Strategic Integration: Competing in the Age of Capabilities', *California Management Review,* vol. 42, no. 3, pp. 118-147.

Gallegos, Fredrick, "Decision Support Systems: Areas of Risk," *Information Strategy,* 15(2), (1999), pp. 46-48.

Galliers, R. D. 1991, 'Choosing Information Systems Research Approaches: A Revised Taxonomy', in *Contemporary Approaches and Emergent Traditions,* eds. H. E. Nissen,

Garceau, Linda R., "Internet Fraud," *OHIO CPA Journal*, 59(3), (2000), pp. 50-55.

Gartner 2001, *Gartner Annual Research Report*, Gartner Group, USA, CT.

Gengler, Barbara (2002) Intrusion Detection System New to Market, Computers Fraud & Security, Issue (5), May, pp. 4.

Geppert, Linda, "Reborn Memory may put Flash in Shade," *IEEE Spectrum*, 39(3), (2002), pp. 20-22.

Gibbs, Jeff (1998), "Going Live With SAP," *Internal Auditor*, June, 70-75.

Gill, Tony (2003) Competitive Strategic Dynamics, Systems Dynamics Review, 19 (3), pp. 265.

Glover, S. M., Prawitt, D. F. & Romney, M. B. 1999, 'Implementing ERP', *Internal Auditor*, vol. 40-46, no. 56.

Glover, Steven M.; Douglas F. Prawitt; and Marshall B. Romney (1999), "Implementing ERP," *Internal Auditor*, Aug., 47-53.

Good, David & Roberta Schultz (2003) E-Commerce Strategies for B2B Service Firm in the Global Environment, American Business Review, West Heaven, June, 20 (2), pp. 111-119.

Good, David J. and Roberta Schultz, "E-Commerce Strategies for Business-to- Business Service Firms in the Global environment," *American Business Review*, 20(2), (2002), pp. 111-118.

Goold, M., Pettifer, D. & Young, D. 2001, 'Redesigning the Corporate Centre', *European Management Journal*, vol. 19, no. 1, pp. 83-91.

Grant, R. M. 1996, 'Toward a Knowledge-based Theory of the Firm', *Strategic Management Journal*, vol. 17, no. Winter Special Issue, pp. 109-122.

Graziano, Cheryl deMesa, "XBRL: Streamlining Financial Reporting," *Financial Executive*, 18(8)(2002), p. 52-55.

Green, Duncan L., Litigation Risk for Auditors and the Risk Society," *Critical Perspectives on Accounting*, 10(3), (1999), pp. 339-353.

Grint, K. 1995, *Management - A Sociological Introduction*, Polity Press, Cambridge.

Guan, Sheng-Uei and Yang Yang ,"AFE: Secure Agent Roaming for e-Commerce," *Computers & Industrial Engineering*, 42(2-4), (2002), pp. 481-493.

Gupta, A. 2000, 'Enterprise Resource Planning: the emerging organisational value systems', *Industrial Management & Data Systems*, vol. 100, no. 3, pp. 114-118.

Halley Alain and Jean Nollet, "The supply chain: The weak link for some preferred suppliers?" *Journal of Supply Chain Management*; 38(3), (2002), pp. 39-47.

Hammer, M. & Champy, J. 1993, *Reengineering the Corporation*, Harper Collins Book, New York

Hansen, M. T. 1999, 'What's your Strategy to Management Knowledge', *Harvard Business Review*, vol. 77, no. 2, pp. 106-111.

Harding, Andrews (2003) SSL Virtual Private Networks, Computers & Security, 22 (5), pp. 416.

Harmanson, Heather M, Mary C. Hill and Susan H. Ivancevich, "Who are We Hiring?" *The CPA Journal*, 72(8), (1999), pp. 67-69.

Harris, J. 1999, 'Designing Change Management Strategies for ERP Systems: Observation of Alameda County, California', *Government Finance Review*, no. 15, pp. 29-31.

Harrison, R. & Leitch, C. M. 2000, 'Learning and Organization in the Knowledge-base Information Findings from a Participatory Action Research Case Study', *British Journal of Management*, vol. 11, no. 2, pp. 103-119.

Hayman, L. 2000, 'ERP in the Internet Economy', *Information System Frontiers*, vol. 2, no. 2, pp. 137-139.

Heidorn, Mark (2002)," The Importance of Design Data Management," Printed Circuit Design (San Fransisco), 19:7, pp. 8-10+.

Heikkila, Jussi , "From Supply to Demand Chain Management: Efficiency and Customer Satisfaction," *Journal of Operations Management*, 20(6), (2002), pp. 747- 767.

Helms, Glen I. and Mancino Jane , "The Electronic Auditor," *Journal of Accountancy*, 185(4), (1998), pp. 45-48.

Helms, Glen I. and Mancino Jane, "Information Technology Issues for the Attest, Audit and Assurance Service Functions," *The CPA Journal*, 69(5), (1999), pp. 62-64.

Helms, Glen L and Fred L Lilly, "Case Study on Auditing in an Electronic Environment," *The CPA Journal*, 70(4), (2000), pp. 52-54.

Helms, Glen L., "Traditional and Emerging Methods of Electronic Assurance," *The CPA Journal*, 72(3), (2002), pp. 26-31.

Helms, Glen L; J Gregory Bushong and Linda Nelms, "Security in Internet e- Commerce," *OHIO CPA Journal*, 61(3), (2002), pp. 12-15.

Hennel, Michael J (2002)," Forecasting Demands Begin with Integration," B to B (Chicago), 87:11, pp. 9.

Herman, Jim, "Creating a Business Architecture," *Business Communications Review*, 31(12), (2001), pp. 22-23.

Hillison, William; Carl Pacini and David Sinason, "Electronic Signatures and Encryption," *The CPA Journal*, 71(8), (2001), pp. 20-25.

Hirt, S. G. & Swanson, E. B. 1999, 'Adopt SAP at Siemens Power Corporation', *Journal of Information Technology*, vol. 14, pp. 243-251.

Holland, C. & Light, B. 1999a, 'Global Enterprise Resource Planning Implementation', in *Hawaii International Conference on System Science*, Hawaii.

Holland, C. P. & Light, B. 1999b, 'A Critical Success Factor Model for ERP Implementation', *IEEE Software*, no. May/June.

Holland, C. P. & Light, B. 2001, 'A Stage Maturity Model for Enterprise Resource Planning Systems Use', *The Database for Advances in Information*, vol. 32, no. 2, pp. 34-45.

Hondo, M; N Nagaratnam and A Nadalin, "Securing Web Services," *IBM Systems Journal*, 41(2), (2002), pp. 228-241.

Huang, Jeffrey, "Future Space: A Blue Print for Business Architecture," *Harvard Business Review*, 79:4, (2001), pp.149-158.

Huang, Z. 2001, 'ERP Implementation Issues in Advanced and Developing Countries', *Business Process Management*, vol. 7, no. 3, pp. 276-284.

Huber, G. P. 1991, 'Organisational Learning: The Contributing Processes and the Literatures', *Organisation Science*, vol. 2, no. 1, pp. 88-115.

Hucklesby, Mark and Josef Macdonald, "XBRL in Action: Banking," *Chartered Accountant Journal of New Zealand*, 81(10), (2002), pp. 55-56.

Ian, M. & Yen, C. 2000, 'SAP and Business Process Re-engineering', *Business Process Management*, vol. 6, no. 2, pp. 113-121.

IDC, "How Users Think about Integrating Applications across Business Solution Domains," *Analyst's Brief by International Data Corporation*, September, (2002), pp. 1-13.

IIA (1978)," Standards for the Professional Practice of Internal Auditing," Altamonte Springs, Institute of Internal Auditors, FL

IIA (1991)," Systems Auditability and Control, Institute of Internal Auditing Inc., Alta Monte springs, FL.

IIA (1994)," Systems Auditability and Control, Institute of Internal Auditing Inc., Alta Monte springs, FL.

Ingram Thomas, Raymond W LaForge and Thomas W Leigh, "Selling in the New Millennium: A Joint Agenda," *Industrial Marketing Management*, 31(7), (2002), pp. 559.

Irani, Zahir, "Invited View Point: Critical Evaluation and Integration of Information Systems," *Business Process Management Journal*, 8(4), (2002), pp. 314-317.

ISACAF (1996)," Control Objectives for Information and Related Technologies, Rolling Meadows, IL, Information Systems Audit and Control Foundation.

Issabella, Lynn A, "Managing an Alliance is Nothing Like Business as Usual," *Organizational Dynamics*, 31(3), (2002), pp. 47.

Jacob, G. & Wagner, T. 1999, 'Rapid ERP Implementation: The Tuolumne County, California Experience', *Government Finance Review*, no. 15, pp. 28-33.

Jahng, J.J; H Jain and K Ramamurthy, "Personality Traits and Effectiveness of Presentation of Product Information in e-Business Systems," *European Journal of Information Systems*, 11(3), (2002), pp. 181-195.

Jan, D. 2001, 'The Tools and Technologies Needed for Knowledge Management', *Information Management Journal*, vol. 35, no. 1, pp. 64-67.

Janzen, W. 1999, 'Tapping ERP to Extend Value Chain Benefits', *Enterprise System Journal*, no. September 1999, pp. 50-52.

Jensen, M. C. & Meekling, W. H. 1995, 'Specific and General Knowledge, and Organizational Structure', *Journal of Applied Corporate Finance*, vol. 8, no. 2 (summer), pp. 4-18.

Jones, R. A. 2002, 'Spotlight on Midlevel ERP Software', *Journal of Accountancy*, vol. 193, no. 5, pp. 24-45.

Kalakota, R. & Whinston, A. B. 1997, *Electronic Commerce: a Manager's Guide*, Addison-Wesley, Reading, Mass.

Kampmeier, Curt, "Business Intelligence Using Smart Techniques," *Consulting to Management*, 13(3), (2002), pp. 62.

Kang, Namo and Sangyong Han, "Agent-based e-Marketplace System for More Fair and Efficient Transaction," *Decision Support Systems*, 34:2, (2003), pp. 157-165.

Kanter, Howard A, "Systems Auditing in a Paperless Environment," *OHIO CPA Journal*, 60(1), (2001), pp. 43-47.

Kanter, R. M. 1988, 'When a Thousand Flowers Bloom: Structural, Collective and Social Conditions for Innovation in Organisations', *Research in organisational Behaviour*, vol. 10, pp. 169-211.

Keith, Levi , "A Goal-driven Approach to Enterprise Component Identification and Specification," *Communications of Association of Computing Machinery*, 45(10), (2002), pp. 45.

Kelley, R. & Caplan, J. 1993, 'How Bell Labs Creates Star Performers', *Harvard Business Review*, vol. 71, no. 4, pp. 128-139.

Kemme, Bettina & Gustavo Alonso (2000)," A New Approach to Developing and Implementing Eager Database Replication Protocols," *ACM Transactions on Database Systems*, 25:3, pp.333-379.

Kennerley, M. & Neely, A. 2001, 'Enterprise Resource Planning: Analysing the Impact', *Integrated Manufacturing*, vol. 12, no. 2, pp. 103-113.

Kent, Donald D and Acton, Daniel, "Practioners' Views on CPA WebTrust," *OHIO CPA Journal*, 60(1), (2001), pp. 64-65.

Khan, M Riaz and Motiwalla, Luvai, "The Influence of E-Commerce initiatives on Corpoarte Performance: An Empirical Investigation in US," *International Journal of Management*, 19(3), (2002), pp. 503-510.

Kim, H. M. 2000, 'Enabling Integrated Decision Making for Electronic Commerce by Modeling an Enterprise's Sharable Knowledge', *Internet Research: Electronic Networking Applications and Policy,* vol. 10, no. 5, pp. 418-423.

Kim, W. C. & Renee, M. 1999, 'Strategy, Value Innovation, and the Knowledge Economy', *Sloan Management Review,* vol. 40, no. 3, pp. 41-54.

Kini, Ranjan B., "Peer-to-Peer Technology- A Technology Reborn," *Information Systems Management*, 19(3), (2002), pp. 74-84.

Kirschmer, M. 1999, Business Process Oriented Implementation of Standard Software, Springer-Verlag, Berlin.

Klaus, H., Rosemann, M. & Gable, G. 2000, 'What is ERP?' *Information System Frontiers,* vol. 2, no. 2, pp. 141-162.

Klein, H. K. & Myers, M. D. 1999, 'A Set of Principles for Conducting and Evaluating Interpretive Field Studies in Information Systems', *MIS Quarterly,* vol. 23, no. 1, pp. 67-94.

Knight, Gary A and Liesch, Peter W., "Information Internationalization in Internationalizing Firms," *Journal of Business Research*, 55(12), (2002), pp. 981-995.

Koch, C. 2001a, 'BPR and ERP: Realising a Vision of Process with IT', *Business Process Management,* vol. 7, no. 3, pp. 258-265.

Koch, C. 2001b, 'Enterprise Resource Planning: Information Technology as a Steamroller for Management Politics?' *Journal of Organisational Change,* vol. 14, no. 1, pp. 64-78.

Kogut, B. & Zander, U. 1992, 'Knowledge of the Firm, Combinative Capabilities, and the Replication of Technology', *Organizational Science,* vol. 3, no. 3, pp. 383-397.

Koldzinski, Oscar, "Cyber Insurance Issues: Managing Risk by Tying Network Security to Business Goals," *The CPA Journal*, 72(11), (2002), pp. 10-11.

Kotter, J. P. 1996, *Leading Change,* Harvard Business School, Boston, Massachusetts.

Kovar SE, Burke KG, Kovar BR (2000)," Consumer responses to the CPA WebTrust assurance," Journal of Information Systems, 14;1, pp.17-36.

Kremer, M. & Van Dissel, H. 2000, 'Enterprise Resource Planning: ERP system Migrations', *Communication of the ACM,* vol. 43, no. 4, pp. 53-56.

Kresner, Richard M , "Building a Knowledge Portal: A Case Study in Web-enabled Collaborations," *Information Strategy*, 19(2), (2003), pp. 13-36.

Krumbholz, M., Galliers, J., Coulianos, N. & Maiden N.A.M. 2000, 'Implementing Enterprise Resource Planning Packages in Different Corporate and National Cultures', *Journal of Information Technology,* vol. 15, pp. 267-279.

Kudyba, Stephen and Donald Vitaliano, "Information Technology and Corporate Profitability: A Focus on Operating Efficiency," *Information Resources Management Journal*, 16(1), (2003), pp. 1-13.

Kumar, K. & Hillegersberg, J. v. 2000, 'ERP Experience and Evolution', *Communications of the ACM,* vol. 43, no. 4, pp. 23-26.

Kushner, David, "Living in the Limelight," *IEEE Spectrum*, 39(9), (2002), pp. 76-79.

Lacity, M. & Janson, M. A. 1994, 'Understanding Qualitative Data: A Framework of Text Analysis Methods', *Journal of Management Information System,* vol. 11, no. 2, pp. 137-155.

Lainhart, John W. (1996)," Arrival of COBIT Helps Refine the Valuable Role of IS Audit and Control in the Enterprise," Information Systems Control Journal, Vol. 4, pp. 20-23.

Landry, John T., "No Collar: The Humane Workplace and its Hidden Costs," *Harvard Business Review,* 81(1), (2003), pp. 22.

Larsen, M. A. & Myers, M. D. 2000, 'When Success Turns Into Failure: a Park age driven Business', *Journal of Strategic Information System,* vol. 8, no. 1999, pp. 395-417.

Laughlin, S., P 1999, 'An ERP Game Plan', *The Journal of Business Strategy,* vol. 20, no. 1, pp. 32-37.

Lee, J. S. K. 1992, 'Qualitative Versus Quantitative Research Methods', *Asia Pacific. Journal of Management,* vol. 9, no. 1, pp. 87-94.

Lee, Younghwa; Jintae Lee and Zoonky Lee, "Integrating Software Life Cycle Process Standards with Security Engineering," *Computers & Security,* 21(4), (2002), pp. 345-355.

Lessor, Victor; Bryan Horling; Klassner Frank; Anita Raja; Thomas Wagner; Zhang Thomas & XQ Shelley (2000)," BIG: An Agent for Resource-bounded Information Gathering & Decision making," Artificial Intelligence, 118: 1-2, pp. 197-244.

Levi, Keith and Arsanjani, Ali, "A Goal Driven Approach to Enterprise Component Identification and Specification," *Communication of Association of Computing Machinery,* 45(10), (2002), pp. 45.

Levitt, B. & March, J. G. 1988, 'Organisational Learning', *Annual Review of Sociology,* vol. 14, pp. 319-340.

Li, Xiaotong and John D Johnson, "Evaluate IT Investment Opportunities Using Real Option Theory," *Information Resources Management Journal,* 15(3), (2002), pp. 32- 48.

Liebmann, Lenny (2002),"Rethinking Remote Management," *Communication News,* 39:6, pp. 54.

Ling, Liu; Piu Calton & Han Wei (2001)," An XML enabled Data Extraction Toolkit for Web Sources," Information Systems, 26:8, pp. 563-583.

Lipsey, John, "Relationship Intelligence," *The CPA Journal,* 72(11), (2002), pp. 14.

Litsikas, Mary (1997) Electronic Downloads Eliminate Inspection Audits, Quality, 36 (1), pp. 50-51.

Liu, Bin; Chen Songting & Elke A Rundensteiner (2002),' Data Warehousing & OLAP: Batch Data Warehouse Maintenance in Dynamic Environments," Proceedings of the 11th International Conference on Information and Knowledge Management, Nov. pp. 68-75. (http://doi.acm.org/10.1145/584792.584807)

Lofland, J. & Lofland, L. H. 1995, Analysing Social Settings - A Guide to Qualitative Observation and Analysis, Wadworth Publishing Company.

Long, Ju, Andrew B Whinston and Kerem Tomak, "Calling All Customers," *Marketing Research,* 14(3), (2002), pp. 28 33.

Louis Scott, Lucila Carvalho, Ross Jeffrey, John D'Ambra, Ulrike Becker-Kornstaedt (2002) Understanding the use of an electronic process guide, Information and Software Technology, Vol. 44, Iss. 10; p. 601

Maccoby, M. 1999, 'Building Cross-Functional Capability: What It Really Takes', *Research Technology Management,* vol. 27, pp. 56-58.

Madden, Garry and Coble-Neal, Grant, "Internet Economics and Policy: An Australian Perspective," *Economic Record,* 78(242), (2002), pp. 343-357.

Majchrzak, A. 2000, 'Computer-mediated Inter-organizational Knowledge-sharing: Insights from a Virtual Team Innovating using a Collaborative Tool', *Information Resources Management Journal.*

Malladi, Rajeshwari and Agarwal, Dharma, "Current and Future Application of Mobile and Wireless Networks," *Communication of Association of Computing Machinery*, 45(10), (2002), pp. 144.

Manville, Brook and Ober, Josiah, "Beyond Empowerment: Building a Company of Citizens," *Harvard Business Review*, 81(1), (2003), pp. 48-53.

Markus, M. L. & Keil, M. 1994, 'If We Build it, they will come: Designing Information Systems that People Want to Use', *Sloan Management Review*, vol. 35, pp. 11-25.

Markus, M. L. & Tanis, C. 1999, 'The Enterprise Systems Experience - From Adoption to Success', In R.W. Zmud (Ed.), *Framing the Domains of IT Research: Glimpsing the Future Through the Past*, Cincinnati, OH: Pinnaflex Educational Resources, Inc.: 173-207

Markus, M. L., Petrie, D. & Axline, S. 2000, 'Bucking the Trends: What the future may Hold for ERP Packages', *Information System Frontiers*, vol. 2, no. 2, pp. 181-193.

Markus, M. L., Tanis, C. & Fenema, P. C. 2000, 'Multi-site ERP Implementations – The Meaning of "Enterprise" and "Site" vary Depending on Unique Organisational Circumstances', *Communication of the ACM*, vol. 43, no. 4, pp. 42-46.

Marlin, Steven (1999)," Enterprise Systems Management: Banks Look to get a grip on IT," Bank Systems & Technology, 36:11, pp. 42-48.

Marquardt, M. J. & Reynolds, A. 1994, 'The Global Learning Organisation', ed. B. Ridge, ill, Irwin.

Marshall, Jaffrey, "Consolidation Looms in BI Field," *Financial Executive*, 18(3), (2002), pp. 48-49.

Martinov, Nonna and Roebuck, Peter, "The Assessment of Integration of Materiality and Inherent Risk: An Analysis of Major Firms' Audit Practices," *International Journal of Auditing*, 2(2), (1998), pp. 103-126.

Martinsons, Maris G., "Electronic Commerce in China: Emerging Success Stories," *Information & Management*, 39(7), (2002), pp. 571-579.

Matherne, Louise J and Mackler, Erin P., "Privacy Framework Helps CPAs Protect Consumers," *Journal of Accountancy*, 194(2), (2002), pp. 79-81.

Maxy, Daisy (2001) E-Commerce (A Special Report); Cover Story- The People Behind the Sites: Expedia; Testing, Testing, Wall Street Journal (Eastern), Dec 10, pp. R-8.

McCann, G. 2000, 'Making ERP Spell ROI', *Charter*, vol. 71, no. 2, pp. 56-57.

McCollum, Tim, "Application Control," *The Internal Auditor*, 59(2), (2002), pp. 23- 25.

McGuire, Craig (1999)," Internet Financial Networks Sign with First Call," Wall Street & Technology, 17:8, pp.62.

Millard, Elizabeth, "Peer-to-Peering into the Future," *ABA Journal*, Vol. 88, (2002), pp. 66.

Miller, C. 1999, 'A look at European Shared Service Centers', *The Internal Auditor*, vol. 56, no. 5, pp. 44-48.

Minghua, He and Ho Fung Leung , "Agents in e-Commerce: State of the Art," *Knowledge & Information Systems*, 4(1), (2002), pp. 257-282.

Mirani, Robert, Moore, Deanne and Weber , John A., "Emerging Technologies for Enhancing Supplier Reseller Partnerships," *Industrial Marketing Management*, 30(2), (2001), pp. 101-114.

Moeller, Robert and Herbert N. Witt (1999), "*Brink's Modern Internal Auditing*," 5th Ed., John Wiley and Sons.

Morgan, John and Stocken, Philip, "The Effect of Business Risk on Audit Pricing," *Review of Accounting Studies*, 3(4), (1998), pp. 365-385.

Morhar Merher, Milan (2001)," Evolving Storage Integration opportunities," Computer Technology Review, 21:10, pp. 30-31.

Morrison, Rees W.,"Developing Knowledge-based Client Relationships: The Future of Professional Services," *Consulting to Management*, 13(4), 2002, pp. 61-63.

Mullin, Rick, "Who Needs E-Commerce?" *Chemical week*, 164(19), (2002), pp. 7.

Myers, P. S. 1996, *Knowledge Management and Organizational Design*, Butterworth-Heinemann, Boston, Mass.

Nah, F. F.-H. & Lee-Shang, L. 2001, 'Critical Factors for Successful Implementation of Enterprise Systems', *Business Process Management*, vol. 7, no. 3, pp. 285-296.

Natraj, Sam and Lee, Jim, "Dot-Com Companies: Are They All Hype?" *S.A.M. Management Journal*, 67(3), (2002), pp. 10-14.

Neef, D. 1998, *The Knowledge Economy*, Butterworth-Heinemann.

Neef, D. 2000, 'Hiring and E-team', The Journal of Business Strategy, vol. 21, no. 6, pp. 17-21.

Neuman, L. 1997, Social Research methods: Qualitative and Quantitative Approaches, Allyn & Bacon, MA.

Nevis, E. C., Dibilla, A. J. & Gould, J. M. 1995, 'The Understanding Organisations as Learning Systems', *Sloan Management Review*, vol. Winter, pp. 73-85.

Ng, J. K. C., Ip, W. H. & Lee, T. C. 1999, 'A Paradigm for ERP and BPR Integration', *INT J. Prod. Res.*, vol. 37, no. 9, pp. 2093-2108.

Nolan, R.L. (1979)," Managing the Crisis in Data Processing," Harvard Business Review, March-April, pp. 115-123.

Nonaka, I. & Konno, N. 1998, 'The Concept of 'ba': Building a Foundation for Knowledge Creation', *California Management Review*, vol. 40, no. 3, pp. 40-54.

Nonaka, I. 1991, "The Knowledge-Creating Company", *Harvard Business Review*, vol. November-December, pp. 96-104.

Nonaka, I. 1994, 'A Dynamic Theory of Organizational Knowledge Creation', *Organizational Science,* vol. 5, no. 1, pp. 14-37.

Nonaka, I., Takeuchi, H. & Umemoto, K. 1996, 'A Theory of Organisational Knowledge Creation', *International Journal of Technology Management*, vol. 11, no. 7/8.

Nunamaker, J. F., Chen, M. & Purdin, T. D. M. 1990, 'System Development in Information Research', *Journal of Management of Information System*, vol. 7, no. 3, pp. 89-106.

O'Connor, David, "Keeping Information Technology off the Balance Sheet," *AFP Exchange*, 22(2), (2002), pp. 38-45.

O'Toole, Thomas (2003) E-Relationships: Emergence & the Small Firm, Marketing Intelligence & Planning, 21 (2), pp. 115.

O'Connor, J. T. & Dodd, S. C. 2000, 'Achieving Integration on Capital Projects with Enterprise Resource Planning Systems', *Automation in Construction,* vol. 9, pp. 515- 524.

Opie, Justin, "Integration is Key: An Introduction to EAI Technology," *Management Services*, 46(9), (2002a), pp. 18-19.

Opie, Justin, "The Next Big Thing- Web Services," *Management Services*, 46(10), (2002b), pp. 22-23.

O'Reilly, C. A. & Pfeffer, J. 2000, Hidden Value: How Great Companies Achieve Extraordinary Result with Ordinary People, Harvard Business School Press, Boston.

Orlikowski, W. 1993, 'Case told as Organisational Change: Investigating Incremental and Radical Changes in System Development', *MIS Quarterly,* vol. 7, no. 3, pp. 309- 340.

Orr, J. 1990, 'Sharing Knowledge, Celebrating Identity: War Stories and Community Memory in a Service Culture', in *Collective Remembering: Memory in Society*, eds. D. S. Middleton & D. Edwards, Sage Publication, Beverly Hills, CA.

Osheroff, Mike, "ABC and SAP," Strategic Finance, 84(5), (2002), pp. 23-25.

Pace, Don, "Assurance in the Electronic Commerce Environment," *Pennsylvania CPA Journal*, 70(3), (1999), pp. 1-5.

Pacini, Carl and Sinason , David, "Auditor Liability for Electronic Commerce Transaction Assurance: The CPA/CA WebTrust," *American Business Law Journal*, 36(3), (1999), pp. 479-514.

Pagano, P, "Knowledge Management & Business Model Innovation," *European Journal of Information Systems*, 11(4), (2002), pp. 296-297.

Pan, S. L., Newell, S., Huang, J. & Wan, K. C. 2001, 'Knowledge Integration as a Key Problem in an ERP Implementation', in *22nd Annual International Conference on Information Systems*, ICIS, New Orleans, pp. 321-328,

Pan, Shan & Jae-Nam Lee (2003) Using e-CRM for a Unified View of the Customer, Communications of ACM, 46 (4), pp. 95.

Paper, David, "What the Next IT Revolution Should Be?" *Information Resources Management Journal*, 16(1), (2003), pp. 1-5

Parker, Marilyn M. and Benson, Robert J. (1988), Information Economics: Linking Business Performance to Information technology, Englewood Cliffs, NJ, Prentice-Hall.

Parkhe, A. 1993, 'Messy Research, Methodological Predispositions, and Theory Development in International Joint Ventures, *Academy of Management Review,* vol. 8, no. 2, pp. 227-268.

Parr, A. & Shanks, G. 2000, 'A Model of ERP Project Implementation', *Journal of Information Technology,* vol. 15, pp. 289-303.

Pathak, Jagdish & Amelia Baldwin (2003) Generation-X Technology & Auditors: A Paradigm Shift, Proceedings of 12th Annual Research Workshop of Artificial Intelligence/Emerging Technology Section, American Accounting Association, Honolulu, Hawaii (USA): 2003-08-02.

Pathak, Jagdish & Mary Lind (2003) Audit Risk, Complex Technology and Auditing Processes, EDPACS, XXXI, No 5 (Nov 2003), pp.1-9.

Pathak, Jagdish (2000) E-Commerce: A Website Audit Review Program, Chartered Accountant, Institute of Chartered Accountants of India, New Delhi, March, pp.25-29.

Pathak, Jagdish (2003) Internal Audit and e-Commerce Controls, INTERNAL AUDITING JOURNAL, Thompson/RIA Press, NY, USA, 18 (2).

Pathak, Jagdish, "EDI: Getting Rid off the Paper Trail," Accountancy SA, January, (2001), pp. 3-4.

Paton, N. W., Goble, C. A. & Bechhofer, S. 2000, 'Knowledge Based Information Integration Systems', *Information and Software Technology,* vol. 42, no. 5, pp. 299-312.

Patton, M. Q. 1990, *Qualitative Evaluation and Research Methods*, 2nd Edition, Sage, London.

Peak, John E., "Long Term Profits, Broad Business Benefits," *AFP Exchange*, 22(6), (2002), pp. 34-39.

Peak, Martha H (1996), "Dynamic Duo: SAP and Reengineering," *Management Review*, 85(12), 7.

Peeples, Donna K, "Instilling Consumer Confidence in e-Commerce," *S.A.M. Advanced Management Journal*, 67(4), (2002), pp. 26-31.

Perlow, L. A. 1999, 'The Time Famine: Toward a Sociology of Work Time', *Administrative Science Quarterly*, vol. 44, no. 1, pp. 57-72.

Peter, J. B. & Martin, J. C. 1999, 'Managing Cross-border Complementary Knowledge', *International Studies of Management & Organization*, vol. 29, no. 1, pp. 80-104.

Petrely, Nicholas (2002)," Open Rules for e-Business," Computer World, 36:25, pp. 48.

Pettigrew, A. 1985, 'Contextualist Research and the Study of Organisational Change Processes', in *Research Methods in Information Systems*, ed. E. Munford et. al., Holland: Amsterdam.

Pfleeger, Charles (1997). *Security in Computing*, 2nd edición Prentice Hall.

Pisano, G. 1994, 'Knowledge Integration and the Locus of Learning: An Empirical Analysis of Process Development', *Strategic Management Journal*, vol. 15, no. Winter Special Issue, pp. 85-100.

Poliski, Iris, "Joining the Third Generation," *Research & Development*, 44(8), (2002), pp. 28-29.

Prahalad, C. K. & Hamel, G. 1990, 'The Core Competence of the Corporation', *Harvard Business Review*, vol. 68, no. 3, p. 79-91.

Pravica, Danica (1999)," Centralized Systems Help Reduce Risks," Computing Canada, 25:30, pp. 23-24.

Primoff WM (1998),"Electronic commerce and WebTrust," CPA Journal, November *http://www.nysscpa.org/cpajournal/1998/1198/Features/f141198.html*.

Primoff, Walter (1998) Electronic Commerce & Web Trust, The CPA Journal, 68 (11), pp. 11-19.

Pugliese, Anthony and Halse, Ronald, "SysTrust & WebTrust: Technology Assurance Opportunity," *The CPA Journal*, 70(11), (2000), pp. 28-34.

Ranganathan, C. and Ganapathy, Shobha ,"Key Dimensions of Business-to-Consumer websites," *Information & Management*, 39(6), (2002) pp. 457-465.

Ratcliffe, Thomas A. and Munter, Paul, "Information Technology, Internal Control and Financial Statement Audit," *The CPA Journal*, 72(4), (2002), pp. 40-44.

Ratliff, Richard L.; Wanda A. Wallace; Glenn E. Summers; William G. McFarland; and James K. Loebbecke (1996), "*Internal Auditing: Principles and Techniques*," 2nd Ed., The Institute of Internal Auditors.

Ratliff, Richard, L., Wallace, Wanda, A., Summers, Glen, E. McFarland, William, G., and Loebbecke, James, K. (1996), Internal Auditing: Principles & Techniques, Altamonte Springs, Institute of Internal Auditors, FL.

Rayport, J. F. & Sviokla, J. J. 1995, 'Exploiting the Virtual Value Chain', *Harvard Business Review*, vol. 73, no. 6, p. 75-85.

Reimers, Jane, "*Financial Accounting: A Business Process Approach*, Ist Edition, Prentice-Hall, 2003.

Rezaee, Zabihollah; Sharbatoghlie, Ahmad; and Elam, Rick, and McMickle, Peter L., "Continuous Auditing: Building Automated Auditing Capability," *Auditing: A Journal of Practice and Theory*, 21(1), (2002) pp. 147-163.

Richard, D. 1991, 'Flying Against the Wind? Culture Management Development in South East Asia', *Journal of Management Development*, vol. 10, no. 6, pp. 7-21.

Riper, K. & Durham, M. 1999, 'Phased ERP Implementation: the City of Des Moines Experience', *Government Finance Review*, no. 15, pp. 37-43.

Rizzi, A. & Zamboni, R. 2000, 'Efficiency Improvement in Manual Warehouses through ERP Systems Implementation and Redesign of the Logistic Processes', *Logistic Information Management*, vol. 12, no. 5, pp. 367-377.

Robert, Michael, "Adding Value to Customer Relationships," *Chemical Week*, 161:11, (1999), pp. 2.

Roberts, J. 2000, 'From Know-how to Show-how? Question the Role of Information and Communication Technologies in Knowledge Transfer', *Technology Analysis & Strategic Management*, vol. 12, no. 4, pp. 429-443.

Robinson, Teri (1999)," Think Big Picture- Incorporating e-Commerce Sites into Core Business Systems has made Processing More Important Than Ever," Internet Week, 772, pp. PG-37.

Rohner, R. P. 1977, 'Advantages of the Comparative Method of Anthropology', *Behavioural Science Research*, vol. 12, pp. 117-144.

Ronen, Joshua and Cherny, Julius,"Is Insurance a Solution to the Auditing Dilemma," *National Underwriter*, 106(32), (2002), pp. 26-29.

Rosemann, M. & Wiese, J. 1999, 'Measuring the performance of ERP Software – a Balanced Scorecard Approach', in *Proceedings of the 10th Australian Conference on Information systems*, pp. 773-784

Rosemann, M. 2000, 'Using Reference Models within The Enterprise Resource Planning Lifecycle', *Australian Accounting Review*, vol. 10, no. 3, pp. 19-45.

Ross, J. W. 1999b, 'Surprising Facts about Implementing ERP', *IT Professional, IEEE*, vol. Aug., pp. 65-68.

Ross, J.W. & Vitale, M. R. 2000, 'The ERP Revolution: Surviving Versus Thriving', *Information system Frontiers*, vol. 2, no. 2, pp. 233-241.

Ross, J.W. 1999a, 'Dow Corning Corporation: Business Processes and Information Technology', *Journal of Information Technology*, vol. 1999, no. 14, pp. 253-266.

Salazar, Angel; Ray Hackney & Jeromy Howells (2003) The Strategic Impact of Internet Technology in Bio-Technology & Pharmaceutical Firms: Insights from Knowledge Management Perspective, Information Technology & Management, 4 (2&3), pp. 289.

Sangjae, Lee & Gyoo Gum Lim (2003) The Impact of Partnership Attributes on EDI Implementation Issues, Information & Management, 41 (2), pp. 135.

Saracevic, Tefko (1999)," Information Science," Journal of the American Society for the Information Science, 50;12, pp. 1051-1063.

Saran, Amitabh; Divyakant Agarwal; Amer El Abbadi; Terrence R Smith & Jianwen Su (1996)," Scientific Modeling Using Distributed Resources," Proceedings of the 4th ACM Workshop on Advances in Geographic Information Systems, pp. 68-75.

Savage, J. 2000, 'Participative Observation: Standing in the Shoes of Others', *Qualitative Health Research*, vol. 10, no. 3, pp. 324-340.

Sawyer, S. 2000, 'Packaged Software: Implications of the Differences from Custom Approaches to Software Development', *European Journal of Information Systems*, vol. 9, no. 1, pp. 47-58.

Scheer, A.-W. & Habermann, F. 2000, 'Enterprise Resource Planning: Making ERP a Success', *Communication of the ACM*, vol. 43, no. 4, pp. 57-61.

Schein, E. 1993, 'On Dialogue, Culture, and Organisational Learning', *Organizational Dynamics*, vol. 22, pp. 40-51.

Schneier, B.(1996). Applied Cryptography. *Protocols, Algorithms and Source code in C.* 2nd edition. John Wiley.

Schoderbek, Peter P., Schoderbek, Charles G. and Kefalas, Asterios G. (1990), Management Systems: Conceptual Considerations, Homewood, IL, IRWIN

Schroder, Monika and McEachern, Movren,"ISO-9001 as an Audit Frame for Integrated Quality Management in Meat Supply Chain," *Managerial Auditing Journal*, 17(1/2,) (2002), pp. 79-85.

Scott, J., E. 1999, 'The FoxMeyer Drugs' Bankruptcy: Was it a Failure of the ERP?' in *American Conference for Information System*, pp. 223-225.

Scott, J., E. 2000, 'Facilitating Inter-organizational Learning with Information technology', *Journal of Management Information Systems*, vol. 17, no. 2, pp. 81-113.

Scott, Robert W., "Making Payments Online," *Accounting Technology*, 18:9, (2002), pp. 45-47.

Seewald, Nancy, "Manufacturers Seek Better ERP Plant Links," *Chemical Week*, 164(44), (2002), pp. 31.

Senge, P., M. 1990, The Fifth Discipline - the Art and Practice of the Learning Organisation, Doubleday/Currency, New York.

Senge, P., M., Goran, C. & Patrick, L. P. 2001, 'Innovating Our Way to the Next Industrial Revolution', *Sloan Management Review*, 42 Vol., pp. 24-38.

Simpson, Paul (2001),"The International e-Commerce Evolution," World Trade, 14:6, pp. 66-68. Simpson, Paul (2001),"The International e-Commerce Evolution," World Trade, 14:6, pp. 66-68.

Siragher, N. 1999, 'Insight from Industry: Enterprise Resource Planning - the End of the Line for the Sales Automation Market and a Major Step Towards Sales Process Definition Standards?' *Supply Chain Management*, vol. 4, no. 1, pp. 11-13.

Siriginidi, S. R. 2000, 'Enterprise Resource Planning in Reengineering Business', *Business Process Management*, vol. 6, no. 5, pp. 362-391.

Slywotzky, A. J., Chrstensen, C. M., Tedlow, R. S. & Carr, N. G. 2000, 'The Future of Commerce', *Harvard Business Review*, vol. 78, no. 1.

Smith, K. & Berg, D. 1987, Paradoxes of Group Life: Understanding Conflict, Paralysis, and Movement in Group Dynamics, San Francisco.

Smith, Richard E.(1997). *Internet Cryptography*. Addison-Wesley. Massachusetts.

Soh, C., Sia, S. K. & Tay-Yap, J. 2000, 'Enterprise Resource Planning: Culture Fits and Misfits: is ERP an Universal Solution', *Communication of the ACM*, vol. 43, no. 4, pp. 47-51.

Soliman, F. & Youssef, M. 1998, 'The role of SAP Software in Business Process Reengineering', *International Journal of Operations & Production Management*, vol. 18, no. 9/10, pp. 886-894.

Spender, J. C. 1996, Competitive Advantage from Tacit Knowledge? Unpacking the Concept and its Strategic Implications, Sage, London.

Sprague, R. H. 2000, 'Researching Organisational Systems Using Social Network Analysis', in *Thirty-third Annual Hawaii International Conference on System Science*, Maui, Hawaii.

Sprott, D. 2000, 'Componentizing the Enterprise Application Packages', *Communication of the ACM*, vol. 43, no. 4, pp. 63-69.

Stal Michael, "Web Services: Beyond Component-based Computing," *Communication of Association of Computing Machinery*, 45(10), (2002), pp. 71-76.

Stallings, William (1994). *Network and Internetwork Computer Security*, Prentice-Hall, IEEE Press.

Stephen, Ferg (1986)," Data Independence & the Relational DBMS," Datamation, 32:11, pp. 103-105.

Stern, D. 1996, 'Human Resource Development in the Knowledge-Based Economy: roles of Firms, Schools and Government', *OECD*.

Stieren, Carl (1999)," Add One Egg, A Cup of Milk, and Stir: Single Source Documentation for Today," Proceedings of the 15th Annual International Conference on Computer Documentation, pp. 255-262. (http://doi.acm.org/10.1145/263367.263400)

Storck, J. & Hill, P. A. 2000, 'Knowledge Diffusion through Strategic Communities', *Sloan Management Review*, vol. 41, no. 3, pp. 63-74.

Strickland, Lee & Jennifer Willard (2002),"Re-Engineering the Immigration Systems: A Case for Data mining & Information Assurance to Enhance Home land Security: Part-1-Identifying the Current Problems," Bulletin of the American Society of Information Science & Technology, (Oct/Nov), pp. 16-21.

Subramani, Mani and Walden, Eric, "The Impact of e-Commerce Announcements on the Market Value of the Firm," *Information Systems Research*, 12(2), (2001), pp. 135-154.

Suh, Christine, "Virtual Images for Real Security," *Research & Development*, 44(7), (2002), pp. 48.

Sumner, M. 1999, 'Critical Success Factors in Enterprise Wide Information Management Systems Projects', *American Conference on Information Systems*, pp. 232- 234.

Sumner, M. 2000, 'Risk Factors in Enterprise-wide/ERP projects', *Journal of Information Technology*, vol. 15, pp. 317-327.

Sunny, B. 1999, 'Global E-commerce, Local Problems', *Journal of Business Strategy*, vol. 20, no. 4, pp. 32-38.

Sutton, Steve & Clark Hampton (2003) Risk Assessment in an Extended Enterprise Environment: Redefining the Audit Model, International Journal of Accounting Information Systems, 4 (1), pp. 37-73.

Szulanski, G. 2000, 'The Process of Knowledge Transfer: A Diachronic Analysis of Stickiness', *Organisational Behavior and Human Decision Processing*, vol. 82, no. 1, pp. 9-27.

Tarasewich, Peter and Warkentin, Merrill, "Information Everywhere," *Information Systems Management*, 19(1), (2002), pp. 8-13.

Taylor, J. C. 1998, 'Participative Design: Linking BPR and SAP with an STS Approach', *Journal of Organisational Change Management*, vol. 11, no. 3, pp. 233-245.

Teece, D., Pisano, G. & Shuen, A. 1997, 'Dynamic Capabilities and Strategic Management', *Strategic Management Journal*, vol. 18, no. 7, pp. 509-533.

The Security of Network Systems. Five Report (A Study on Behalf of the Commission of the European Communities). Coopers and Lybrand. 1998.

Themistocleous, M. & Irani, Z. 2001, 'Benchmarking the Benefits and Barriers of Application Integration', *Benchmarking: An International Journal*, vol. 8, no. 4, pp. 317-331.

Thomas, R. R. 2000, 'The Global E-economy: Can your ERP handle it?' *The Journal of Corporate Accounting & Finance*, vol. 11, no. 6, pp. 15-18.

Triplett, A. & Scheumann, J. 2000, 'Managing Shared Services with ABM', *Strategic Finance*, vol. 81, no. 8, pp. 40-45.

Tushman, M. L. & Romanelli, E. 1985, 'Organisational Evolution: A Metamorphosis Model of Convergence and Reorientations', *Research in Organisational Behavior*, vol. 7, pp. 171-222.

Van Everdingen, Y., Hillegersberg, V. & Waarts, E. 2000, 'ERP Adoption by European Midsize Companies', *Communications of the ACM*, vol. 43, no. 4, pp. 27-31.

Van Stijin, E. & Wensley, A. 2001, 'Organisational Memory and Completeness of Process Modelling in ERP systems: Some concerns, methods and directions for future research', *Business Process Management,* vol. 7, no. 3, pp. 181-204.

Vandermerwe, S. 2000, 'How Increasing Value to Customers Improves Business Results', *Sloan Management Review,* vol. 42, no. 1, pp. 27-37.

Vasarhelyi, Miklos A; Kogan, Alexander; and Alles, Michael, "Would Continuous Auditing Have Prevented the ENRON Mess?" *The CPA Journal,* 72(7), (2002). pp. 80.

Venkatraman, N. & Henderson, J. C. 1998, 'Real Strategies for Virtual Organisation', *Sloan Management Review,* vol. 40, no. 1, pp. 33-48.

Vice, Patrick, "Online: E-ffective Risk Management," *Risk Management,* 48(12), (2001), pp. 38-42.

Viehland, Dennis, "The Internet for Accountants," *Chartered Accountants Journal of New Zealand,* 78(5), (1999), pp. 30.

Vinten Gerald (2001) Corporate governance and the sons of Cadbury, Corporate Governance. Vol. 1, Iss. 4; p. 4-9

Von Krogh, G. & Cusumano, M. A. 2001, 'Three Strategies for Managing Fast Growth', *Sloan Management Review,* vol. 42, no. 2, pp. 53-61.

Vosburg, J. & Kumar, A. 2001, 'Managing Dirty Data in Organisations using ERP: Lessons from a Case Study', *Industrial Management & Data Systems,* vol. 101, no. 1, pp. 21-31.

Waddington, D G & H Hutchison (1999)," Resource Partitioning in General Purpose Operating Systems: Experimental Results in Windows NT," ACM SIGOPS Operating Systems Review, 33:4, pp. 52-74.

Wagle, D. 1998, 'The Case for ERP Systems', *The Mckinsey Quarterly,* pp. 130-138.

Wagner, Christian and Turban, Efraim; (2002),"Are Intelligent e-Commerce Agents Partners or Predators?" *Communication of Association of Computing Machinery,* 45(5), (2002), pp. 84-90.

Walid, Ben-Ameur & Herve Kerivin (2003) New Economical Virtual Private Networks, Communications of ACM, June, 46 (6), pp. 69.

Walsh, Brian, "The Future of Audit," *Accountancy Ireland,* 34(5), (2002), pp. 5.

Walsham, G. 1993, *Interpreting Information Systems in Organizations,* Wiley, Chichester, West Sussex, England ; New York.

Wan, K. C., Pan, S. L. & Huang, J. 2001a, 'Barriers to ERP Implementation: An Action Research', in *Pacific Asia Conference for Information System,* Korea, Seoul, pp. 1126-1140.

Wan, K. C., Pan, S. L. & Huang, J. 2001b, 'Knowledge Management in E-commerce: the Next Step after Implementation', in *American Conference for Information System,* Boston, USA, pp. 1037-1042.

Weber, Richard M, "Technology and its Role in Our Ethical Relationships," *Journal of Financial Services Professionals,* 56(6), (2002), pp. 39-40.

Weber, Ron (1988) EDP Auditing: Conceptual Foundations & Practice, McGraw-Hill, New York, USA.

Wei, C.P, P.J. Hue & Y-X Dong (2002) Managing Document Categories in e-Commerce Environments: An Evolution-based Approach, European Journal of Information Systems, 11 (3), pp. 208-218.

Wenger, E. 2000, 'Communities of Practice', *Harvard Business Review,* vol. 78, no. 1, pp. 139-145.

Wigand, R. T. 1997, 'Electronic Commerce: Definition, Theory, and Context', *Information Society,* vol. 13, no. 1, pp. 1-16.

Wil, M. & Vandlee, A. 1999, 'Process-Oriented Architectures for Electronic Commerce & Inter-organizational Workflow', *Information Systems,* vol. 24, no. 8, pp. 639-671.

Willcocks, L. P. & Sykes, R. 2000, 'Enterprise Resource Planning: the Role of the CIO and it Function in ERP', *Communication of the ACM,* vol. 43, no. 4, pp. 32-38.

William, Kathy (1997) AICPA Launches Electronic Commerce Seal, Strategic Finance, October, 79 (4), pp. 16.

Williams, Lisa; Terry Esper & John Ozment (2002) The Electronic Supply Chain: Its Impact on the Current & Future Structure of Strategic Alliances, Partnerships & Logistic Leadership, International Journal of Physical Distribution & Logistic Management, 32 (8), pp. 703-720.

Wolf, Jonathan, "The Next Big Hurdle for the Internet," *Communication News,* 38(2), (2001), pp. 12.

Wood, T. & MCaldas, M. P. 2001, 'Reductionism and Complex Thinking during ERP Implementation', *Business Process Management Journal,* vol. 7, no. 5, pp. 387-393.

Wright, Arnold, "Forum on Continuous Auditing & Assurance," *Auditing: A Journal of Practice and Theory,* 21(1), (2002), pp. 123.

Wu, Ing-Long (2003) Understanding Senior Management's Behavior in Promoting the Strategic Role of IT in Process Re-engineering: The Use of the Theory of Reasoned Actions, Information & Management, 41 (1), pp. 1.

Yu, Chien-Chih et al, "The Impact of e-Commerce on Auditing Practices," *International Journal of Intelligent Systems in Accounting, Finance & Management,* 9(3), (2000), pp. 195-216.

Yusuf, Yahia Y; Little, David and Omuh, Spencer O, "Multiple Case Studies of Total Enterprise Integration Programs: Lessons & Benefits," *International Journal of Manufacturing technology & Management,* 4(3-4), (2002), pp. 283-302

Glossary of IT Auditing Terms

The definitions in this glossary are drawn from several sources, including this book, certain IBM and other manuals, and the documents and sources listed in the bibliography.

ABEND: (short for abnormal ending) An unexpected processing termination that may indicate that coding was incorrectly performed and that earlier testing was not adequate or not adequately controlled.

Acceptance testing: Final testing by users to decide whether they accept a new system.

Access control facility (CA-ACF2): An access control software package marketed by Computer Associates International, Inc.(CA).

Access control software (CA-ACF2, RACF, CA-TOP SECRET): This type of software, which is external to the operating system, provides a means of specifying who has access to a system; who has access to specific resources, and what capabilities authorized users are granted. Access control software can generally be implemented in different modes that provide varying degrees of protection such as denying access for which the user is not expressly authorized, allowing access which is not expressly authorized but providing a warning, or allowing access to all resources without warning regardless of authority.

Access control: Controls designed to protect computer resources from unauthorized modification, loss, or disclosure. Access controls include both physical access controls, which limit access to facilities and associated hardware, and logical controls, which prevent or detect unauthorized access to sensitive data and programs that are stored or transmitted electronically.

Access method: The technique used for selecting records in a file for processing, retrieval, or storage.

Access path: Sequence of hardware and software components significant to access control. Any component capable of enforcing access restrictions or any component that could be used to bypass an access restriction should be considered part of the access path. The access path can also be defined as the path through which user requests travel, including the telecommunications software, transaction processing software, application program, etc.

Access privileges: Precise statements that define the extent to which an individual can access computer systems and use or modify the programs and data on the system, and under what circumstances this access will be allowed.

Accountability: The existence of a record that permits the identification of an individual who performed some specific activity so that responsibility for that activity can be established.

ACF2: See access control facility.

ADABAS: A relational database system developed by Software AG and implemented on mainframe and UNIX platforms. It uses relational attributes and also non-relational techniques, such as multiple values and periodic groups. It has its own language called Natural.

American Standard Code for Information Interchange (ASCII): A standard seven-bit code for representing 128-characters that was adopted by the American Standards Association to achieve compatibility between data devices.

APF: See authorized program facility.

Application: A computer program designed to help people perform a certain type of work, including specific functions, such as payroll, inventory control, accounting, and mission support. Depending on the work for which it was designed, an application can manipulate text, numbers, graphics, or a combination of these elements.

Application controls: Application controls are directly related to individual applications. They help ensure that transactions are valid, properly authorized, and completely and accurately processed and reported.

Application programmer: A person who develops and maintains application programs, as opposed to system programmers who develop and maintain the operating system and system utilities.

Application programs: See application.

ASCII: See American standard code for information interchange.

Assembly language: A low-level procedural programming language in which each program statement corresponds directly to a single machine instruction. Assembly languages are thus specific to a given processor.

Assertion: Financial statement assertions are management representations that are embodied in financial statement components. The assertions can be either explicit or implicit and can be classified into the following broad categories: existence or occurrence (an entity's assets or liabilities exist at a given date and recorded transactions have occurred during a given period), completeness (all transactions and accounts that should be presented in the financial statements are so included), rights and obligations (assets are the rights of the entity, and liabilities are the obligations of the entity at a given date), valuation or allocation (asset, liability, revenue, and expense components have been included in the financial statements at appropriate amounts), and presentation and disclosure (the particular components of the financial statements are properly classified, described, and disclosed).

Audit risk: The risk that information or financial reports will contain material errors that the auditor may not detect.

Audit software (ACL, IDEA) Generic audit software consists of a special program or set of programs designed to audit data stored on computer media. Audit software performs functions such as data extraction and reformatting, file creation, sorting, and downloading. This type of audit software may also be used to perform computations, data analysis, sample selection, summarization, file stratification, field comparison, file matching, or statistical analysis. (Panaudit, EDP Auditor, CA-EXAMINE) The term audit software may also refer to programs that audit specific functions, features, and controls associated with specific types of computer systems to evaluate integrity and identify security exposures.

Audit trail: A program feature that automatically keeps a record of transactions enabling auditors to find the origin of specific figures in an accounting package. In computer systems, it is a step-by-step history of a transaction, especially a transaction with security sensitivity including source documents, electronic logs, and records of accesses to restricted files.

Authentication: The act of verifying the identity of a user and the user's eligibility to access computerized information. It is designed to protect against fraudulent activity.

Authorized program facility: It is an operating system facility that controls which programs are allowed to use restricted system functions.

Backdoor: An undocumented way to gain access to a program, data, or an entire computer system, often known only to the programmer who created it. Backdoors can be handy when the standard way of getting information is unavailable, but they usually constitute a security risk.

Backup: Any duplicate of a primary resource function, such as a copy of a computer program or data file. This standby is used in case of loss or failure of the primary resource.

Backup procedures: A regular maintenance procedure that copies all new or altered files to a backup storage medium, such as a tape drive.

Bandwidth: The amount of data that can be transmitted via a given medium of communication channel (such as a computer network) in a given unit of time (generally one second).

Batch processing: This is a mode of operation in which transactions are accumulated over a period of time, such as a day, week, or month, and then processed in a single run. In batch processing, users do not interact with the system while their programs and data are processing as they do during interactive processing.

Biometric authentication: The process of verifying or recognizing the identity of a person based on physiological or behavioural characteristics. Biometric devices include fingerprints, retina patterns, hand geometry, speech patterns, and keystroke dynamics.

BLP: See bypass label processing.

Bridge: A device that allows two networks, even ones dissimilar in topology, wiring, or communications protocols, to exchange data.

Browsing: This is an act of electronically perusing files and records without authorization.

Bug: A flaw in a computer program that causes it to produce incorrect or inappropriate results.

Bypass label processing (BLP): A technique of reading a computer file while bypassing the internal file/data set label. This process could result in bypassing security access controls.

CA-ACF2: See access control facility.

CA-EXAMINE: An audit software package marketed by Computer Associates International, Inc. (CA) that can help identify and control MVS security exposures, viruses, Trojan horses, and logic bombs that can destroy production dependability and circumvent existing security mechanisms.

CA-TOP SECRET: See TOP SECRET.

CAAT: See computer-assisted audit technique.

CD-ROM: See compact disk-read only memory.

Central processing unit (CPU): The computational and control unit of a computer; the device that interprets and executes instructions.

Checkpoint: The process of saving the current state of a program and its data, including intermediate results to disk or other non-volatile storage, so that if interrupted the program could be restarted at the point at which the last checkpoint occurred.

Chip (also referred to as a microchip): Usually a silicon wafer on which circuit elements have been imprinted.

CICS: See customer information control system.

Cipher key lock: A lock with a key pad-like device that requires the manual entry of a predetermined code for entry.

Client/server model: A design model used on a network where individual workstations (clients) and shared servers work together to process applications. In this model, certain functions are allocated to the client workstations and the server. Typically, the server provides centralized, multi-user services, whereas the client workstations support user interaction.

CLIST (short for command list): In TSO/E, CLISTS are programs that perform given tasks or groups of tasks. The most basic CLIST is a list of TSO/E commands. However, two command languages available in TSO/E (CLIST and REXX) provide the programming tools needed to create structured applications or manage programs written in other languages.

COBIT: See, Control Objectives for Information and Related Technology.

COBOL: See common business-oriented language.

Code: Instructions written in a computer programming language. (See, object code and source code.)

Cold site: An IS backup facility that has the necessary electrical and physical components of a computer facility, but does not have the computer equipment in place. The site is ready to receive the necessary replacement computer equipment in the event that the user has to move from their main computing location to an alternative computing location.

Command: A job control statement or a message, sent to the computer system, that initiates a processing task.

Common business-oriented language (COBOL): A high-level programming language specially designed for business applications.

Communications program: A program that enables a computer to connect with another computer and exchange information by transmitting or receiving data over telecommunications networks.

Communications protocol: The standards that govern the transfer of information among computers on a network.

Compact disc-read only memory (CD-ROM): Compact Disc (CD)-Read Only Memory (ROM) is a form of optical rather than magnetic storage. CD-ROM devices are generally read-only.

Compatibility: The capability of a computer, device, or program to function with or substitute for another make and model of computer, device, or program and also, the capability of one computer to run the software written to run on another computer. Standard interfaces, languages, protocols, and data formats are critical to achieving compatibility.

Compensating control: This is an internal control that reduces the risk of an existing or potential control weakness that could result in errors or omissions.

Compiler: A program that reads the statements in a human-readable programming language and translates them into a machine-readable executable program.

Component: A single resource with defined characteristics, such as a terminal or printer. These components are also defined by their relationship to other components.

Computer architecture: A general term referring to the structure of all or part of a computer system. The term also covers the design of system software, such as the operating system, as well as refers to the combination of hardware and basic software that links the machines on a computer network. Computer architecture refers to an entire structure and to the details needed to make it functional. Thus, computer architecture covers computer systems, circuits, and system programs, but typically does not cover applications, which are required to perform a task but not to make the system run.

Computer-assisted audit technique (CAAT): Any automated audit technique, such as generalized audit software, test data generators, computerized audit programs, and special audit utilities.

Computer facility: A site or location with computer hardware where information processing is performed or where data from such sites are stored.

Computer operations: The function responsible for operating the computer and peripheral equipment, including providing the tape, disk, or paper resources as requested by the application systems.

Computer processing location: See computer facility.

Computer resource: See resource.

Computer room: This is a room within a facility that houses computers and/or telecommunication devices.

Computer system: A complete computer installation, including peripherals, in which all the components are designed to work with each other.

Computer-related controls: Computer-related controls help ensure the reliability, confidentiality, and availability of automated information. They include both general controls, which apply to all or a large segment of an entity's information systems, and application controls, which apply to individual applications.

Confidentiality: Ensuring that transmitted or stored data are not read by unauthorized persons.

Configuration management: The control and documentation of changes made to a system's hardware, software, and documentation throughout the development and operational life of the system.

Console: Traditionally, a control unit such as a terminal through which a user communicates with a computer. In the mainframe environment, a console is the operator's station.

Contingency plan: Management policy and procedures designed to maintain or restore business operations, including computer operations, possibly at an alternate location, in the event of emergencies, system failure, or disaster.

Contingency planning: See contingency plan.

Control environment: The control environment is an important component of an entity's internal control structure. It sets the "tone at the top" and can influence the effectiveness of specific control techniques. Factors that influence the control environment include management's philosophy and operating style, the entity's organizational structure, methods of assigning authority and responsibility, management's control methods for monitoring and following up on performance, the effectiveness of the Inspector General and internal audit, personnel policies and practices, and influences external to the entity.

Control Objectives for Information and Related Technology (COBIT): A framework, control objectives, and audit guidelines developed by the Information Systems Audit and Control Foundation (ISACF) as a generally applicable and accepted standard for good practices for controls over information technology.

Control risk: Risk that a material misstatement that could occur in an assertion will not be prevented, or detected and corrected on a timely basis by the entity's internal control structure.

Cooperative processing: A mode of operation in which two or more computers, such as a mainframe and a microcomputer, can carry out portions of the same program or work on the same data. It enables computers to share programs, workloads, and data files.

CPU: See, central processing unit.

Cryptographic algorithm: A mathematical procedure used for such purposes as encrypting and decrypting messages and signing documents digitally.

Cryptographic system: The hardware, software, documents, and associated techniques and processes that together provide a means of encryption.

Cryptography: The science of coding messages so they cannot be read by any person other than the intended recipient. Ordinary text—or plain text—and other data are transformed into coded form by encryption and translated back to plain text or data by decryption.

Customer information control system (CICS): An IBM communications system used for production applications in a mainframe environment. It facilitates the development of on-line applications and handles the concurrent processing of transactions entered from different terminals.

DASD: See, direct access storage device.

Data: Facts and information that can be communicated and manipulated.

Data access method: See, access method.

Data administration: The function that plans for and administers the data used throughout the entity. This function is concerned with identifying, cataloging, controlling, and coordinating the information needs of the entity.

Database: A collection of related information about a subject organized in a useful manner that provides a base or foundation for procedures, such as retrieving information, drawing conclusions, or making decisions. Any collection of information that serves these purposes qualifies as a database, even if the information is not stored on a computer.

Database administrator (DBA): The individual responsible for both the design of the database, including the structure and contents, and the access capabilities of application programs and users to the database. Additional responsibilities include operation, performance, integrity, and security of the database.

Database management: Tasks related to creating, maintaining, organizing, and retrieving information from a database.

Database management system (DBMS): (DB2, IMS, IDMS) A software product that aids in controlling and using the data needed by application programs. DBMSs organize data in a database, manage all requests for database actions—such as queries or updates from users—and permit centralized control of security and data integrity.

Data center: See, computer facility.

Data communications: The transfer of information from one computer to another through a communications medium, such as telephone lines, microwave relay, satellite link, or physical cable.

Data communications systems: See, data communications.

Data control: The function responsible for seeing that all data necessary for processing is present and that all output is complete and distributed properly. This function is generally responsible for reconciling record counts and control totals submitted by users with similar counts and totals generated during processing.

Data definition: Identification of all fields in the database, how they are formatted, how they are combined into different types of records, and how the record types are interrelated.

Data dictionary: A repository of information about data, such as its meaning, relationships to other data, origin, usage, and format. The dictionary assists company management, database administrators, systems analysts, and application programmers in effectively planning, controlling, and evaluating the collection, storage, and use of data.

Data diddling: Changing data with malicious intent before or during input to the system.

Data encryption standard (DES): A NIST Federal Information Processing Standard and a commonly used secret-key cryptographic algorithm for encrypting and decrypting data.

Data file: See, file.

Data owner: See, owner.

Data processing: The computerized preparation of documents and the flow of data contained in these documents through the major steps of recording, classifying, and summarizing.

Data processing center: See, computer facility.

Data security: See, security management function.

Data validation: Checking transaction data for any errors or omissions that can be detected by examining the data.

Data warehouse: A generic term for a system used to store, retrieve, and manage large amounts of data. A database, often remote, containing recent snapshots of corporate data that can be used for analysis without slowing down day-to-day operations of the production database.

DBA: See, database administrator.

DBMS: See, database management system.

Debug: With software, to detect, locate, and correct logical or syntactical errors in a computer program.

Decision support system (DSS): An information system or analytic model designed to help managers and professionals be more effective in their decision-making.

Delete access: This level of access provides the ability to erase or remove data or programs.

DES: See, data encryption standard.

Detection risk: The risk that the auditor will not detect a material misstatement that exists in an assertion.

Dial-up access: This is a mean of connecting to another computer, or a network like the Internet, over a telecommunications line using a modem-equipped computer.

Dial-up security software: It is software that controls access via remote dial-up. One method of preventing unauthorized users from accessing the system through an unapproved telephone line is through dial-back procedures in which the dial-up security software disconnects a call initiated from outside the network via dial-up lines, looks up the user's telephone number, and uses that number to call the user.

Direct access: An access method for finding an individual item on a storage device and accessing it directly, without having to access all preceding records.

Direct access storage devices (DASD): Any storage device, such as a hard disk, that provides the capability to access and/or manipulate data as required without having to access all preceding records to reach it. In contrast to direct or random access, sequential access devices, such as tape drives, require all preceding records to be read to reach the required data.

Disaster recovery plan: A written plan for processing critical applications in the event of a major hardware or software failure or destruction of facilities.

Disk storage: It is a high-density random access magnetic storage devices that store billions of bits of data on round, flat plates that are either metal or plastic.

Diskette: A removable and widely used data storage medium that uses a magnetically coated flexible disk of Mylar enclosed in a plastic case.

Distributed processing: It is a mode of operation in which processing is spread among different computers that are linked through a communications network.

DSS: See, decision support system.

Download Process of transferring data from a central computer to a personal computer or workstation.

Dumb terminal: A terminal that serves only as an input/output mechanism linking a user with the central computer. This type of terminal does not have an internal processor.

Dump: To transfer the contents of memory to a printer or disk storage. Programmers use memory dumps to debug programs.

EBCDIC: See, extended binary-coded decimal interchange code.

EDI, See, electronic data interchange.

Electronic data interchange (EDI): A standard for the electronic exchange of business documents, such as invoices and purchase orders. Electronic data interchange (EDI) eliminates intermediate steps in processes that rely on the transmission of paper-based instructions and documents by performing them electronically, computer to computer.

Electronic signature: A symbol, generated through electronic means, that can be used to (1) identify the sender of information and (2) ensure the integrity of the critical information received from the sender. An electronic signature may represent either an individual or an entity. Adequate electronic signatures are (1) unique to the signer, (2) under the signer's sole control, (3) capable of being verified, and (4) linked to the data in such a manner that if data are changed, the signature is invalidated upon verification. Traditional user identification code/password techniques do not meet these criteria.

Encryption: The transformation of data into a form readable only by using the appropriate key, held only by authorized parties.

End user computing: Any development, programming, or other activity where end users create or maintain their own systems or applications.

Environmental controls: This subset of physical access controls prevents or mitigates damage to facilities and interruptions in service. Smoke detectors, fire alarms and extinguishers, and uninterruptible power supplies are some examples of environmental controls.

Execute access: This level of access provides the ability to execute a program.

Exit: A predefined or in-house written routine that receives controls at a predefined point in processing. These routines provide an entity with flexibility to customize processing, but also create the opportunity to bypass security controls.

Extended Binary-Coded Decimal Interchange Code (EBCDIC): It is an eight-bit code developed by IBM for representing 256 characters.

Field: A location in a record in which a particular type of data are stored. In a database, the smallest unit of data that can be named. A string of fields is a concatenated field or record.

File: A collection of records stored in computerized form.

Financial information system: An information system that is used for one of the following functions: (1) collecting, processing, maintaining, transmitting, and reporting data about financial events, (2) supporting financial planning or budgeting activity, (3) accumulating and reporting cost information, or (4) supporting the preparation of financial statements.

Financial management system: Financial information systems and the financial portions of mixed systems (systems that support both financial and non-financial functions) that are necessary to support financial management.

Firewall: Firewalls are hardware and software components that protect one set of system resources (e.g., computers, networks) from attack by outside network users (e.g., Internet users) by blocking and checking all incoming network traffic. Firewalls permit authorized users to access and transmit privileged information and deny access to unauthorized users.

Floppy disk: A removable and widely used data storage medium that uses a magnetically coated flexible disk of Mylar enclosed in a plastic envelope.

Flowchart: A diagram of the movement of transactions, computer functions, media, and/or operations within a system. The processing flow is represented by arrows between symbolic shapes for operation, device, data file, etc. to depict the system or program.

Flow-charter: Software that allows the user to prepare flowcharts. (See, flowchart.)

Gateway: In networks, a computer that connects two dissimilar local area networks, or connects a local area network to a wide area network, minicomputer, or mainframe. A gateway may perform network protocol conversion and bandwidth conversion.

General controls: General controls are the structure, policies, and procedures that apply to an entity's overall computer operations. They include an entity-wide security program, access controls, application development and change controls, segregation of duties, system software controls, and service continuity controls.

General support system: An interconnected set of information resources under the same direct management control that shares common functionality. Normally, the purpose of a general support system is to provide processing or communication support.

Hacker: A person who attempts to enter a system without authorization from a remote location.

Hardware: The physical components of information technology, including the computers, peripheral devices such as printers, disks, and scanners, and cables, switches, and other elements of the telecommunications infrastructure.

High level programming language: A programming language that provides a certain level of abstraction from the underlying machine language through the use of declarations, control statements, and other syntactical structures. In practice, the term refers to a computer language above assembly language.

Host computer: This is the main computer in a system of computers and terminals connected by communication links.

Hot site: A fully operational off-site data processing facility equipped with both hardware and system software to be used in the event of a disaster.

I/O appendage: See, input/output appendage.

IDMS: This is the brand name of a database management system.

Implementation: The process of making a system operational in the organization.

IMS: See, information management system.

Information: The meaning of data. Data are facts; they become information when they are seen in context and convey meaning to people.

Information Management System (IMS): A general purpose IBM system product that allows users to access a database through remote terminals.

Information resource: See, resource.

Information resource management: See, information systems management.

Information resource owner: See, owner.

Information systems management: The function that directs or manages the activities and staff of the IS department and its various organizational components.

Inherent risk: The susceptibility of an assertion to a material misstatement, assuming that there are no related internal controls.

Initial program load (IPL): A program that brings another program, often the operating system, into operation to run the computer and also, referred to as a bootstrap or boot program.

Input: Any information entered into a computer or the process of entering data into the computer.

Input/output appendage: A routine designed to provide additional controls for system input/output operations.

Integration testing: Testing to determine if related information system components perform to specification.

Integrity: With respect to data, its accuracy, quality, validity, and safety from unauthorized use. This involves ensuring that transmitted or stored data are not altered by unauthorized persons in a way that is not detectable by authorized users.

Interactive processing: A mode of operation in which users interact with the system as their programs and data are processed.

Interface: A connection between two devices, applications, or networks or a boundary across which two systems communicate. Interface may also refer to the portion of a program that interacts with the user.

Internal control (also referred to as internal control structure): A process, effected by agency management and other personnel, designed to provide reasonable assurance that (1) operations, including the use of agency resources, are effective and efficient; (2) financial reporting, including reports on budget execution, financial statements, and other reports for internal and external use, are reliable; and (3) applicable laws and regulations are followed. Internal control also includes the safeguarding of agency assets against unauthorized acquisition, use, or disposition. Internal control consists of five interrelated components that form an integrated process that can react to changing circumstances and conditions within the agency. These components include the control environment, risk assessment, control activities, information and communication, and monitoring.

Internet: When capitalized, the term "Internet" refers to the collection of networks and gateways that use the Transmission Control Protocol/Internet Protocol suite of protocols.

IPL: See, initial program load.

JES2: See, job entry system.

JES3: See, job entry system.

Job: A set of data that completely defines a unit of work for a computer. A job usually includes programs, linkages, files, and instructions to the operating system.

Job accounting software: Software that tracks the computer resources (e.g., processor time and storage) used for each job.

Job control language (JCL): In mainframe computing, a programming language that enables programmers to specify batch processing instructions. The abbreviation JCL refers to the job control language used in IBM mainframes.

Job entry system (JES2, JES3): Software that allows the submission of programs from terminals (usually through on-line program development systems such as TSO to the mainframe computer.

Job scheduling system (CA-7, Manager, Scheduler): Software that queues the jobs submitted to be run on the mainframe. It uses job classes and other information provided by the person submitting the job to determine when the job will be run.

Key: A long stream of seemingly random bits used with cryptographic algorithms. The keys must be known or guessed to forge a digital signature or decrypt an encrypted message.

LAN: See, local area network.

Legacy system: A computer system, consisting of older applications and hardware that was developed to solve a specific business problem. Many legacy systems do not conform to current standards, but are still in use because they solve the problem well and replacing them would be too expensive.

Library: In computer terms, a library is a collection of similar files, such as data sets contained on tape and/or disks, stored together in a common area. Typical uses are to store a group of source programs or a group of load modules. In a library, each program is called a member. Libraries are also called partitioned data sets (PDS). Library can also be used to refer to the physical site where magnetic media, such as a magnetic tape, is stored. These sites are usually referred to as tape libraries.

Library control/ management: The function responsible for controlling program and data files that are either kept on-line or are on tapes and disks that are loaded onto the computer as needed.

Library copier: Software that can copy source code from a library into a program. Library management software: Software that provides an automated means of inventorying software, ensuring that differing versions are not accidentally misidentified, and maintaining a record of software changes.

Loader: A utility that loads the executable code of a program into memory for execution.

Load library: A partitioned data set used for storing load modules for later retrieval.

Load module: The results of the link edit process. An executable unit of code loaded into memory by the loader.

Local area network (LAN): A group of computers and other devices dispersed over a relatively limited area and connected by a communications link that enables a device to interact with any other on the network. Local area networks (LAN) commonly include microcomputers and shared (often expensive) resources such as laser printers and large hard disks. Most modern LANs can support a wide variety of computers and other devices. Separate LANs can be connected to form larger networks.

Log: With respect to computer systems, to record an event or transaction.

Log off: The process of terminating a connection with a computer system or peripheral device in an orderly way.

Log on: The process of establishing a connection with, or gaining access to, a computer system or peripheral device.

Logging file: See, log.

Logic bomb: In programming, a form of sabotage in which a programmer inserts code that causes the program to perform a destructive action when some triggering event occurs, such as terminating the programmer's employment.

Logical access control: The use of computer hardware and software to prevent or detect unauthorized access. For example, users may be required to input user identification numbers (ID), passwords, or other identifiers that are linked to predetermined access privileges.

Logical security: See, logical access control.

Machine code: The program instructions that are actually read and executed by a system processing circuitry.

Mainframe computer: A multi-user computer designed to meet the computing needs of a large organization. The term came to be used generally to refer to the large central computers developed in the late 1950s and 1960s to meet the accounting and information management needs of large organizations.

Maintenance: Altering programs after they have been in use for a while. Maintenance programming may be performed to add features, correct errors that were not discovered during testing, or update key variables (such as the inflation rate) that change over time.

Major application: It is defined as an application that requires special attention due to the risk and magnitude of the harm resulting from the loss, misuse, or unauthorized access to or modification of information in the application.

Management controls: The organization, policies, and procedures used to provide reasonable assurance that (1) programs achieve their intended result, (2) resources are used consistent with the organization's mission, (3) programs and resources are protected from waste, fraud, and mismanagement, (4) laws and regulations are followed, and (5) reliable and timely information is obtained, maintained, reported, and used for decision-making.

Master console: In MVS environments, the master console provides the principal means of communicating with the system. Other multiple console support (MCS) consoles often serve specialized functions, but can have master authority to enter all MVS commands.

Master file: In a computer, the most currently accurate and authoritative permanent or semi-permanent computerized record of information maintained over an extended period.

Material weakness: A material weakness is a reportable condition in which the design or operation of the internal controls does not reduce to a relatively low level the risk that losses, noncompliance, or misstatements in amounts that would be material in relation to the principal statements or to a performance measure or aggregation of related performance measures may occur and not be detected within a timely period by employees in the normal course of their assigned duties.

Materiality: An auditing concept regarding the relative importance of an amount or item. An item is considered as not material when it is not significant enough to influence decisions or have an effect on the financial statements.

Merge access: This level of access provides the ability to combine data from two separate sources.

Microchip: See, chip.

Microcomputer: Any computer with its arithmetic-logic unit and control unit contained in one integrated circuit, called a microprocessor.

Microprocessor: An integrated circuit device that contains the miniaturized circuitry to perform arithmetic, logic, and control operations (i.e. contains the entire CPU on a single chip).

Midrange computer: A medium-sized computer with capabilities that fall between those of personal computers and mainframe computers.

Migration: A change from an older hardware platform, operating system, or software version to a newer one.

Modem (Short for modulator-demodulator):.A device that allows digital signals to be transmitted and received over analog telephone lines. This type of device makes it possible to link a digital computer to the analog telephone system. It also determines the speed at which information can be transmitted and received.

Multiple virtual storage (MVS): It is an IBM mainframe operating system. It has been superseded by OS/390 for IBM 390 series mainframes.

MVS: See, multiple virtual storage.

Naming conventions: Standards followed for naming computer resources, such as data files, program libraries, individual programs, and applications.

Network: A group of computers and associated devices that are connected by communications facilities. A network can involve permanent connections, such as cables, or temporary connections made through telephone or other communications links. A network can be as small as a local area network consisting of a few computers, printers, and other devices, or it can consist of many small and large computers distributed over a vast geographic area.

Network administration: The function responsible for maintaining secure and reliable network operations. This function serves as a liaison with user departments to resolve network needs and problems.

Network architecture: The underlying structure of a computer network, including hardware, functional layers, interfaces, and protocols (rules) used to establish communications and ensure the reliable transfer of information. Because a computer network is a mixture of hardware and software, network architectures are designed to provide both philosophical and physical standards for enabling computers and other devices to handle the complexities of establishing communications links and transferring information without conflict. Various network architectures exist, among them the internationally accepted seven-layer open systems interconnection model and International Business Machine (IBM) Systems Network Architecture. Both the open systems interconnection model and the Systems Network Architecture organize network functions in layers, each layer dedicated to a particular aspect of communication or transmission and each requiring protocols that define how functions are carried out. The ultimate objective of these and other network architectures is the creation of communications standards that will enable computers of many kinds to exchange information freely.

Network master control system: Software that controls the network providing monitoring information for reliability, stability, and availability of the network and traffic control and errors. These may also involve the use of special hardware.

Networked system: See, network.

Node: In a local area network, a connection point that can create, receive, or repeat a message. Nodes include repeaters, file servers, and shared peripherals. In common usage, however, the term node is synonymous with workstation.

Non-repudiation: The ability to prevent senders from denying that they have sent messages and receivers from denying that they have received messages.

Object code: The machine code generated by a source code language processor such as an assembler or compiler. A file of object code may be immediately executable or it may require linking with other object code files, e.g., libraries, to produce a complete executable program.

Off-the-shelf software: Software that is marketed as a commercial product, unlike custom programs that are privately developed for a specific client.

On-line: A processing term that categorizes operations that are activated and ready for use. If a resource is on-line, it is capable of communicating with or being controlled by a computer. For example, a printer is on-line when it can be used for printing. An application is classified as on-line when users interact with the system as their information is being processed as opposed to batch processing.

On-line coding facility: See, on-line program development software.

On-line debugging facility: This is Software that permits on-line changes to program object code with no audit trail. This type of software can activate programs at selected start points.

On-line editors: See, on-line program development software.

On-line program development software: Software that permits programs to be coded and compiled in an interactive mode, e.g. TSO, ROSCOE, VOLLIE, ICCF & ISPF.

On-line transaction monitor: In the mainframe environment, software that provides online access to the mainframe, e.g. IMS/DC, CICS.

On-line transaction processing: On-line transaction processing records transactions as they occur.

Operating system: The software that controls the execution of other computer programs, schedules tasks, allocates storage, handles the interface to peripheral hardware, and presents a default interface to the user when no application program is running.

Operational controls: These controls relate to managing the entity's business and include policies and procedures to carry out organizational objectives, such as planning, productivity, programmatic, quality, economy, efficiency, and effectiveness objectives. Management uses these controls to provide reasonable assurance that the entity (1) meets its goals, (2) maintains quality standards, and (3) does what management directs it to do.

Output: Data/information produced by computer processing, such as graphic display on a terminal or hard copy.

Output Devices: Peripheral equipment (such as a printer or tape drive), that provides the results of processing in a form that can be used outside the system.

Owner: Manager or director with responsibility for a computer resource, such as a data file or application program.

Parameter: A value that is given to a variable. Parameters provide a means of customizing programs.

PARMLIB (Short for SYS1.PARMLIB): The partitioned data set that contains many initialization parameters that are used by an MVS operating system during an initial program load and by other system software components such as SMF that are invoked by operator command.

Partitioned data set (PDS): Independent groups of sequentially organized records, called members, in direct access storage. Each member has a name stored in a directory that is part of the data set and contains the location of the member's starting point. PDSs are generally used to store programs. As a result, many are often referred to as libraries.

Password: A confidential character string used to authenticate an identity or prevent unauthorized access.

PDS: See, partitioned data set.

Performance monitor: Software that tracks and records the speed, reliability, and other service levels delivered by a computer system e.g. Omegamon, Resolve & Deltamon.

Peripheral: A hardware unit that is connected to and controlled by a computer, but external to the CPU. These devices provide input, output, or storage capabilities when used in conjunction with a computer.

Personnel controls: This type of control involves screening individuals prior to their authorization to access computer resources. Such screening should be commensurate with the risk and magnitude of the harm the individual could cause.

Personnel security: See, personnel controls.

Physical access control: This type of control involves restricting physical access to computer resources and protecting these resources from intentional or unintentional loss or impairment.

Physical security: See, physical access control.

Piggy-backing: A method of gaining unauthorized access to a restricted area by entering after an authorized person but before the door closes and the lock resets. Piggy-backing can also refer to the process of electronically attaching to an authorized telecommunications link to intercept transmissions.

Platform: The foundation technology of a computer system, typically, a specific combination of hardware and operating system.

Port: An interface between the CPU of the computer and a peripheral device that governs and synchronizes the flow of data between the CPU and the external device.

Privileges: Set of access rights permitted by the access control system.

Processing: is execution of program instructions by the central processing unit.

PPT: See, program properties table.

Production control and scheduling: The function responsible for monitoring the information into, through, and as it leaves the computer operations area and for determining the succession of programs to be run on the computer. Often, an automated scheduling package is utilized in this task.

Production data: The data that supports the agency's operational I formation processing activities. It is maintained in the production environment as opposed to the test environment.

Production environment: The system environment where the agency performs its operational information processing activities.

Production programs: Programs that are being used and executed to support authorized organizational operations. Such programs are distinguished from "test" programs which are being developed or modified, but have not yet been authorized for use by management.

Profile: A set of rules that describes the nature and extent of access to available resources for a user or a group of users with similar duties, such as accounts payable clerks. (See standard profile and user profile.)

Program: A set of related instructions that, when followed and executed by a computer, perform operations or tasks. Application programs, user programs, system programs, source programs, and object programs are all software programs.

Program library: See, library.

Program properties table (PPT): A facility provided by IBM to identify programs that require special properties when invoked in an MVS environment. Although special properties may be required for an application to run efficiently, certain special properties also have security implications because they may allow the programs to bypass security authorization checking.

Programmer: A person who designs, codes, tests, debugs, and documents computer programs.

Programming library software: These systems allow control and maintenance of programs for tracking purposes. These systems usually provide security, check out controls for programs, and on-line directories for information on the programs. Some of the examples are Panvalet, Librarian & Endeavor.

Proprietary: Privately owned, based on trade secrets, privately developed technology, or specifications that the owner refuses to divulge, thus preventing others from duplicating a product or program unless an explicit license is purchased.

Protocol: In data communications and networking, a standard that specifies the format of data as well as the rules to be followed when performing specific functions, such as establishing a connection and exchanging data.

Prototyping: A system development technique in which a working model of a new computer system or program is created for testing and refinement.

Public access controls: A subset of access controls that apply when an agency application promotes or permits public access. These controls protect the integrity of the application and public confidence in the application and include segregating the information made directly available to the public from official agency records.

Public domain software: Software that has been distributed with an explicit notification from the program's author that the work has been released for unconditional use, including for-profit distribution or modification by any party under any circumstances.

Quality assurance: The function that reviews software project activities and tests software products throughout the software life-cycle to determine if (1) the software project is adhering to its established plans, standards, and procedures, and (2) the software meets the functional specifications defined by the user.

Query: The process of extracting data from a database and presenting it for use.

RACF: See, resource access control facility.

Read access: This level of access provides the ability to look at and copy data or a software program.

Real-time system: A computer and/or a software system that reacts to events before they become obsolete. This type of system is generally interactive and updates files as transactions are processed.

Record: A unit of related data fields. The group of data fields that can be accessed by a program and contains the complete set of information on a particular item are records.

Regression testing: Selective retesting to detect faults introduced during modification of a system.

Reliability: The capability of hardware or software to perform as the user expects and to do so consistently, without failures or erratic behavior.

Remote access: The process of communicating with a computer located in another place over a communications link.

Remote job entry (RJE): With respect to computer systems with locations geographically separate from the main computer center, submitting batch processing jobs via a data communications link.

Report writer software: Software that allows access to data to produce customized reports e.g. Easytrieve, SAS.

Reportable condition: Reportable conditions include matters coming to the auditor's attention that, in the auditor's judgment, should be communicated because they represent significant deficiencies in the design or operation of internal controls, which could adversely affect the entity's ability to meet its internal control objectives.

Resource: Something that is needed to support computer operations, including hardware, software, data, telecommunications services, computer supplies such as paper stock and pre-printed forms, and other resources such as people, office facilities, and non-computerized records.

Resource access control facility (RACF): An access control software package developed by IBM.

Resource owner: See, owner.

Risk assessment: The identification and analysis of possible risks in meeting the agency's objectives that forms a basis for managing the risks identified and implementing deterrents.

Risk management: A management approach designed to reduce risks inherent to system development and operations.

RJE: See, remote job entry.

Router: An intermediary device on a communications network that expedites message delivery. As part of a LAN, a router receives transmitted messages and forwards them to their destination over the most efficient available route.

Run: A popular, idiomatic expression for program execution.

Run manual: A manual that provides application-specific operating instructions, such as instructions on job setup, console and error messages, job checkpoints, and restart and recovery steps after system failures.

SDLC methodology: See, system development life cycle methodology.

Security: The protection of computer facilities, computer systems, and data stored on computer systems or transmitted via computer networks from loss, misuse, or unauthorized access. Computer security, involves the use of management, personnel, operational, and technical controls to ensure that systems and applications operate effectively and provide confidentiality, integrity, and availability.

Security administrator: Person who is responsible for managing the security program for computer facilities, computer systems, and/or data that are stored on computer systems or transmitted via computer networks.

Security management function: The function responsible for the development and administration of an entity's information security program. This includes assessing risks, implementing appropriate security policies and related controls, establishing a security awareness and education program for employees, and monitoring and evaluating policy and control effectiveness.

Security plan: A written plan that clearly describes the entity's security program and policies and procedures that support it. The plan and related policies should cover all major systems and facilities and outline the duties of those who are responsible for overseeing security (the security management function) as well as those who own, use, or rely on the entity's computer resources.

Security profile: See, profile.

Security program: The security program is an entity-wide program for security planning and management that forms the foundation of an entity's security control structure and reflects senior management's commitment to addressing security risks. The program should establish a framework and continuing cycle of activity for assessing risk, developing and implementing effective security procedures, and monitoring the effectiveness of these procedures.

Security software: See, access control software.

Sensitive information: Any information that, if lost, misused, or accessed or modified in an improper manner, could adversely affect the national interest, the conduct of federal programs, or the privacy to which individuals are entitled under the Privacy Act.

Server: A computer running administrative software that controls access to all or part of the network and its resources, such as disk drives or printers. A computer acting as a server makes resources available to computers acting as workstations on the network.

Service continuity controls: This type of control involves ensuring that when unexpected events occur, critical operations continue without interruption or are promptly resumed and critical and sensitive data are protected.

Simultaneous peripheral operations on-line (SPOOL): In the mainframe environment, a component of system software that controls the transfer of data between computer storage areas with different speed capabilities. Usually, an intermediate device, such as a buffer, exists between the transfer source and the destination (e.g., a printer).

Smart card: A credit card sized token that contains a microprocessor and memory circuits for authenticating a user of computer, banking, or transportation services.

SMF: See, system management facility.

Sniffer: Synonymous with packet sniffer. A program that intercepts routed data and examines each packet in search of specified information, such as passwords transmitted in clear text.

Social engineering: A method used by hackers to obtain passwords for unauthorized access. Typically, this involves calling an authorized user of a computer system and posing as a network administrator.

Software: A computer program or programs, in contrast to the physical environment on which programs run (hardware).

Software life cycle: The phases in the life of a software product, b ginning with its conception and ending with its retirement. These stages generally include requirements analysis, design, construction, testing (validation), installation, operation, maintenance, and retirement.

Source code: Human-readable program statements written in a high-level or assembly language, as opposed to object code, which is derived from source code and designed to be machine-readable.

SPOOL: See, simultaneous peripheral operations on-line.

Spooling: A process of storing data to be printed in memory or in a file until the printer is ready to process it.

Stand-alone system: A system that does not require support from other devices or systems. Links with other computers, if any, are incidental to the system's chief purpose.

Standard: In computing, a set of detailed technical guidelines used as a means of establishing uniformity in an area of hardware or software development.

Standard profile: A set of rules that describes the nature and extent of access to each resource that is available to a group of users with similar duties, such as accounts payable clerks.

Substantive testing: Substantive testing is performed to obtain evidence that provides reasonable assurance of whether the principal statements, and related assertions, are free of material misstatement. There are two general types of substantive tests: (1) substantive analytical procedures and (2) tests of details.

Supervisor call (SVC): A supervisor call instruction interrupts a program being executed and passes control to the supervisor so that it can perform a specific service indicated by the instruction.

SVC: See, supervisor call.

System administrator: The person responsible for administering use of a multi-user computer system, communications system, or both.

System analyst: A person who designs systems.

System designer; See, system analyst.

System developer: See, programmer.

System development life cycle (SDLC) methodology: The policies and procedures that govern software development and modification as a software product goes through each phase of its life cycle.

System life cycle: See, software life cycle.

System management facility: An IBM control program that provides the means for gathering and recording information that can be used to evaluate the extent of computer system usage.

System programmer: A person who develops and maintains system software.

System software: The set of computer programs and related routines designed to operate and control the processing activities of computer equipment. It includes the operating system and utility programs and is distinguished from application software.

System start-up: See, initial program load.

System testing: Testing to determine that the results generated by the enterprise's information systems and their components are accurate and the systems perform to specification.

Tape library: The physical site where magnetic media is stored.

Tape management system: These are Software that control and tracks tape files, e.g. CA-1, TMS & EPAT.

Technical controls: See, logical access control.

Telecommunications: A general term for the electronic transmission of information of any type, such as data, television pictures, sound, or facsimiles, over any medium, such as telephone lines, microwave relay, satellite link, or physical cable.

Teleprocessing monitor: In the mainframe environment, a component of the operating system that provides support for on-line terminal access to application programs. This type of software can be used to restrict access to on-line applications and may provide an interface to security software to restrict access to certain functions within the application.

Terminal: A device consisting of a video adapter, a monitor, and a keyboard.

Test facility: A processing environment isolated from the production environment that is dedicated to testing and validating systems and/or their components.

Time-sharing: A technique that allows more than one individual to use a computer at the same time.

Time sharing option (TSO): The time sharing option of MVS allows users to interactively share computer time and resources and also makes it easier for users to interact with MVS.

Token: In authentication systems, some type of physical device (such as a card with a magnetic strip or a smart card) that must be in the individual's possession in order to gain access. The token itself is not sufficient; the user must also be able to supply something memorized, such as a personal identification number (PIN).

TOP SECRET: An access control software package marketed by Computer Associates International, Inc. (CA).

Transaction: A discrete activity captured by a computer system, such as an entry of a customer order or an update of an inventory item. In financial systems, a transaction generally represents a business event that can be measured in money and entered in accounting records.

Transaction file: A group of one or more computerized records containing current business activity and processed with an associated master file. Transaction files are sometimes accumulated during the day and processed in batch production overnight or during off-peak processing periods.

Trojan horse: A computer program that conceals harmful code. A Trojan horse usually masquerades as a useful program that a user would wish to execute.

TSO: See, time-sharing option.

Unit testing: Testing individual program modules to determine if they perform to specification.

UNIX: A multitasking operating system originally designed for scientific purposes which has subsequently become a standard for midrange computer systems with the traditional terminal/host architecture. UNIX is also a major server operating system in the client/server environment.

Update access: This access level includes the ability to change data or a software program.

Upload: The process of transferring a copy of a file from a local computer to a remote computer by means of a modem or network.

User: The person who uses a computer system and its application programs to perform tasks and produce results.

User identification (ID): A unique identifier assigned to each authorized computer user.

User profile: A set of rules that describes the nature and extent of access to each resource that is available to each user.

Utility program: Generally considered to be system software designed to perform a particular function (e.g., an editor or debugger) or system maintenance (e.g., file backup and recovery).

Validation: The process of evaluating a system or component during or at the end of the development process to determine whether it satisfies specified requirements.

Virus A program that "infects" computer files, usually executable programs, by inserting a copy of itself into the file. These copies are usually executed when the "infected" file is loaded into memory, allowing the virus to infect other files. Unlike the computer worm, a virus requires human involvement (usually unwitting) to propagate.

Wide area network (WAN): A group of computers and other devices dispersed over a wide geographical area that are connected by communications links.

WAN: See, wide area network.

Workstation: A microcomputer or terminal connected to a network. Workstation can also refer to a powerful, stand-alone computer with considerable calculating or graphics capability.

Worm: An independent computer program that reproduces by copying itself from one system to another across a network. Unlike computer viruses, worms do not require human involvement to propagate.

ZAP: A generic term used to define a type of program that can alter data and programs directly, bypassing controls. Because of this ability, the ZAP and Super ZAP programs must be secured from casual or unauthorized use.